4/98

ARCHITECTURE AND ORDER

MATERIAL CULTURES

Interdisciplinary studies in the material construction of social worlds

Series Editors
Daniel Miller, Dept of Anthropology, University College London
Michael Rowlands, Dept of Anthropology, University College London
Christopher Tilley, Institute of Archaeology, University College London
Annette Weiner, Dept of Anthropology, New York University

ARCHITECTURE AND ORDER

Approaches to Social Space

Michael Parker Pearson
and Colin Richards

London and New York

First published 1994
by Routledge
11 New Fetter Lane, London EC4P 4EE

Simultaneously published in the USA and Canada
by Routledge
29 West 35th Street, New York, NY 10001

First published in paperback 1997

Typeset in 10/12pt Garamond by Florencetype Limited, Stoodleigh, Devon
Printed and bound in Great Britain by T.J. International Ltd, Cornwall

British Library Cataloguing in Publication Data
Pearson, Michael Parker
Architecture and Order: Approaches to Social Space – (Material Cultures Series)
I. Title II. Richards, Colin III. Series 720.1

Library of Congress Cataloguing in Publication Data
A catalogue record for this book is available from the Library of Congress

ISBN 0-415–06728–6 (hbk)
ISBN 0-415–15743–9 (pbk)

CONTENTS

FIGURES

CONTRIBUTORS

John Barrett is a Senior Lecturer in Archaeology at the University of Glasgow. He writes about archaeological theory.

Annie Bartlett is a forensic psychiatrist at St George's Hospital, London. Her background is in social anthropology.

Ian Hodder is a Reader in Archaeology at the University of Cambridge. He writes about archaeological theory.

Mark Horton is a freelance archaeologist and part-time Lecturer at Bristol University. He has conducted excavations at Shanga in Kenya.

Matthew Johnson is a Lecturer in Archaeology at the University of Durham. He writes about archaeological approaches to the study of vernacular architecture.

Clive Knights is a Lecturer in Architecture at the University of Sheffield. He is interested in design theory.

Paul Lane is a Lecturer in Archaeology at the University of Botswana. He has done much ethnoarchaeology as well as archaeology.

Lisa Nevett is a British Academy Post-Doctoral Fellow in Classical Archaeology.

Mike Parker Pearson is a Lecturer in Archaeology at the University of Sheffield. He writes about later prehistory and archaeological theory.

Colin Richards is a Lecturer in Archaeology at the University of Glasgow. He is interested in archaeological approaches to the use of space.

Todd Whitelaw is a Lecturer in Archaeology at the University of Cambridge. One of his interests is prehistoric Greece.

PREFACE

The idea and incentive for this book arose out of a shared feeling that despite the obsessive practice of recording architecture and physical features in the greatest detail imaginable, archaeologists were somehow missing the point in their substitution of description for understanding. Although this observation could encompass most archaeogical studies of material culture, it was different ways of interpreting architecture and the definition of social space which especially interested us. This was primarily due to a confrontation of these issues in our independent research into prehistoric tombs and houses. As a result of this interest, we both considered it important to examine and experience architecture and order in different cultural settings. Consequently we began our own fieldwork in Bali (CR) and Madagascar (MPP).

The more we considered the problem the clearer it became that through the power of a tradition of practice, archaeologists viewed the materiality of the past in a very peculiar manner. Nowhere has this been more apparent than in the treatment of social space where a contrived objectivity is practised which frequently serves to reduce architecture to a descriptive and definitional level that totally alienates the observer/reader. Here the 'landscape', 'enclosure' or 'house' merely defines units of analysis and unfortunately these constructs are often viewed solely in two dimensions. An experience of space tends never to be considered appropriate because of the inherent subjectivity. Therefore, any understanding of the architecture of the past is quite different and alien from our own experiences of architecture and social practices in the present. We reject this reductionism through the realization of the subjective experience *and* the objective presentation of architecture. We also accept the potential reconstruction of a past which acknowledges that different people who live in different places and times, order and understand their world in very different ways.

In this volume we begin by introducing a number of themes which show how the constructed environment is more than a backdrop to action and is locked in a reflexive relationship with lived experience of the world. Classifications of people and things are physically realized through architecture, thus conceptions of order are constantly confronted from our earliest days and recollections. In some cases the most complex cosmological schemes are manifest in spatial representation. However, it should not be forgotten that the derivation of such meaning is contingent, on people and practice.

The following contributions draw out these themes in a highly original manner. They examine aspects of social space from different disciplinary perspectives, including archaeology, ethnoarchaeology, psychology and philosophy. However, they all share our interest and sympathy in the symbolic power of architecture. As such, although this book is primarily aimed at archaeologists we hope it will have wider appeal and interest in the social sciences. Our main intention of opening a door to a more imaginative and interesting archaeology, however, remains to be seen.

Some of the contributions to this volume were given at a session on 'Architecture and Order' at the Theoretical Archaeology Group conference held at Lampeter in December 1990. We are greatly indebted to those who participated in that session and also those who have written chapters specially for this volume. We would like to thank Hilary Moor at Routledge for her help and patience during the preparation of the volume and Karen Godden and Jane Downes for substantial editorial assistance. Our own views have been clarified and modified through many discussions and seminars with students, postgraduates and colleagues at Sheffield and Glasgow. We would particularly like to thank: Andrew Fleming, John Moreland, Alex Woolf, Gretel Boswijk, Dianne Harris, Carol Mee, Martin Thorburn (MPP) and Patrick Ashmore, John Barrett, Sally Foster, Pam Graves, Alan Leslie and Ross Samson (CR).

1

ORDERING THE WORLD: PERCEPTIONS OF ARCHITECTURE, SPACE AND TIME

Mike Parker Pearson and Colin Richards

From the pavement, I noticed a slight twitch of the curtain and a hint of movement in the corner of the left-hand window. Ahead, there was a token barrier; a small wooden gate which inevitably was stuck and difficult to open. Squeezing past this obstacle I took the left pathway which led towards the front door, ignoring a well-worn path leading around the side of the bungalow. Almost at once the door opened, instantly interrupting the awful harmony of the chiming doorbell, and a cautious face enquired my business. Despite the overwhelming image of a brightly emblazoned van parked behind me announcing the merits of television rental, I had to go through the familiar doorstep ritual. Hesitating a moment, I announced that my presence was in direct response to her urgent plea to restore the family television to working order. At my feet, I noticed a trail of newspaper leading in a neat path from the front doormat, along the hallway and into the sitting room. The reason for this precaution was not immediately clear since the day was sunny and the pathway dry, but obviously her worst fears had been realized. Her half glance directed towards the kitchen, at the rear of the house, transmitted the unspoken annoyance that the rear door had not been used: the tradesman's entrance. Finally, I was invited across the threshold and admitted to the house. By following the newspaper trail I arrived at the television and noted with interest that no such paper path led in from the kitchen, the rear entrance. I soon had the repair completed and, after the mandatory cup of tea, left for my next call.

You may feel the situation described above to be an unusual occurrence, yet it was encountered frequently by one of us in a previous occupation. This brief situation reveals clearly so many aspects of the way we categorize space and associated meanings in given social situations. Here, concepts of

1

'weighted' space, in terms of boundaries and paths of movement, are bound up with classifications of people and notions of cleanliness, dirt and purity. Consider the changes which would have occurred if that bungalow door had been opened to someone other than the humble repair man; perhaps a dinner guest, the local priest, or a tramp.

THE WORST OF ARCHITECTS, THE BEST OF BEES

'The architect builds the cell in his mind before he constructs it in wax' wrote Karl Marx, and this relationship between building and human awareness 'distinguishes the worst architect from the best of bees' (Marx [1867] 1976: 284). Humans are not the only animals that build. Creatures that we classify low down the hierarchy of the animal kingdom – termites, wasps, bees – build elaborate structures; some birds adapt their building techniques as they learn from experience. Other primates build nightly nests of branches (Groves and Sabater Pi 1985). Precisely how we may draw a line between humans and other animals with regard to architecture, is a problem which has been encountered in related discussions of tool use and tool making. Yi-Fu Tuan (1977: 102) has suggested that it is awareness that singles out humans as superior to other animals in architectural achievement.

Philosophers such as Heidegger, Merleau-Ponty and Bachelard have considered that our relation to places consists in dwelling and that dwelling is the basic principle of existence. Our ability to dwell is distinguished from that of a bird living in a nest by our inherent awareness that we are not mere things. Learning to be mortal is the essence of dwelling (Zimmerman 1985). Attempts at a phenomenological architecture or geography have explored how our relationship to the built environment is rooted in experience (Norberg-Schulz 1971; Buttimer and Seamon 1980; Dovey 1985; Seamon and Mugerauer 1985; Lang 1985). Such a perspective may also be linked to approaches which stress the symbolic as well as the functional.

We may never know much about thought in animals other than humans, but the link between human awareness or imagination and the building of structures has been discussed in detail within architecture and the social sciences. People everywhere act on their environment and are aware of that environment, practically and discursively. As in the example of the Australian Aborigines, with the natural landscape formed by mythical ancestors during the Dreaming (Myres 1986), what we select from nature to serve our purposes, we also call architecture (Norberg-Schulz 1971: 37).

PEOPLE, SPACE AND THE BUILT ENVIRONMENT

According to Rapoport (1980: 298), environments are thought before they are built. Equally, we build *in order* to think and act (Preziosi 1983). The relationship is essentially dynamic and reflexive. Winston Churchill said that 'first we shape our buildings and afterwards our buildings shape us'. This relationship is dynamic, subtle and complex since the effects of environment are not direct, passive or readily predictable (Holahan 1978: 1). Giddens' theory of structuration (for example 1984) has provided a useful conceptual approach: social structures (as embodied in traditions and social rules) have a dialectical relationship with human actions. Structures are both the medium and the outcome of social practices (e.g. Duncan 1985; Pader 1988). They are modified continually as the actions that constitute them change. As Gregory and Urry have pointed out, as a result of structuration theory, 'spatial structure is now seen not merely as an arena in which social life unfolds, but rather as a medium through which social relations are produced and reproduced' (Gregory and Urry 1985: 3).

Our experience of the built environment may be both exhilarating and banal. Often we do not examine our surroundings but 'breathe them in' (Day 1990: 10). Great monuments shout their presence and instil feelings of awe and wonder, yet a familiar environment is taken for granted. Architectural discourse can be psychologically persuasive, or experienced inattentively. It may be coercive or indifferent (Eco 1980: 41–2). Within the context of confining institutions such as the prison, coercion is strongly marked. The nineteenth-century design of the panopticon (enabling a supervisor to see into each and every cell from one vantage point) has been described as 'a diagram of a mechanism of power reduced to its ideal form' (Foucault 1973: 207). Yet most constructions exert power in ways that are not so obviously coercive. 'Space commands bodies, prescribing or proscribing gestures, routes and distances to be covered. . . . Monumentality . . . always embodies and imposes a clearly intelligible message. . . . Monumental buildings mask the will to power and the arbitrariness of power beneath signs and surfaces which claim to express collective will and collective thought' (Lefebvre 1991: 143). By building in monumental terms, we attempt the physical embodiment of an eternal and imperishable social order, denying change and transmuting 'the fear of the passage of time, and anxiety about death, into splendour' (ibid.: 221).

'HOUSES ARE BUILT TO LIVE IN AND NOT TO LOOK ON' (FRANCIS BACON)

Our own conception of space may be as a 'container' of material objects, an otherwise empty frame to be filled. Yet this may differ from many people's experience of space. Vere Gordon Childe, writing in a philosophical rather than archaeological vein, said: 'men gradually discover by experiment how things and persons can be arranged spatially, so defining an idea of space. As such it must find a symbolic vehicle and be expressed' (Childe 1956: 76). In other words, our environment exists in terms of our actions and meanings; it is an existential space which is neither external object nor internal experience. Architectural space may be defined as a concretization of this existential space (Norberg-Schulz 1971: 12). Space is perceived only as places. The environment is categorized and named. Through the cultural artefact of a name, undifferentiated *space* is transformed into marked and delimited *place*. Stories and tales may be attached to such places, making them resonate with history and experience. The culturally constructed elements of a landscape are thus transformed into material and permanent markers and authentications of history, experience and values. Although the stories change in the retelling, the place provides an anchor of stability and credibility. The very existence of physical places validates the rewoven histories (Bruner 1984: 5).

If we examine, for example, the conceptualization of 'the forest', we find that it has undergone an historical transformation (Tuan 1974: 109–12; Rapoport 1982: 40). The concept of 'forest' is a cultural artefact. The deep forest wildernesses, rarely penetrated, were once potentially threatening, full of dangerous spirits and wild creatures. Names and stories were associated with the forest – we may still recognize this cultural construction in fairy tales, for example – and it acquired a meaning, a conceptual place in an organized world. People's lived experiences and everyday practices and routines were rooted in such concepts of the world around them. The forest as a place of danger, or more positively as a place of refuge or purgation, was conceptually opposed to the security and order of the town or city. Yet today we invest the forest with attributes of retreat and tranquillity, in opposition to the social evils and stress of the city.

The material environment is rarely neutral; 'it either helps the forces of chaos that make life random and disorganized or it helps to give purpose and direction to one's life' (Csikszentmihalyi and Rochberg-Halton 1981: 16–17). Yet it may be more than that according to structuration theory. Determinations of space may have profound effects on other aspects of society and culture. Such determinations 'play a decisive role in the constitution of the world the society inhabits, which world in its turn plays a role in the constitution of the society. Without their geometrical space for example Europeans would be unable to survey, navigate, calculate stress etc., as they do, and without such activities their economy would not be as it is' (Littlejohn 1967: 334–5). Littlejohn was contrasting the European conception of space with that of the Temne of Sierra Leone. Unlike Europeans, the Temne do not divide their landscapes into the useful and the beautiful. They never go to 'look at the view', nor do they measure distances in the same way. When travelling between two points the distance is measured in numbers of villages passed, regardless of the distance between villages – to the infuriation of European administrators. In Temne society, space is not considered a homogeneous and isotropic entity which can be measured mathematically but is categorized in qualitative terms relating to the ordering of experience (Littlejohn 1963). For example, the cardinal points, of which east is pre-eminent, 'are not mere coordinates for plotting position (the Temne have no maps) but directions of existence' (Littlejohn 1967: 334).

The concept of 'environment' is a cultural artefact, as the example of the Temne world demonstrates. The minds of archaeologists attempting to reconstruct past people's environments have been moulded in a pattern probably very different to that which formed the minds of those people themselves, who named and categorized the world according to concepts and experiences which may be alien to ourselves. Space is practice (our everyday actions); it is also symbol, and we might conceive of architecture as symbolic technology. The meanings that are given to places and the spatial order are not fixed or invariant givens but must be invoked in the context of practice and recurrent usage. Meanings adhere to a spatial frame only through the medium of human activity. However, the capacity to reinterpret and change meanings and ideologies is constrained by the already existing spatial order (Moore 1986: 186–7). In other words, we make history not as we wish but under circumstances not of our own choosing. The relationship between spatial form and human agency is mediated by meaning. People actively give their physical environments meanings, and then act upon those meanings.

Most analysts of space, place and architecture would now reject deterministic formulations of the relationship between people and their built environment. Lawrence and Low (1990) provide an excellent summary of the literature. Architectural determinism proposes two causal relationships (Harris and Lipman 1980): that either behaviour determines the architectural form of an environment ('form follows function'); or that behaviour is the result of environment ('function follows form'). Psychological explanations such as Cooper's (1974) Jungian interpretation of the house as an archetypal symbol of the self, or notions that private property psychologically fulfils a vital need of the soul, may also be criticized for treating as universal law what is in fact an 'ideology surrounding the private ownership of a freestanding house' (Pratt 1981). Sociobiological and behavioural formulations have been similarly challenged for their inability to take into account social and historical context or social structure (N.G. Duncan 1981).

THE SYMBOLIC ARCHAEOLOGY OF THE MODERN HOUSE

For many people the house is synonymous with the home. Equally it may be thought of as a purely practical and functional domain, a 'machine for living in' in Le Corbusier's words. In recent years both these assumptions have been upset. On new housing estates in Britain we see hoardings advertising 'homes' rather than houses. The word 'home' comes from a Germanic root and, for English speakers, may be filled with emotional meaning – reminders of childhood and the roots of our being, or concepts of privacy, freedom and security. The Latin word '*domus*' may be equated to it but there is no linguistic equivalent in Italian, French or Hungarian, for example. What at first glance seems a universal human concept is culturally variable in time and space (Csikszentmihalyi and Rochberg-Halton 1981: 121–2). 'Home' may not mean a house; it might also mean the ancestral land of Australian Aboriginal groups such as the Pintupi (Myres 1986: 54). Home is a concept of order and identity. Since home is an attitude of being, we do not necessarily solve 'homelessness' by building more houses (Heidegger 1978: 161). 'To be at home is to know where you are; it means to inhabit a secure centre and to be oriented in space' (Dovey 1985: 36). Several phenomenologists have remarked on the problems of modern living, where architectural trends are towards a placeless geography, a meaningless pattern of similar buildings, a 'flatscape' (Relph 1976: 117; Seamon 1980). Equally, for many people home is a very restricted and privatized architectural space – a small island within a great void of public and uncontrollable landscape (Dovey 1985: 57). Increasingly throughout the world, people have equated their 'house' with their 'home'. In the words of Csikszentmihalyi and Rochberg-Halton: 'Like some strange race of cultural gastropods, people build homes out of their own essence, shells to shelter their personality. But, then, these symbolic projections react on their creators, in turn shaping the selves they are. The envelope thus created is not just a metaphor' (Csikszentmihalyi and Rochberg-Halton 1981: 138).

The house not only embodies personal meanings but also expresses and maintains the ideology of prevailing social orders (J.S. Duncan 1981: 1). We will look later at how prehistoric and early historic societies organized their space as symbolic creations of cosmic order, but various commentators have pointed out that contemporary space also expresses a cosmic order. Writing of modern America, Constance Perin suggests that the cosmic order expressed is 'of the American heaven and hell in the suburban pull towards salvation and the urban push of social pollution' (Perin 1977: 216). She also shows that principles of social order are translated into settlement patterns by the practices of everyday life, relating to physical proximity, social homogeneity, race relations, form of tenure, housing styles, income levels, privacy and community (ibid.: 210). Others have shown how the ideology of housing as private ownership of dwellings in separate, individualized space according to wealth has fragmented household units within the workings of modern capitalism and its accompanying processes of individualism and privatization (King 1984: 254). The places of work and leisure have become separated and where people live is determined more by their place of employment than by their family roots.

It may be difficult for us to see symbolism and function (or utility) as commingled and conjoined. When we designate an artefact as symbolic, there is often the assumption that it serves no other purpose. We might also consider ourselves 'utilitarian' or 'pragmatic' in outlook, as though our world view had no symbolic principles. Yet the two are linked inextricably.

We take concepts, such as utility or comfort, and consider them to be universal principles although they are culturally specific, relative values. In his influential book *House Form and Culture*, Amos Rapoport (1969: 60–2, 131–2) explained how western notions of comfort, adequate lighting, heating, pleasant smells, absence of smoke, privacy, bathroom hygiene and orientation to the view, beach or sun might not be shared by other cultures. As Nigel Barley (1989: 47) has observed, the British have an obsession with explaining everything in utilitarian terms. He goes on to say that a Toradjan rice farmer would find our own attitudes to houses totally impractical and incomprehensible since, having bought a house, through the loan of an extraordinary sum of money, we then spend most of our time elsewhere, trying to earn the money for repayment (ibid.: 51).

The average English house may be analysed in terms of these, and other, structuring principles. Many people like to consider that their taste or way of living is unique to them, that individuality is a concept that enables each of us to have the freedom to express ourselves uniquely. Yet our uniformity in structuring our domestic shells is predicated by age, gender, class, ethnicity and other aspects of social context. In England, patterns of domestic space have been consistent since the Industrial Revolution (Lawrence 1987: 90). Most houses have been independent dwellings with a 'withdrawing' room or parlour at the front and a kitchen (or scullery until the mid-twentieth century) at the back. The living room was likewise toward the rear of the house. Bedrooms are normally located upstairs (if there is an upstairs), with separate lavatory and bath at the back and upstairs (after World War I). Rooms and spaces within the house are strongly demarcated according to use and objects contained. Rooms for daytime living and for night-time sleeping are rigidly differentiated. Traditionally, the parlour or drawing room was a shrine-like room which contained ancestral furniture and ornaments, photographs and heirlooms. This 'public' room was used for those special occasions – the rites of passage such as christenings, marriage and funeral gatherings or Sunday tea when formality in behaviour and dress were to be observed. The pragmatist might account for the siting of kitchen, bathroom and toilet at the rear in terms of utility of plumbing, and explain the demarcation of rooms as stemming from the need to prevent messy practices such as food preparation from ruining smart furniture and carpets. Viewed from within the structuring principles of comfort, utility and hygiene, these are no doubt sensible and practical strategies. But when we stand back and ask why the plumbing is not at the front of the house (nearer to the sewer and mains supply running under the street) or why we need smart furniture, we begin to grasp the cultural particularity of the situation.

Roderick Lawrence has taken the approach of the social anthropologist and shown that the vast majority of English dwellings conform to a set of codes or rules which are articulated by a series of oppositions. These are front/back, clean/dirty, day/night, public/private, male/female and

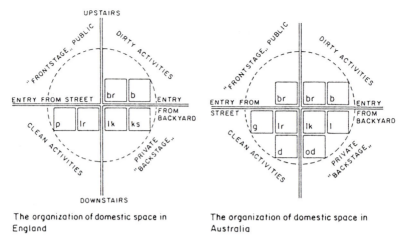

The organization of domestic space in England

The organization of domestic space in Australia

br = bedroom, lr = living room, d = dining room, lk = dining/kitchen, b = bathroom, l = laundry, od = outdoor dining, g = garden, p = parlor, ks = kitchen/scullery

Figure 1.1 The organization of domestic space in Australia and England according to the notions of private/public, clean/dirty, and front/back (from R.J. Lawrence 1987, by kind permission of the author and Wiley & Sons)

symbolic/secular or sacred/profane (ibid.: 103–7). Space within the house is organized as a gradient or hierarchy of rooms within each opposition (Figure 1.1). For example, as one proceeds through the house from front to back or from downstairs to upstairs, one moves along a 'privacy gradient' from most public to most private spaces.

Lawrence shows how sets of oppositions may be articulated (ibid.: 90). For example:

$$\frac{\text{Front}}{\text{Back}} = \frac{\text{Symbolic}}{\text{Secular}} = \frac{\text{Parlour}}{\text{Kitchen}} = \frac{\text{Special occasion}}{\text{Daily routines}}$$

He also demonstrates that the internal organization of domestic space is different in England and Australia. While both apply similar oppositional principles, the configurations are slightly different. For example, Australians are more likely to have their dining rooms at the front of the house. Sub-cultures make the situation more complex. In northern English cities, such as Sheffield, the traditions of working-class community dictate that visitors approach the back, and not the front, door. In total contrast, the apartments of the Swiss and French do not utilize these binary oppositions but are based on very different notions of organizing domestic space (Lawrence 1990).

Lawrence is also interested in the boundedness, conceptual and physical, of the house. He observes that the space around dwelling units is treated in particular ways. Likewise, boundaries between rooms might be important. For example, he found gender role differentiation far stronger in English than in Australian homes, and many of his English interviewees were concerned to screen off from the living room the smells and sights of dirty utensils and food in preparation.

We have come a long way from medieval conceptions of the house as a large semi-public structure, with its central and large hall for receiving visitors, for feasting and other commonly shared activities. During the late medieval and post-medieval periods, private space expanded at the expense of such areas (Fairclough 1992) until today we end up with the vestigial, obligatory 'hall' – a tiny room or passageway just inside the front door, where visitors are received, boots removed and coats hung up. Now only a boundary zone with the outside world, such space seems ludicrous when we consider its medieval origins. Yet its transformation encapsulates the increasing privacy of the domestic house and the erosion of communal and semi-public space. As a result, we now inhabit small islands, isolated and secured, within a great void (Dovey 1985: 57).

As cultural gastropods we should be very much in control of our domestic domains, particularly when many feel that it is the one setting for relationships that we feel we can manipulate. And yet a small but growing number of people have considerable problems living normal lives in such surroundings, or spend many hours in rituals and routines of domestic purification or the instilling of a sense of order in their homes. The disabling obsessive behaviours that may result (Bartlett, this volume) can prevent people even from entering their own homes for fear of rendering them impure. People may also have considerable trouble negotiating boundaries (such as moving from sitting down to standing up, crossing thresholds or stepping off a kerb) and become helplessly enthralled by elaborate private rituals. The link between sacredness and cleanliness was touched on by Lord Raglan (1964: 42), who interpreted the cleaning and tidying of western homes as a modern version of preserving the sanctity of the house by keeping it free from symbolic pollution, a concept explored by Mary Douglas (1966).

Houses in western society are also status symbols and the hierarchical social order is encapsulated in their variety. The ranking of 'detached', 'semi-detached', 'terrace' and 'flat' in Britain indicates the amount of space, garden area and privacy which are indicators of social position (Sircar 1987). In Britain the ideology of house-ownership is stronger than in other countries in Europe, and the distinction between owned and rented accommodation (the latter typified by council housing) is another feature of the class hierarchy. The match between social classes and house types may not be absolute, but the hierarchical classification of dwellings acts as a totemic system of moral and social taxonomies for the British class structure, both exemplifying and reinforcing it.

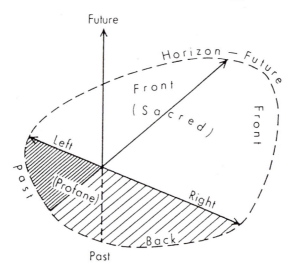

Figure 1.2 Upright human body, space and time. Space projected from the body is biased toward the front and right. The future is ahead and 'up'. The past is behind and 'below' (from Tuan 1977, by kind permission of Edward Arnold)

THE COSMOS: PUTTING OUR HOUSE IN ORDER

Humans are expert classifiers and categorizers (Humphrey 1984: 143–5). The world around us, as created and lived, may be divided up and made sense of in many different ways. Often very complex systems of classification may derive from simple principles, as social anthropologists have found in studying traditional small-scale societies. Through classification, order is imposed upon the world, not simply an ordering of everything in its place, but an order of morality, social relations, space, time, and the cosmos. One of the most important generators of these ordering principles is the human body. We move through space and time; we experience our surroundings through our bodies and, by our mere presence, impose a schema on space whether we are aware of it or not (Tuan 1977: 36). The human body's potential divisions (top/bottom, left/right, front/back, vertical/horizontal, male/female) provide a simple framework, which we impose on the world linked to concepts such as sacred/profane, future/past, and good/evil (Figure 1.2). In addition, the body can also represent any bounded system (like a house, a territory, a group). 'Its boundaries can represent any boundaries which are threatened or precarious. The body is a complex structure. The functions of its different parts and their relation afford a source of symbols for other complex structures' (Douglas 1966: 115).

Other organizing principles may be derived from our environments. The concentric structuring of space into a centre and a periphery (or a set of concentric zones) and diametric organization according to one or more axes (such as the four cardinal directions) are also common elements of an underlying system of rules or conventions (Lévi-Strauss 1963: 132–63). Through the imposition and articulation of these various underlying principles, humans create order (cosmos) out of the primeval disorder (chaos).

The creation of order (or construction of cosmologies) has been a feature of all human societies and we may perceive its first physical manifestations in the tool assemblages of early hominids, and more obviously in the dwellings and burials of the Lower and Middle Palaeolithic. As we have seen, not all communities seek that sense of order in physically modifying the environment, nor do all seek it in the elaboration of a coherent cosmic system. On the other hand, people may devise elaborate cosmologies which permeate all aspects of life. 'The characteristic that distinguishes a traditional society is order, the sense of coherence in every aspect of life. This order or coherence derives from a shared knowledge of origins and gives validity to every event. In a traditional society the creation myth normally serves as the basis for the organization of society, territory, dwelling and family. The myth embodies a metaphysical doctrine and inspires every act and every artefact' (Khambatta 1989: 257).

This stress on the importance of the creation myth is an example of cosmogonic structure, whereby a linear and unidirectional mythic narrative can be employed to order society. It may be contrasted to an astronomic approach, in which mythic time is cyclical and conforms to the natural cycles of day and night, lunar months and solar years. These may be differentiated from human time – the linear and unidirectional course of a life. Tuan (1977: 131–2) has suggested that cosmogonic time is weakly symbolized (or even ignored) where astronomic time is prominently articulated, and that astronomic time, in contrast, is easily mapped onto a spatial frame. Khambatta's subject matter, the Hindu dwelling and its cosmic symbolism, seems to contradict Tuan's proposal. We should also bear in mind that many cosmologies embody both cosmogonic and astronomic principles.

The incorporation of any of or all these underlying codes into the physical organization of the human environment has been called 'sacred architecture'. William Lethaby wrote: 'The main purpose and burthen of sacred architecture – and all architecture, temple, tomb or palace, was sacred in the early days – is thus inextricably bound up with a people's thoughts about God and the universe' (Lethaby [1891] 1974: 2). Whilst his writings are flawed in his search for an ancient all-embracing magic cosmology, free of particular historical contexts, he did identify a number of important structuring principles used variously in the architecture of prehistoric, early historic and traditional societies.

11

FOCUS IN ARCHITECTURE

If the world is to be lived in, it must be founded.

(Eliade 1959: 22)

Mircea Eliade considered that human dwelling required the revelation of a sacred space to obtain a fixed point and hence acquire orientation in the chaos of homogeneity. By 'founding the world' we fix the limits and establish order (ibid.: 23). He noted that in many societies there is a tradition that a particular place is considered to be the centre of the world, or *axis mundi*. The centre of the world might be replicated in temples or even in domestic dwellings. Examples of the former are the Temple of Jerusalem, the centre of the Christian world in the medieval period, and the Ka'aba, considered by Muslims to be the point on earth closest to heaven. For Hindus the cosmic mountain Mount Meru is considered to be a similar *axis mundi*. This concept of a cosmic mountain is found in many societies from ancient Mesopotamia to contemporary Madagascar. The latter notion of a domestic architectural representation of the *axis* may be found in societies such as the Kwakiutl of the north-west coast of America, the Nad'a of Indonesia, the ancient Romans and Saxons, in the Canary Islands, and India.

These replicas of the centre of the cosmos could form part of a wider domain. The temple of Jerusalem was not only the centre of the world but also an image of the universe (an *imago mundi*). The navel of the earth (or *omphalos*) for the ancient Greeks might be found in every temple or sanctuary, or in every dwelling. The hearth within the houses of the Atoni (Cunningham 1973), of the Tewa (Ortiz 1969), and within the *hogan* of the Navajo (Witherspoon 1977), symbolizes the centre of the world. Within the Mongolian *yurt* tent (Humphrey 1974) the fire is considered as a protective deity, integrating Buddhist principles of male and female (the square of the hearth within the circle of the yurt) and the five elements (fire, the wood of the hearth frame, the earth of the floor, the iron of the tripod and the water in the kettle). In these and many other cases the hearth of the dwelling is considered to be a pivotal point, literally a *focus* (from the Latin for hearth or fire; through French it has also given us the word 'foyer'; Raglan 1964: 79).

This principle of concentricity may be found within settlement layouts (Figure 1.3). For example, the villages of the Bororo of Amazonia were arranged in a circle (Figure 1.4), with the men's house and ceremonial area at the centre (Figure 1.5) (Lévi-Strauss [1955] 1973: 284–90). Lévi-Strauss (1963: 132–9) also pointed to the concentric structure of the Trobriand village and the Winnebago Indian village. In the latter case he noted that individual perceptions of the village structure varied according to the status of the inhabitants. The higher-status clan members considered themselves part of a hierarchical concentric structure (high status at the centre). Lower-status people regarded the village as split into two diametrically organized and equal clans.

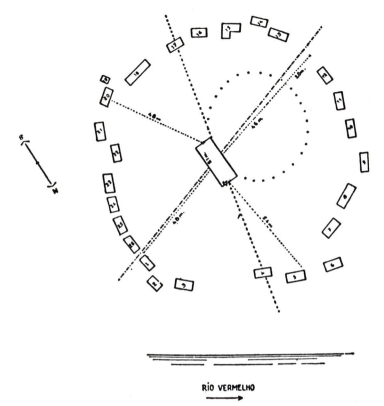

RÍO VERMELHO

Figure 1.3 Plan of Kejara village (from Lévi-Strauss [1955] 1973, by kind permission of the author, Librairie Plon and Jonathan Cape)

Inhabited space can be transformed into an *imago mundi* by projection of two or four horizons from a central point, or by a construction ritual which is based on the paradigmatic actions of myth. Christine Hugh-Jones's (1979) study of the Barasana of Amazonia indicates how the interrelationship of the organizational principles of concentricity, diametricity and creation myth creates the form of the long house. The front entrance faces east; it faces the 'water door' of the Milk River (Amazon), up which the ancestral anaconda journeyed. This door is the men's entrance, whilst the women have an access to the rear. The men's circle and dance area forms a central focus within the house while the family units and female domain are located against its walls and at the back. The house forms a microcosm of the whole world (above are the roof/sky and the posts/mountains, below is the underworld where the dead are buried). It is also a homology of the human body, of the womb and of its environmental setting. Hugh-Jones's very detailed account shows how astronomic and cosmogonic structuring principles can be used together (Figure 1.6).

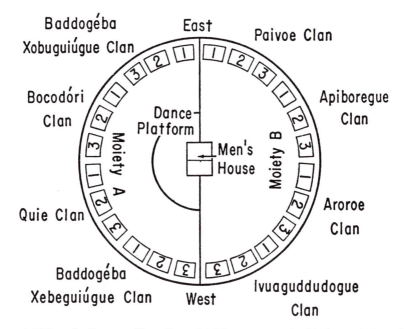

Figure 1.4 Plan of a Bororo village (from Lévi-Strauss 1963, by kind permission of HarperCollins)

The cities of ancient China, ancient Rome, Mesopotamia, the Aztecs and Incas utilized diametric and concentric structures. From the palace at the centre led the roads along the four cardinal directions, leaving the city through elaborate city gates 'where power generated at the *axis mundi* flowed out from the confines of the ceremonial complex towards the cardinal points of the compass' (Wheatley 1971: 435).

THE MEANING OF ORIENTATION

In many societies the east, the direction of the rising sun, is considered auspicious and often the most significant of the cardinal points. Among most of the ethnic groups of Madagascar, the house is traditionally aligned north–south. West is profane in relation to the sacred east, north is high status and south is low. For the highland Betsileo and Merina (Kus and Raharijaona 1990), the Sakalava (Feeley-Harnik 1980) and the Bara (Huntington 1988), the doorway is located on the west side towards the south. In the seating arrangements at formal occasions the male head of the household is seated in the north-east corner (which may have a small shrine) with men of lesser seniority ranged along the east wall towards the south. In the south part of the house sit the women and children. As one enters the

14

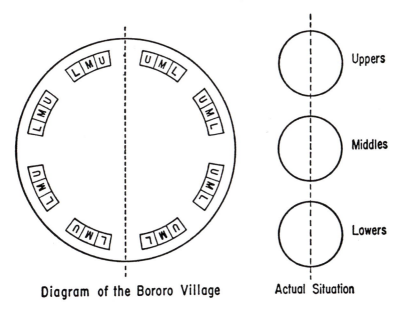

Diagram of the Bororo Village   Actual Situation

Figure 1.5 The organization of upper, middle and lower clans in a Bororo village (from Lévi-Strauss 1963, by kind permission of HarperCollins)

house through the door one moves towards the auspicious domain. Traditionally this house layout also functioned as a zodiacal calendar, using Arabic-derived notation. The layout of the house is also mirrored by the organization of the settlement. The senior households are to the north-east. New houses are built in the south-west so, over time, the village gradually migrates from north-east to south-west. In other parts of Madagascar the system is different. Amongst the Antandroy of the south, the doorway is on the north side and the men sit towards the south end, away from the hearth which is located just inside the door. Equally, status within the settlement declines from the south to the north.

The importance of east as a cardinal point for us is evident in the very word 'orientation' – a looking to the rising sun (Lethaby [1891] 1974: 53) – which we use today to express the general notion of 'direction'. Some cultures, however, are 'occidented'. For example, the ancient Tarascan state religion in Central America employed a concept of four quarters of the earth associated with the four cardinal directions emerging from the centre. North was equated with right and south with left – seen from the vantage of the rising sun (Pollard 1991: 168). Cunningham's (1973) classic study of the Atoni house in Indonesian Timor – south of the equator – illustrates an interesting variant on orientation (that is 'facing east'). Whilst the Atoni are 'oriented' – making prayers towards the east which is their direction of origin – it is forbidden to 'orient' the door, since the sun must not enter the

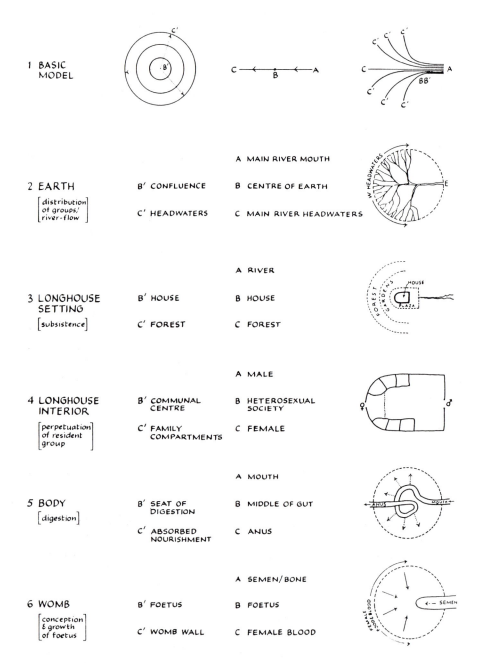

1 BASIC MODEL		
2 EARTH [distribution of groups,/ river-flow]	B' CONFLUENCE	A MAIN RIVER MOUTH
		B CENTRE OF EARTH
	C' HEADWATERS	C MAIN RIVER HEADWATERS
3 LONGHOUSE SETTING [subsistence]	B' HOUSE	A RIVER
		B HOUSE
	C' FOREST	C FOREST
4 LONGHOUSE INTERIOR [perpetuation of resident group]	B' COMMUNAL CENTRE	A MALE
		B HETEROSEXUAL SOCIETY
	C' FAMILY COMPARTMENTS	C FEMALE
5 BODY [digestion]	B' SEAT OF DIGESTION	A MOUTH
		B MIDDLE OF GUT
	C' ABSORBED NOURISHMENT	C ANUS
6 WOMB [conception & growth of foetus]	B' FOETUS	A SEMEN/BONE
		B FOETUS
	C' WOMB WALL	C FEMALE BLOOD

Figure 1.6 The Barasana long house: models of horizontal space-time (from Hugh-Jones 1979, by kind permission of the author and Cambridge University Press)

house. The direction of the door is called *ne'u* (meaning south and right). This might seem reasonably straightforward, except that Cunningham observed that houses might be aligned in various directions though rarely directly east–west (ibid.: 206–7). Whether this incongruence, between the actual position of a door and the conceptual naming of that position, had developed over time or had been apparent for centuries, we do not know. An alternative dislocation between meaning and building can be found in situations where the traditional orientation of buildings is maintained yet the discursive and apparent meaning for this is lost.

The Atoni house, as a model of the cosmos, expresses explicitly the order of the human, natural and supernatural world (ibid.: 234–5) and its organizational principles are invoked in politics and other aspects of daily life. Moreover, it is not simply analogous to the cosmos, but is integrated within it. It is constructed according to concentric and diametric principles. The four cardinal points organize the locations of the key internal features: sleeping platform, main platform and water jar (Figure 1.7). The door is at the south. The north or left side is the interior and associated with female space, while the right side includes the outer area, inside the door and the front yard, a male domain. The house's corner posts and the interior posts that support the rafters form two other axes, north-east to south-west and south-east to north-west (Figure 1.8). The roof, with its upper regions associated with the spiritual and male spheres, may also be contrasted with the lower, female and secular. Concentric order moves out from the hearth to the interior posts, to the door, to sleeping platforms at the east and west, and the fixed water jar at the north, and to the corner posts. An outside area beyond them is further defined, not only as the front yard but also as a further 'outside'. Order in the Atoni house expresses the twin concerns of unity and difference, and their continual interpretation. The wall and roof represent the unity of the house and its social group, while the internal divisions symbolize and articulate the structured social groupings which are pervaded by the premise of inequality (ibid.: 232).

A similar concern with the four cardinal points is found among the Tewa (Pueblo Indians) of New Mexico (Ortiz 1969). Each direction is marked by a sacred mountain, on top of which is an 'earth navel' marked by an arrangement of stones. The sacred centre of the village is marked by a circle of stones and is another earth navel. This is located in the south plaza, considered to be the first of the four plazas of the village. Today the kiva, the communal ritual house, is incorporated into one of the village houseblocks but supposedly in earlier villages the earth navel was in the centre of the kiva floor. The cardinal directions are also marked by four shrines, comprising piles of large stones or single stones. Around the village there are many shrines where the souls dwell. Three are located in the middle of refuse dumps – the artefacts of the past are sacred because of their association with

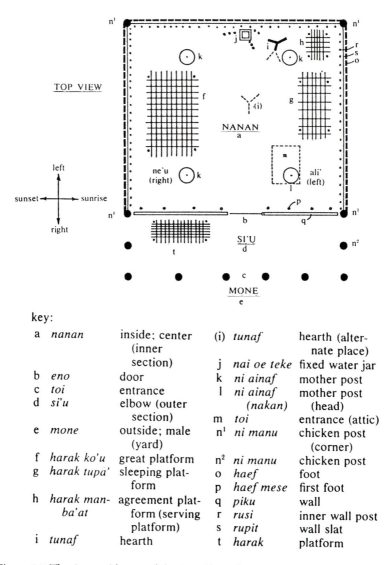

key:

a	*nanan*	inside; center (inner section)	(i)	*tunaf*	hearth (alternate place)
			j	*nai oe teke*	fixed water jar
b	*eno*	door	k	*ni ainaf*	mother post
c	*toi*	entrance	l	*ni ainaf*	mother post
d	*si'u*	elbow (outer section)		*(nakan)*	(head)
			m	*toi*	entrance (attic)
e	*mone*	outside; male (yard)	n¹	*ni manu*	chicken post (corner)
f	*harak ko'u*	great platform	n²	*ni manu*	chicken post
g	*harak tupa'*	sleeping platform	o	*haef*	foot
h	*harak man-ba'at*	agreement platform (serving platform)	p	*haef mese*	first foot
			q	*piku*	wall
			r	*rusi*	inner wall post
i	*tunaf*	hearth	s	*rupit*	wall slat
			t	*harak*	platform

Figure 1.7 The Amarasi house of the Atoni in Indonesian Timor: plan of the interior (from Cunningham 1973, by kind permission of University of Chicago Press)

souls and with the sacred past. Since 1600, and possibly earlier, the village has been divided into quarters, just as the Tewa have classified their physical world into quarters. With multiple *axes mundi*, the Tewa structuring of concentricity is complex.

18

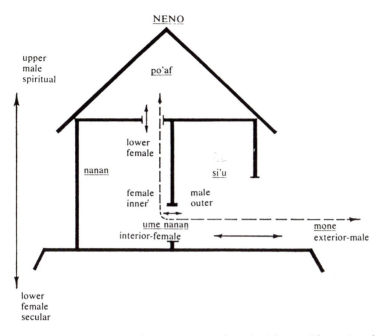

Figure 1.8 The Amarasi house of the Atoni in Indonesian Timor: side section (from Cunningham 1973, by kind permission of University of Chicago Press)

GENDER, ACTIVITY AND CLASSIFICATION

We have looked at some examples of concentric structuring (centres and peripheries), diametric structuring, involving east–west, north–south, left/right, up/down and front/back, and their combinations. Bourdieu's (1973) analysis of the Berber Kabyle house shows how gender and activity associations are embodied by similar principles. The main door, to the east, is male while opposite is the smaller female entrance. The wife's loom is placed against this west wall. The attached stable, a dark place associated with sex, death and birth, is a female space, while the higher, lighter, living space is associated with the nobility and honour of the patrilineal head of the household. The house in general terms is the women's domain while men spend their daylight hours outside. Bourdieu identified an additional structuring principle, one of reversal. Whilst men are associated with light and women with darkness in the house, the loom is propped against the 'Wall of Light', illuminated by the light of the east door. Although geographically west, this wall is considered to be the 'east' wall internally whilst the opposite wall – the 'Wall of Darkness' – is associated with 'west'. Thus the orientation within the house, the world of women, is a reversal of the outside world, the world of men. This structuring of organization and order

19

should be understood more in terms of degrees of accessibility and exclusion, rather than the absolute categories implied by Bourdieu (Mitchell 1988: 50–6).

In north-eastern Thailand the house (Figure 1.9), is similarly oriented (Tambiah 1969; 1985). East is auspicious and sacred, the place of the Buddha shelf. East is considered to be on the right hand, associated with maleness. West represents death, impurity, the left hand and the female sex. While south is neutral, north is auspicious and associated with the elephant, an animal with mythical and royal associations. In the sleeping room, at the north of the house, the parents sleep in the east and the married daughter and son-in-law sleep to the west. The house is entered from the south, the visitor facing north, while the kitchen and the wash place must always be on the west side. Additionally, each room is at a different level, a vertical repetition of the horizontal order. The wash place is lowest, followed by the kitchen and entrance. Higher up is the guest room and highest is the sleeping room. Tambiah found that in some cases the positions of the entrance and sleeping room were reversed but never were any of the rooms rearranged east–west.

Perhaps most interesting about Tambiah's analysis is his recognition that the organization of house space is generally, if not precisely, homologous to the systems of classification of marriage rules and of animals. For example, the buffalo and ox are important as work animals, are cared for and are the prime ceremonial food. They are penned under the sleeping room. Pigs are also killed on ritual occasions but pork is a second preference to beef. Other domestic animals are ducks (not eaten at ceremonial feasts) and chickens (eaten as ordinary food or at feasts). Pigs, ducks and chickens are kept under the guest room.

Some of the most elaborate conceptions of space are embodied in the Chinese practice of *feng-shui*, developed as an integrated theory of geomancy from the tenth century AD, and the Japanese directional system of *hogaku*, which are summarized elsewhere (Oliver 1987: 167–9). We have touched on Hindu conceptions of space and dwelling. A well-documented variant is found among the traditional courtyard-houses of Kerala in south-west India (Moore 1989).

HOUSES, PEOPLE AND METAPHORS

The classic interpretation of the Dogon house of West Africa is that its plan represents that of a man (Griaule and Dieterlen 1954; Griaule 1965). This example of anthropomorphic symbolism has been widely employed in a number of texts (Oliver 1971; Orme 1981: 228–32). Yet this interpretation now seems erroneous (van Beek 1991, 148). It is especially pertinent since Griaule's work was one of the first of such symbolic studies, whilst the example has also been used to illustrate the difficulties an archaeologist would meet if attempting to interpret the heterogeneous and irregular

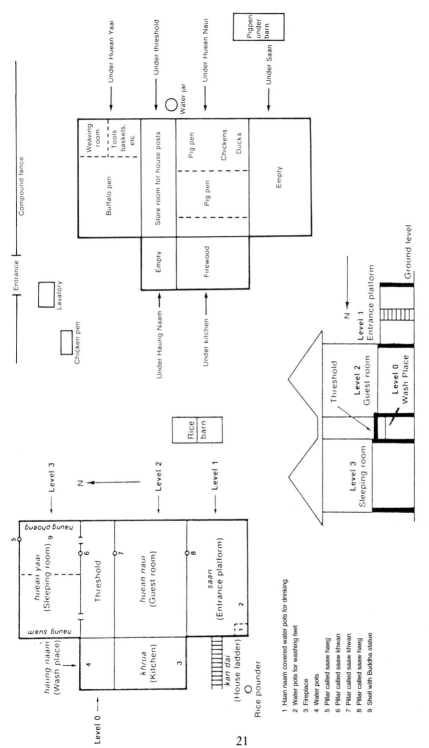

21

Figure 1.9 Profile and plan of a Thai house (living space on a raised floor over the animal pens) (from Tambiah 1969, by kind permission of *Ethnology*. © *Ethnology*)

1 Haan naam covered water pots for drinking
2 Water pots for washing feet
3 Fireplace
4 Water pots
5 Pillar called saaw haeg
6 Pillar called saaw khwan
7 Pillar called saaw khwan
8 Pillar called saaw haeg
9 Shell with Buddha statue

Dogon house compounds as a standard anthropomorphic design from the physical evidence alone.

One of the most impressive studies of architectural metaphor has been Suzanne Preston Blier's (1987) analysis of the houses of the Batammaliba (literally 'those who are the real architects of earth'), not far from the Dogon in the northern parts of Togo and Benin. As we have seen in other examples, Batammaliba architectural representations act as mnemonic aids and as permanent and concrete expressions of the principles on which their cosmogony rests (ibid: 36). Key expressions connected with the house are building the earth, fabricating humans, setting the sun in motion, shaping the sky, building the underworld and creating the gods. The house is a metaphor at many levels, and Preston Blier has described it as an architecture of therapy, easing the trauma of life crises, forming a source of knowledge with regard to psychological problems, and capable of modification to solve daily problems of living (ibid.: 135–9).

Preston Blier proposes a useful classification of social representation in architectural form, which should have wider applicability:

Nesting: the transposing of a series of elements or ideas into a nest of parts. For example, the Batammaliba house, the shrine, tomb, the fonio mound (on the roof), and the village all present parallels with the original creation. Whilst each emphasizes particular aspects of the creation myth, together they incorporate the principal features of Kuiye's act of creation.

Silhouetting: defining an object through its distinctive profile such as the circular shapes of house, tomb and village layout representing the earth.

Skeuomorph: using a material other than the original. For example, a calabash is associated with human creation and represents the female womb. Plants, calabashes and wood carvings reinforce metaphors of regeneration and growth.

Synecdoche: where elements of the house or the whole house stand for the essential features of, or the whole cosmos. For example, the egg or a ball of earth, through their identity with the Batammaliba house, convey the creation themes of regeneration and growth.

Reversal: especially for death, when the impact of imagery is heightened. For example, when the deceased is laid out in the Batammaliba house, the head is positioned to the west, the reversal of the sleeping position in life.

Condensed metaphor: when a larger idea is condensed into a compact miniature, such as the house as *imago mundi*, with the ground floor as underworld, roof as earth and granary roofs as sky.

The Batammaliba house (Figure 1.10) possesses the anatomy of both sexes and is treated like a human. For instance, it is 'dressed up' in cloths for

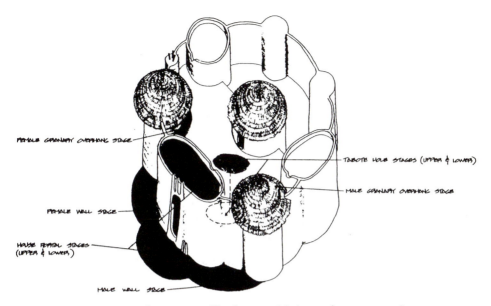

Figure 1.10 Diagram of a Batammaliba house with its performance staging areas (from Preston Blier 1987, by kind permission of the author and Cambridge University Press)

funerals and it is cicatrized, like a young girl, towards the end of construction. Through the middle of the house and linking the ground floor and upper storey is an access known as the *tabote* hole, under which take place funeral rites and birth. The *tabote* is sealed with a flat circular stone (*kubotan*) which symbolizes the continuum of life, death and rebirth, the power of the gods Kuiye and Butan, and the life force of the house. When the male elder of the house dies this stone is taken to close his tomb. Resting places for the souls of deceased ancestors are constructed in and around the house, placed according to sex and status.

The moulded clay 'horns of the entrance' above the door divide the house into its male and female areas. These horns have multiple meanings which vary according to their context of use. They are altars to Kuiye, testicles of fertilizing sperm, husband and wife, and the succession of generations, the protection and power associated with hunted game, the movement of the sun each day and each year, death and liminal resting places for the dead soul. Beyond the house, the village is perceived as oval (though it is more irregular) and seen to represent a person through the distribution of shrines to Butan (the goddess of earth). The village landscape is ordered by paths, which represent destiny and the pathways of the gods. The cemetery is a model of the settlement and the tomb locations mirror the house locations in a village. As an abode of the dead, the tomb incorporates in minature the

23

elements of the house – terrace, roof, portal, and *tabote* hole.

Within the sociological and anthropological literature, there are many more examples of architecture as cosmic homology. Examples are known from south-west Africa to the Mediterranean (literally 'middle of the earth'), throughout the Americas, from the Near East to China and India, Australasia and the circumpolar regions of Asia and Europe.[1]

BOUNDEDNESS, PURITY AND DECORATION

The creation of boundaries as physical features is often associated with needs of defence, territory, shelter and containment. Entrances and physical barriers, such as walls or earthworks, mark differences in domains and thus restrict and control access between them. By physically dividing up and demarcating space we may classify and control places and relationships more readily. Walls, gateways and entrances serve to mark transitions between domains such as inside/outside, sacred/profane, female/male, public/private, enemy/friend, elite/commoner or initiate/uninitiate. We have to acknowledge the functional aspects of defensive circuits around territories or cities but we must also bear in mind that they contribute to the very definition of those territorial or urban entities. Eliade (1959: 49) suggested that city fortifications began by being magical defences and noted that the European city walls of the Middle Ages were regularly consecrated in defence against the devil, sickness and death. Whilst we need not postulate a hypothetical evolution from magical to functional purpose, we should appreciate that the symbolic and the functional are intertwined. Fairclough's (1992) consideration of English medieval military defences as symbolic entities is one example of this approach. Of course, many boundaries are perceptual and are not physically marked on the ground. For example, English parish boundaries exist as physical entities only on maps or during the 'beating of the bounds', a traditional Rogation Day procession around the boundary. As Rapoport notes: 'very simple environments may be highly divided conceptually and these divisions may be indicated either not at all physically – or only in very subtle ways' (Rapoport 1980: 298–9). He suggests that the internal organization of the Kabyle Berber house is an example of the former and that the distinction of swept and unswept areas within Australian Aborigine camps is an example of the latter.

Whilst the archaeologist has to admit that the absence of a physical boundary need not imply the absence of a conceptual division between domains, as we have seen, there is a reflexive though not deterministic relationship between the physical and the conceptual. Within a historical sequence the construction of a city wall where there was none before, other than a conceptual understanding of the urban/suburban transition, is going to have a profound impact on conceptual schemata relating to the city and its definition.

Boundaries and transitions between domains can be marked in many ways other than simple physical features. We have already mentioned Mary Douglas's (1966: 115) insight into the modelling of the human body as a symbol of society. Okely's (1983) description of Gypsy life in Britain uses this formulation to explore the insider/outsider relationship of this ethnic minority (Gypsies) to the rest of society (Gorgios). She demonstrates homologies of this relationship in the treatment of animals, separation of washing facilities and organization of encampment space. For example, in the treatment of the body the washing of the outside (clothing, use of soap, etc.) must never be mixed with the washing of items associated with the inside (the crockery and cutlery). Gypsy trailers are very clean and elaborately ornamented, yet Gypsy sites are notorious for their litter and untidiness. The inner area (trailer interior and, to a lesser extent, the circle of trailers) is kept clean whilst the outside accumulates rubbish. Okely also suggests that, once they feel secure about tenure or access, the Gypsies will extend their spatial boundary to the edge of the camp and push rubbish over the hedge or fence on the outer rim of the circle. 'The inner/outer boundary of dirt and cleanliness is thus completed in territorial space' (ibid.: 89). Order is affirmed through this inside/outside principle but it comes into conflict with the concepts of order maintained by the dominant society, notably through the 'pollution' of rubbish and excrement in the countryside and the Gypsy resistance to the placing of caravans in rows of straight lines.

Thresholds, whether spatial or temporal (such as rites of passage), are liminal zones, 'betwixt and between', or transitions where danger lies. As people pass from one state (physical, psychological, social) to another so they encounter danger which must be controlled through rituals that protect against pollution. The doors of traditional Jewish households are protected by the *mezuzah*, a small prayer case secured to the doorpost. In many cultures all over the world, the transition rites of marriage nuptials and entering of the marital home are marked by the carrying of the bride over the threshold (not always by the husband). As we mentioned earlier, people suffering from compulsive-obsessive disorders may devise elaborate private rituals to negotiate thresholds and boundaries. The danger and pollution that awaits in transitional and marginal zones is often considered a necessary social phenomenon. Initiates in a rite of separation from society (for example, in coming of age) may be expected to become anti-social or non-social. 'Dirt, obscenity and lawlessness are as relevant symbolically to the rite of seclusion as other ritual expressions of their condition' (Douglas 1966: 97). Profanity and sacredness must exist as a duality and often corruption is enshrined in sacred places and times (ibid.: 179).

Purification is one method of negotiating transitional zones; particularly where there is a sharp gradient between profane and sacred. It may be achieved through appropriate clothing, gestures, or incantations. Fire, smoke or water may also be used as purificatory agencies. For example, the

25

purificatory and transformative powers of water and fire in religious obser-vances at Hindu temples (Lewandowski 1980: 127) may have been employed for millennia in the Indian subcontinent (Miller 1985: 60).

Cleanliness is one manifestation of the striving for order and the preser-vation of sanctity. It may be a principle that extends from bodily to public space and, as we have seen, may vary cross-culturally in its meaning and application. In his study of the Tswana house, Hardie (1985) noted that the concern for clean compounds, attributed by the inhabitants to a fear of snakes, was due to a desire for order and remembrance of the ancestors, snakes being liminal creatures between the underworld and the world of the living. Cleanliness may be used as an instrument of power, coercion and even oppression. For example, the rise of the Zulu state in the nineteenth century was accompanied by major changes in the organization of space in these terms. The concept of the circular and hierarchical kraal (with first wife's family on the right-hand side and those of other wives on the left) was employed in the design of circular layouts for very large populations. The Zulu city was an indigenous adaptation of the homestead (Biermann 1971: 99). The need for cleanliness was no doubt a functional requirement for the strains on services and sanitation imposed by a dense population but it formed an element of an increasingly authoritarian ideology. 'The re-organization of society on military lines was accompanied by a new ethos. . . . A pride amounting almost to arrogance and an indifference to human life were accompanied by a sense of discipline, order and cleanliness . . . at the same time political loyalty was enhanced to a high degree, and came to be regarded as an absolute value' (Omer-Cooper 1966: 37, quoted in Biermann 1971: 99).

In his book *The Public Culture*, Donald Horne noted: 'I was so struck by the wording of the following sign in one country I was visiting that I wrote it down. It said: "There is one road to freedom. Its milestones are obedience, diligence, honesty, order, cleanliness, temperance, truth, sacrifice, and love of country." The place I saw this was in the administration block of the concentration camp at Dachau' (Horne 1986: 76). We may thus compare the German Nazi ideology of racial purity with the practical circumstances of the genocide of 'impure' races and social categories such as Jews, Gypsies and homosexuals. The meticulously planned despatching of millions took place in environments which were carefully ordered and controlled. Concentration camps were kept meticulously clean by the inmates, at the command of the camp guards. Douglas suggests that such callous and racist attitudes develop out of a quest for purity, when purity is no longer a symbol but something lived: 'Purity is the enemy of change, of ambiguity and compromise' (Douglas 1966: 162).

Relationships between men and women are, in many societies, ordered by male fears and proscriptions concerning the alleged impurity of women in some cases and the need to maintain their purity in others. The organization of village space in many New Guinea villages is ordered, in large part, by the segregation and marginalization of the women's realm from the men's. For example, in a Bomagai village, the central area is a male domain and women live in peripheral houses, with a menstruation hut located some distance away (Clarke 1971; Orme 1981: 95–7). Whilst the symbolic impurity of women is expressed in an extreme form in New Guinea society, such gender ideologies are encountered in many societies (MacCormack and Strathern 1980; Ardener 1981). Moore's study of the Marakwet of Kenya (1986) explains how the spatial organization of houses, burials and refuse appeals to the structural hierarchy implicit in the male/female distinction. For example, the spatial association of ash heaps with women's houses and piles of goat dung with men's relates to an opposition between the fertility of goats and the fertility of women, who are linked to cooking and to ash.

An interesting proposal on the ritual marking of physical boundaries and transitions is that such zones may be elaborated or decorated. Braithwaite (1982) suggested that decoration may be used as a ritual marker for ambiguities in the social order where hidden meanings are necessary for group interests. She showed that, among the Azande, decoration was used to mark transactions between women and men (which also included transformations between raw and cooked, and mixing of other conceptual categories). For example, pots used for serving beer, cooking porridge and drinking water all involved women giving them to men. The only undecorated style of pot was a small porous vessel from which men drank, which was kept in the men's huts. The use of decoration marked situations where the discreteness and distinction of opposed categories of people such as men and women were threatened with dissolution. Hodder's (1986: 107–20) study of decoration on the milk calabashes of Ilchamus (or Njemps) cattle pastoralists comes to a similar conclusion about the negotiation of power between women and men; the making of milk and childcare 'beautiful' through decoration was part of the process of extending female control. Both of these studies have involved portable objects rather than fixed architectural features. However, they do relate to, and derive their meaning from, the architectural situations in which gender relations are played out.

The study of the Mesakin and Moro tribal groups of the Nuba in southern Sudan (Hodder 1982: 125–84) shows how different strategies involving decoration and cleanliness are used to solve 'pollution' dilemmas in male and female interaction within domestic compounds. The Nuba in general are concerned with sex pollution and each of these two tribal groups have developed particular ways of dealing with it, some of which involve architectural elements. Amongst the Moro the central courtyard – the main eating, cooking and living area – is kept clean. Amongst the Mesakin the walls of this central compound are decorated with male symbols, particularly around the entrance to the huts, the female area. In contrast to the Moro, the Mesakin courtyard is frequently covered in dung, straw and household rubbish. Hodder suggests that activities in the Mesakin courtyard are symbolically 'cleaned' by the decoration of its boundaries.

Within the eighteenth- and nineteenth-century Swahili traders' houses on the island of Lamu, off the Kenyan coast, decoration was an important device for maintaining the purity of women and to protect both sexes from defiling activities within the house (Donley 1982). Women were considered sexually polluting and, conversely, were to be kept 'pure' as the reproductive means of the elite trading class. Many lived lives of almost total seclusion within the house. The various activities involving bodily defilement – birth, death, sexual intercourse and body wastes – took place in the innermost rooms of the house (the *ndani*). In Swahili culture, objects and decoration are seen as a source of protection and purification; the front door of the house is protected by charms and carved Koranic inscriptions. A household prayer niche (women are excluded from the mosque) is also decorated and traditional houses are additionally aligned north–south on the correct direction to Mecca. The toilet pit is decorated like the prayer niche (but in contrast is constructed on an east–west axis, away from the Mecca axis) whilst the wall of the *ndani* is decorated with elaborate plaster niches and ornamented with porcelain plates.

We have already seen how the decoration of horns above the entrance to the Batammaliba house serves similar purposes in stressing a multitude of sexual and supernatural category distinctions. In south India the gates of temples are monumental as well as decorated, and are considerably larger than the central sanctuary. They are images of the *axis mundi* Mount Meru and are made of replicas of themselves (Lewandowski 1980: 130). Similarly the walls of ancient cities, according to Wheatley (1971: 435), also incorporated over-elaborate gateways.

Of course, there are no universal laws on the use and meaning of decoration. Each case must be explored within the limits of its social and historical context. In many situations, decoration may relate to different structuring principles, may change its meaning over time, or may become culturally irrelevant. A good example of the latter are the decorated houses of Pyrghi, on the Greek island of Chios (Politis 1975). Traditional houses are elaborately painted with geometric motifs on their plasterwork. At the time of fieldwork, Politis was unable to identify the original meaning and symbolism of house decoration but she noticed that the designs maintained the continuity, symmetry and unity of the village and suggested links between styles of house decoration, costume and music (ibid.: 144–6). For many villagers the significance of the decoration had gone completely and many of these traditional houses were being demolished.

To summarize, the various organizational principles involved in the social production of architecture include gender and sex pollution, kinship and moiety patterning, linking of the cosmos and the earth, and segregating individuals by age and rank and status. These may be achieved by many different mechanisms: structured oppositions, establishment of an *axis mundi* and an *imago mundi*, concentric and diametric structuring, reversal of enclosed space, homologies of body and cosmos, boundedness, decoration and cleanliness. Perhaps the simplest way of illustrating many of these principles and, most importantly, their mobilization in context, is to quote Paul Wheatley's description of Persepolis, the ancient Persian capital begun in 518 BC and sacked by Alexander in 330 BC:

> With its acres of buildings, with a reception hall open on all sides to symbolize the diffusion of divine authority to the four quarters, and its triple wall, itself symbolic but further strengthened by symbolic defensive signs and enormous supernatural figures standing guard before its gates, with its sacred groves in stone, its man-headed and lion-slaying bulls, sphinxes with paws uplifted in adoration before the Tree-of-Life, throneroom scenes, and all-pervading symbolic emblems, Persepolis constituted a magnificent demonstration of abundance, the contribution of the Persian people to the maintenance of harmony between the heavens and the earth.
>
> (Wheatley 1971: 439)

SPACE SYNTAX AND SPACE SEMANTICS

The approaches outlined so far constitute an exploration of meaning in architectural symbolism. Such an approach is concerned with semantic architectural codes (Eco 1980: 38–39). These involve denotative and connotative meanings, such as denotative functions (roof, window), and connotative functions (triumphal arch, tympanum, palace) and connotative ideologies (dining room, menstruation hut). Syntactic codes involve spatial types such as circular plan, high-rise and panopticon. Eco considered that the study of syntax and semantics should be pursued jointly but conceded that the study of purely syntactic codifications was an appropriate pursuit as well. 'Finding such codifications and defining them with precision, we might be in a better position to understand and classify, at least from the point of view of semiotics, objects whose once denoted functions can no longer be ascertained, such as the menhir, the dolmen, the Stonehenge construction' (ibid.: 35–6).

Similarly pessimistic observations on the difficulties of recovering the semantic codes, as discussed so far, were made by Mary Douglas: 'The organization of thought and of social relations is imprinted on the landscape. But, if only the physical aspect is susceptible of study, how to interpret this pattern would seem to be an insoluble problem' (Douglas 1972: 513).

The study of space syntax, along with other approaches such as architectural semiology, formal analysis, EBS (environment-building studies) and 'architectronics' have been developed (e.g. Hillier et al. 1976; Fletcher 1977;

Hillier and Hanson 1984; Rapoport 1990) and applied to archaeological situations, often with some success. Foster's (1989a; 1989b) application of network analysis to Iron Age broch settlements in Orkney, Chapman's (1991a; 1991b) study of evolving social hierarchy in south-eastern Europe in the Copper Age and Fairclough's (1992) study of the medieval castle's development are all excellent examples.[2] Preziosi's (1983) study of Minoan architectural design identifies the components and significative units which form the larger entities of the palace settlements. From a modular analysis of ground plans, he identifies the rules of Minoan spatial syntax. Glassie's (1975) study of Middle Virginian folk housing similarly identifies the rule sets for house design and their transformations over time.

Formal analysis of space syntax, however, has come in for strong criticism (Leach 1978; Hodder 1986: 39–41; Lawrence 1987: 52–3). By ignoring symbolic meanings we overlook the possibility that design structures have different meanings in different cultural contexts. The approach may also ignore differing cultural strategies of privacy regulation. Unwarranted assumptions about relative depth of space as equivalent to ease of access are implicitly made, while it rarely yields any information on the meaning and uses of specific spaces. Moreover, such analysis has been described as highly codified and mechanistic involving the systematic extraction of symbols from their historical and social context (Lawrence 1987: 48, citing Knox 1984).

Despite these reservations, there is no doubt that space syntax will continue to serve as a useful device in the archaeologist's toolkit. Recent studies (notably Fairclough's and Chapman's) indicate that, when linked to the study of meaning and context, such approaches may be very fruitful. However, it is not our concern in this volume to integrate the two approaches. Instead we will concentrate on the study of symbolism and meaning, since this approach has been regarded as nigh impossible for the archaeologist and because we consider that it is a critical area of study for understanding past architectural schemes and their transformations.

NOTES

1 Good examples are the Ainu of Sakhalin (Ohnuki-Tierney 1972), Japan (Critchlow 1975; Bognar 1989), rural China (Knapp 1986), Korea (Lee 1989), the Mongols (Humphrey 1974), Tibetan cities (Peiper 1975), Indian Hindus (Beck 1976; Khambatta 1989), the Karen (Hamilton 1987), Indonesia (Feldman 1989) including the Nage of Indonesia (Forth 1991), the Balinese (James 1973) and Java (Tjahjono 1989), Fiji (Sahlins 1976: 32–46; Tanner 1991), the Maori (Linzey 1989), the Kwakiutl and other north-west coast native Americans (Vastokas 1978), the Mistassini Cree of Canada (Tanner 1991), the Sioux (Niehardt 1961), the Pueblo culture (Saile 1985), the highland Maya (Deal 1987), the Hausa (Nicolas 1966), the Yoruba (Kamau 1976), the Iraqw (Thornton 1980), Madagascar (Feeley-Harnik 1980; Coulaud 1982; Dahl 1982; Kus 1982; Kus and Raharijaona 1990), Greece

(Pavlides and Hesser 1989), and the Saami (or Lapps) of northern Scandinavia (Yates 1989).

2 Many other applications may be found in *The Social Archaeology of Houses* (Samson 1990), *Domestic Architecture and the Use of Space – an Interdisciplinary Cross-cultural Study* (Kent 1990), *Social Space: Human Spatial Behaviour in Dwellings and Settlements* (Grøn, Engelstad and Lindblom 1991), *Engendering Archaeology: Women and Prehistory* (Gero and Conkey 1991), and in a special issue of the journal *Environment and Planning B* – renamed *Design and Planning* – (Boast and Steadman 1987).

BIBLIOGRAPHY

Altman, I. (1979) 'Privacy as an interpersonal boundary process', in M. von Cranach, K. Foppa, W. Lepenies and D. Ploog (eds), *Human Ethology: Claims and Limits of a New Discipline*, Cambridge: Cambridge University Press.

Ardener S. (ed.) (1981) *Women and Space: Ground Rules and Social Maps*, London: Croom Helm.

Barley, N. (1989) *Native Land*, London: Viking Press.

Beck, B.E.F. (1976) 'The symbolic merger of body, space, and cosmos in Hindu Tamil Nadu', contributions to *Indian Sociology* (n. s.) 10: 213–43.

Biermann, B. (1971) 'Indlu: the domed dwelling of the Zulu', in P. Oliver (ed.), *Shelter in Africa*, London: Barrie & Jenkins.

Boast, R. and Steadman, P. (eds) (1987) 'Guest editorial: analysis of building plans in history and prehistory', *Environment and Planning B: Planning and Design* 14: 359–484.

Bognar, B. (1989) 'The place of no-thingness: the Japanese house and the oriental world view of the Japanese', in J.P. Bourdier and N. Alsayyad (eds), *Dwellings, Settlements and Tradition: Cross-cultural Perspectives*, Lanham, Maryland: University Press of America.

Bourdier, J.P. and Alsayyad, N. (eds) (1989) *Dwellings, Settlements and Tradition: Cross-cultural Perspectives*, Lanham, Maryland: University Press of America.

Bourdieu, P. (1973) 'The Berber house', in M. Douglas (ed.), *Rules and Meanings*, Harmondsworth: Penguin.

Braithwaite, M. (1982) 'Decoration as ritual symbol: a theoretical proposal and an ethnographic study in southern Sudan', in I. Hodder (ed.), *Symbolic and Structural Archaeology*, Cambridge: Cambridge University Press.

Bruner, E.M. (1984) 'Introduction: the opening up of anthropology', in E.M. Bruner (ed.), *Text, Play, and Story: the Construction and Reconstruction of Self and Society*, Proceedings of the American Ethnological Society 1983: 1–16.

Buttimer, A. and Seamon, D. (eds) (1980) *The Human Experience of Space and Place*, London: Croom Helm.

Chapman, J. (1991a) 'The creation of social arenas in the Neolithic and Copper Ages of SE Europe: the case of Varna', in P. Garwood, D. Jennings, R. Skeates and J. Toms (eds), *Sacred and Preface: Proceedings of a Conference on Archaeology, Ritual and Religion*, Oxford 1989, Oxford: Oxford University Committee for Archaeology.

——(1991b) 'The early Balkan village', in O. Grøn, E. Engelstad and I. Lindblom (eds), *Social Space: Human Spatial Behaviour in Dwellings and Settlements*, Odense: Odense University Press.

Childe, V.G. (1956) *Society and Knowledge*, Westport, Conn.: Greenwood.

Clarke, W.C. (1971) *Place and People: an Ecology of a New Guinean Community*, Berkeley: University of California Press.

Cooper, C. (1974) 'The house as symbol of the self', in J. Lang, C. Burnett, W. Moleski and C. Vachon (eds), *Designing for Human Behavior*, Stroudsberg: Dowden, Hutchinson & Ross.

Coulaud, D. (1982) 'The Zafimaniry house: a witness of the traditional houses of the highlands of Madagascar', in K.G. Izikowitz and P. Sørensen (eds), *The House in East and South-east Asia*, London: Curzon.

Critchlow, K. (1975) 'Niike: the siting of a Japanese rural house', in P. Oliver (ed.), *Shelter, Sign and Symbol*, London: Barrie & Jenkins.

Csikszentmihalyi, M. and Rochberg-Halton, E. (1981) *The Meaning of Things: Domestic Symbols and the Self*, Cambridge: Cambridge University Press.

Cunningham, C.E. (1973) 'Order in the Atoni house', in R. Needham (ed.), *Right and Left: Essays on Dual Symbolic Classification*, Chicago: University of Chicago Press.

Dahl, O.C. (1982) 'The house in Madagascar', in K.G. Izikowitz and P. Sørensen (eds), *The House in East and South-east Asia*, London: Curzon.

Day, C. (1990) *Places of the Soul: Architecture and Environmental Design as a Healing Art*, Wellingborough: Aquarian Press.

Deal, M. (1987) 'Ritual space and architecture in the Highland Maya household', in D.W. Ingersoll and G. Bronitsky (eds), *Mirror and Metaphor: Material and Social Constructions of Reality*, Lanham, Maryland: University Press of America.

Donley, L.W. (1982) 'House power: Swahili space and symbolic markers', in I. Hodder (ed.), *Symbolic and Structural Archaeology*, Cambridge: Cambridge University Press.

Douglas, M. (1966) *Purity and Danger: an Analysis of the Concepts of Pollution and Taboo*, London: Routledge & Kegan Paul.

——(1972) 'Symbolic orders in the use of domestic space', in P.J. Ucko, R. Tringham and G.W. Dimbleby (eds), *Man, Settlement and Urbanism*, London: Duckworth.

Dovey, K. (1985) 'Home and homelessness', in I. Altman and C.M. Werner (eds), *Home Environments. Human Behavior and Environment: Advances in Theory and Research Vol. 8*, New York: Plenum.

Duncan, J.S. (1981) 'Introduction', in J.S. Duncan (ed.), *Housing and Identity: Cross-cultural Perspectives*, London: Croom Helm.

——(1985) 'Individual action and political power: a structuration perspective', in R.J. Johnson (ed.), *The Future of Geography and Geography in the Future*, London: Methuen.

Duncan, N.G. (1981) 'Home ownership and social theory', in J.S. Duncan (ed.), *Housing and Identity: Cross-cultural Perspectives*, London: Croom Helm.

Eco, U. (1980) 'Function and sign: the semiotics of architecture', in G. Broadbent, R. Bunt and C. Jencks (eds), *Signs, Symbols and Architecture*, Wiley: Chichester.

Eliade, M. (1959) *The Sacred and the Profane: the Nature of Religion*, New York: Harcourt, Brace and World.

Fairclough, G. (1992) 'Meaningful constructions – spatial and functional analysis of medieval buildings', *Antiquity* 66: 348–66.

Feeley-Harnik, G. (1980) 'The Sakalava house (Madagascar)', *Anthropos* 75: 559–85.

Feldman, J. (1989) 'The design of the great chief's house in South Nias, Indonesia', in J.P. Bourdier and N. Alsayyad (eds), *Dwelling, Settlements and Tradition: Cross-cultural Perspectives*, Lanham, Maryland: University Press of America.

Fletcher, R. (1977) 'Settlement studies (micro and semi-micro)', in D. Clarke (ed.), *Spatial Archaeology*, New York: Academic Press.

Forth, G. 1991. 'Nage directions: an eastern Indonesian system of spatial orientation', in O. Grøn, E. Engelstad and I. Lindblom (eds), *Social Space: Human Spatial Behaviour in Dwellings and Settlements*, Odense: Odense University

Press.

Foster, S. (1989a) 'Transformation in social space: the Iron Age of Orkney and Caithness', *Scottish Archaeological Review* 6: 34–55.

——(1989b) 'Analysis of spatial patterns in buildings (access analysis) as an insight into social structure: examples from the Scottish Atlantic Iron Age; *Antiquity* 63: 40–50.

Foucault, M. (1973) *Discipline and Punish: the Birth of the Prison*, trans. A. Sheridan, London: Tavistock.

Gero, J. and Conkey, M. (eds) (1991) *Engendering Archaeology: Women and Prehistory*, Oxford: Blackwell.

Giddens, A. (1984) *The Constitution of Society: Outline of the Theory of Structuration*, London: Polity.

Glassie, H. (1975) *Folk Housing in Middle Virginia*, Knoxville: University of Tennessee Press.

Gregory, D. and Urry, J. (1985) 'Introduction', in D. Gregory and J. Urry (eds), *Social Relations and Spatial Structures*, Basingstoke: Macmillan.

Griaule, M. (1965) *Conversations with Ogotemmili*, Oxford: Oxford University Press.

Griaule, M. and Dieterlen, G. (1954) 'The Dogon of the French Sudan', in D. Forde (ed.), *African Worlds*, Oxford: Oxford University Press.

Groves, C.P. and Sabater Pi, J. (1985) 'From ape's nest to human fix-point', *Man* 20: 22–47.

Grøn, O., Engelstad, E. and Lindblom, I. (eds) (1991) *Social Space: Human Spatial Behaviour in Dwellings and Settlements*, Odense: Odense University Press.

Hamilton, J.W. (1987) 'This old house: a Karen ideal', in D.W. Ingersoll and G. Bronitsky (eds), *Mirror and Metaphor: Material and Social Constructions of Reality*, Lanham, Maryland: University Press of America.

Hardie, G.J. (1985) 'Continuity and change in the Tswana's house and settlement form', in I. Altman and C.M. Werner (eds), *Home Environments. Human Behavior and Environment: Advances in Theory and Research Vol. 8*, New York: Plenum.

Harris, H. and Lipman, A. (1980) 'Social symbolism and space usage in daily life', *Sociological Review* 28: 415–28.

Heidegger, M. (1978) 'Building, dwelling, thinking', in M. Heidegger, *Basic Writings: from 'Being and time' (1927) to 'The task of thinking' (1964)*, trans. and ed. D.F. Krell, London: Routledge & Kegan Paul.

Hillier, B. and Hanson, J. (1984) *The Social Logic of Space*, Cambridge: Cambridge University Press.

Hillier, B., Leaman, A., Stansall, P. and Bedford, M. (1976) 'Space syntax', *Environment and Planning Series B* 3: 147–85.

Hodder, I. (1982) *Symbols in Action: Ethnoarchaeological Studies of Material culture*, Cambridge: Cambridge University Press.

——(1986) *Reading the Past: Current Approaches to Interpretation in Archaeology*, Cambridge: Cambridge University Press.

Holahan, C.J. (1978) *Environment and Behavior: a Dynamic Perspective*, New York: Plenum.

Horne, D. (1986) *The Public Culture: the Triumph of Industrialism*, London: Pluto.

Hugh-Jones, C. (1979) *From the Milk River: Spatial and Temporal Processes in North-west Amazonia*, Cambridge: Cambridge University Press.

Humphrey, C. (1974) 'Inside a Mongolian tent', *New Society* 630: 273–5.

Humphrey, N. (1984) *Consciousness Regained: Chapters in the Development of Mind*, Oxford: Oxford University Press.

Huntington, R. (1988) *Gender and Social Structure in Madagascar*, Bloomington: Indiana University Press.

James, J. (1973) 'Sacred geometry on the island of Bali', *Journal of the Royal Asiatic Society* 2: 141–54.

Kamau, L.J. (1976) 'Conceptual patterns in Yoruba culture', in A. Rapoport (ed.), *The Mutual Interaction of People and their Built Environment*, The Hague: Mouton.

Kent, S. (ed.) (1990) *Domestic Architecture and the Use of Space: an Interdisciplinary Cross-cultural Study*, Cambridge: Cambridge University Press.

Khambatta, I. (1989) 'The meaning of residence in traditional Hindu society', in J.P. Bourdier and N. Alasayyad (eds), *Dwellings, Settlements and Tradition: Cross-cultural Perspectives*, Lanham, Maryland: University Press of America.

King, A.D. (1984) *The Bungalow: the Production of a Global Culture*, London: Routledge & Kegan Paul.

Knapp, R.G. (1986) *China's Traditional and Rural Architecture: a Cultural Geography of the Common House*, Honolulu: University of Hawaii.

Knox, P. (1984) 'Symbolism, styles and settings: the built environment and the imperatives of urbanized capitalism', *Architecture and Behaviour* 2(2): 107–22.

Kus, S. (1982) 'Matters material and ideal', in I. Hodder (ed.), *Symbolic and Structural Archaeology*, Cambridge: Cambridge University Press.

——(1987) ' "The Blue Height" and the "Village of a Thousand" ', in D.W. Ingersoll and G. Bronitsky (eds), *Mirror and Metaphor: Material and Social Constructions of Reality*, Lanham, Maryland: University Press of America.

Kus, S. and Raharijaona, V. (1990) 'Domestic space and the tenacity of tradition among some Betsileo of Madagascar', in S. Kent (ed.), *Domestic Architecture and the Use of Space: an Interdisciplinary Cross-cultural Study*, Cambridge: Cambridge University Press.

Lang, R. (1985) 'The dwelling door: towards a phenomenology of transition', in D. Seamon and R. Mugerauer (eds), *Dwelling, Place and Environment: Towards a Phenomenology of Person and World*, New York: Columbia University Press.

Lawrence, D.L. and Low, S.M. (1990) 'The built environment and spatial form', *Annual Review of Anthropology* 19: 453–505.

Lawrence, R.J. (1987) *Housing, Dwellings and Homes: Design Theory, Research and Practice*, Chichester: Wiley.

——(1990) 'Public collective and private space: a study of urban housing in Switzerland', in S. Kent (ed.), *Domestic Architecture and the Use of Space: an Interdisciplinary Cross-cultural Study*, Cambridge: Cambridge University Press.

Leach, E. (1978) 'Does space syntax really "constitute the social"?', in D. Green, C. Haselgrove and M. Spriggs (eds), *Social Organization and Settlement: Contributions from Anthropology, Archaeology and Geography*, Oxford: BAR Int. Series (Suppl.) 47.

Lee, S.H. (1989) 'Siting and general organization of traditional Korean settlements', in J.P. Bourdier and N. Alsayyad (eds), *Dwellings, Settlements and Tradition: Cross-cultural Perspectives*, Lanham, Maryland: University Press of America.

Lefebvre, H. (1991) *The Production of Space*, trans. D. Nicholson-Smith, Oxford: Blackwell.

Lethaby, W. [1891] (1974) *Architecture, Mysticism and Myth*, London: The Architectural Press.

Lévi-Strauss, C. (1963) *Structural Anthropology*, trans. C. Jacobson and B.G. Schoepf, New York: Basic.

——[1955] (1973) *Tristes tropiques*, Paris: Librairie Plon, trans. J. & D. Weightman, London: Jonathan Cape.

Lewandowski, S. (1980) 'The Hindu temple in south India', in A.D. King (ed.), *Buildings and Society: Essays on the Social Development of the Built Environment*, London: Routledge & Kegan Paul.

Linzey, M. (1989) 'Speaking to and talking about: Maori architecture', in J.P. Bourdier and N. Alsayyad (eds), *Dwellings, Settlements and Tradition: Cross-cultural Perspectives*, Lanham, Maryland: University Press of America.

Littlejohn, J. (1963) 'Temne space', *Anthropological Quarterly* 36(1): 1–17.

——(1967) 'The Temne house', in J. Middleton (ed.), *Myth and Cosmos: Readings in Mythology and Symbolism*, New York: Natural History Press.

MacCormack, C. and Strathern, M. (eds) (1980) *Nature, Culture and Gender*, Cambridge: Cambridge University Press.

Marx, K. [1867] (1976) *Capital: a Critique of Political Economy. Volume 1*, Harmondsworth: Penguin.

Miller, D. (1985) 'Ideology and the Harappan civilization', *Journal of Anthropological Archaeology* 4: 34–71.

Mitchell, T. (1988) *Colonizing Egypt*, Cambridge: Cambridge University Press.

Moore, H.L. (1982) 'The interpretation of spatial patterning in settlement residues', in I. Hodder (ed.), *Symbolic and Structural Archaeology*, Cambridge: Cambridge University Press.

——(1986) *Space, Text and Gender: an Anthropological Study of the Marakwet of Kenya*, Cambridge: Cambridge University Press.

Moore, M.A. (1989) 'The Kerala house as a Hindu cosmos', *Contributions to Indian Sociology* (n.s.) 23: 169–202.

Morgan, L.H. (1881) *Houses and House-life of the American Aborigines*, Chicago: University of Chicago Press.

Myres, F.R. (1986) *Pintupi Country, Pintupi Self: Sentiment, Place, and Politics among Western Desert Aborigines*, Washington: Smithsonian Institution Press.

Nicolas, G. (1966) 'Essai sur les structures fondamentales de l'espace dans la cosmo-logie Hausa', *Journal de la Societé des Africanistes* 36: fasc. I.

Niehardt, J.G. (1961) *Black Elk Speaks: being the Life Story of a Holy Man of the Oglala Sioux*, London: Abacus.

Norberg-Schulz, C. (1971) *Existence, Space and Architecture*, London: Studio Vista.

Ohnuki-Tierney, E. (1972) 'Spatial concepts of the Ainu of the northwest coast of Southern Sakhalin', *American Anthropologist* 74: 426–57.

Okely, J. (1983) *The Traveller-Gypsies*, Cambridge: Cambridge University Press.

Oliver, P. (ed.) (1971) *Shelter in Africa*, London: Barrie & Jenkins.

——(ed.) (1975) *Shelter, Sign and Symbol*, London: Barrie & Jenkins.

——(1987) *Dwellings: the House across the World*, Oxford: Phaidon.

Omer-Cooper, J.D. (1966) *The Zulu Aftermath*, London: Longmans.

Orme, B. (1981) *Anthropology for Archaeologists*, London: Duckworth.

Ortiz, A. (1969) *The Tewa World: Space, Time, Being, and Becoming in a Pueblo Society*, Chicago; University of Chicago Press.

Pader, E.J. (1988) 'Inside spatial relations', *Architectural Behavior* 4: 251–68.

Pavlides, E. and Hesser, J. (1989) 'Sacred space, ritual and the traditional Greek house', in J.P. Bourdier and N. Alasayyad (eds), *Dwellings, Settlements and Tradition: Cross-cultural Perspectives*, Lanham, Maryland: University Press of America.

Peiper, J. (1975) 'Three cities of Nepal', in P. Oliver (ed.), *Shelter, Sign and Symbol*, London: Barrie & Jenkins.

Perin, C. (1977) *Everything in its Place: Social Order and Land Use in America*, Princeton: Princeton University Press.

Politis, E. (1975) 'Decorated houses of Pyrghi, Chios', in P. Oliver (ed.), *Shelter,*

Sign and Symbol, London: Barrie & Jenkins.

Pollard, H.P. (1991) 'The construction of ideology in the emergence of the prehispanic Tarascan state', *Ancient Mesoamerica* 2: 167–79.

Pratt, G. (1981) 'The house as an expression of social worlds', in J.S. Duncan (ed.), *Housing and Identity: Cross-cultural Perspectives*, London: Croom Helm.

Preston Blier, S. (1987) *The Anatomy of Architecture: Ontology and Metaphor in Batammaliba Architectural Expression*, Cambridge: Cambridge University Press.

Preziosi, D. (1983) *Minoan Architectural Design: Formation and Signification*, Berlin: Mouton.

Raglan, A. (1964) *The Temple and the House*, London: Routledge & Kegan Paul.

Rapoport, A. (1969) *House Form and Culture*, Englewood Cliffs: Prentice-Hall.

——(1980) 'Vernacular architecture and the cultural determinants of form', in A.D. King (ed.), *Buildings and Society: Essays on the Social Development of the Built Environment*, London: Routledge & Kegan Paul.

——(1982) *The Meaning of the Built Environment: a Non-verbal Communication Approach*, Beverley Hills: Sage.

——(1990) *History and Precedent in Environmental Design*, New York: Plenum.

Relph, E. (1976) *Place and Placelessness*, London: Pion.

Sahlins, M. (1976) *Culture and Practical Reason*, Chicago: University of Chicago Press.

Saile, D.G. (1985) 'Many dwellings: views of a Pueblo world', in D. Seamon and R. Mugerauer (eds), *Dwelling, Place and Environment: Towards a Phenomenology of Person and World*, New York: Columbia University Press.

Samson, R. (ed.) (1990) *The Social Archaeology of Houses*, Edinburgh: Edinburgh University Press.

Seamon, D. (1980) 'Body-subject, time-space routines, and place-ballets', in A. Buttimer and D. Seamon (eds), *The Human Experience of Space and Place*, London: Croom Helm.

Seamon, D. and Mugerauer, R. (eds) (1985) *Dwelling, Place and Environment: Towards a Phenomenology of Person and World*, New York: Columbia University Press.

Sircar, K. (1987) 'The house as a symbol of identity', in D.W. Ingersoll and G. Bronitsky (eds), *Mirror and Metaphor: Material and Social Constructions of Reality*, Lanham, Maryland: University Press of America.

Tambiah, S.J. (1969) 'Animals are good to think and good to prohibit', *Ethnology* 8: 423–59.

——(1985) *Culture, Thought, and Social Action: an Anthropological Perspective*, Cambridge, Mass.: Harvard University Press.

Tanner, A. (1991) 'Spatial organization in social formation and symbolic action: Fijian and Canadian examples', in O. Grøn, E. Engelstad and I. Lindblom (eds), *Social Space: Human Spatial Behaviour in Dwellings and Settlements*, Odense: Odense University Press.

Thornton, R.J. (1980) *Space, Time and Culture among the Iraqw of Tanzania*, New York: Academic Press.

Tjahjono, G. (1989) 'Centre and duality in the Javanese dwelling', in J.P. Bourdier and N. Alsayyad (eds), *Dwellings, Settlements and Tradition: Cross-cultural Perspectives*, Lanham, Maryland: University Press of America.

Tuan, Y.F. (1974) *Topophilia: a Study of Environmental Perception, Attitudes, and Values*, Englewood Cliffs: Prentice-Hall.

——(1977) *Space and Place: the Perspective of Experience*, London: Edward Arnold.

van Beek, W.E.A. (1991) 'Dogon restudied: a field evaluation of the work of Marcel Griaule', *Current Anthropology* 32: 139–67.

Vastokas, J.M. (1978) 'Cognitive aspects of Northwest Coast art', in M. Greenhaugh and J.V.S. Megaw (eds), *Art in Society*, London: Duckworth.

Wheatley, P. (1971) *The Pivot of the Four Quarters: a Preliminary Enquiry into the Origins and Character of the Ancient Chinese City*, Edinburgh: Edinburgh University Press.

Witherspoon, G. (1977) *Language and Art in the Navajo Universe*, Ann Arbor: University of Michigan.

Yates, T. (1989) 'Habitus and social space: some suggestions about meaning in the Saami (Lapp) tent ca. 1700–1900', in I. Hodder (ed.), *The Meanings of Things: Material Culture and Symbolic Expression*, London: Unwin Hyman.

Zimmerman, M.E. (1985) 'The role of spiritual discipline in learning to dwell on earth', in D. Seamon and R. Mugerauer (eds) *Dwelling, Place and Environment: Towards a Phenomenology of Person and World*, New York: Columbia University Press.

2

ARCHITECTURE AND ORDER: SPATIAL REPRESENTATION AND ARCHAEOLOGY

Mike Parker Pearson and Colin Richards

By now, it should be apparent to the archaeologist that the structuring of space incorporates cosmological and symbolic principles in many situations. The problem lies in their detection and recovery without textual or iconographic representations, or at least with only minimal sources other than material remains alone. For some, the attempt to move from post-holes to symbolic orders is simply too difficult. Undoubtedly, the quality of evidence, as embodied in the variety of available contexts and degree of preservation, is very important. But the exploration of early historical and even prehistoric cosmologies is by no means too daunting. There has already been a number of archaeological studies of architecture and classification, cosmological and social. Some have drawn on written sources and others have relied solely on artefactual evidence.[1] The study of ancient city-states, such as China, Rome, and Egypt, relies on textual evidence which is otherwise unavailable to the prehistorian. From integrated analysis of cosmology as inscribed in religious texts and fixed in architecture, we may be able to recover symbolic meaning to some degree. The following examples present some broad indicators of ancient cosmologies. We will turn later to the difficulties and possibilities of interpreting prehistoric cosmologies, by taking two case studies, one from the Neolithic of Orkney and the other from the Iron Age in southern Britain.

The symbolism of the ancient Chinese town is encapsulated in microcosm in building tiles, such as those of the Han dynasty (Chang 1983: 21). Their square shape and cardinal directions (each linked to four directional animals) are duplicated in town layouts. An approximately square perimeter was delimited by a massive wall. At the centre of a series of cardinal alignments and axes was the palace, 'the pivot of the four quarters'.

> The capital of Shang was a city of cosmic order
> The pivot of the four quarters.
> Glorious was its renown,
> Purifying its divine power,

Manifested in longevity and tranquility
And the protection of us who came after.
(Ancient poem quoted in Wheatley 1971: 450)

The ancient Roman city possessed an elaborate and geometrical structure (Rykwert 1976). The foundation of Rome was permanently enshrined in monuments which anchored commemorative rituals to place. For example, Rykwert illustrates how the Temple of Vesta served as a 'focus', or symbolic hearth, for the whole city. The orthogonal city grid was based on the order of the universe with its four cardinal directions. Left was north and right was south; behind was west. The *decumani* streets were set in line with the sun's axis and the *cardines* followed the axis of the pole star. The term *cardo* means 'axis', 'axle', 'hinge' or 'pole' (ibid.: 91). For the Roman city, the boundaries, traditionally marked by the ploughing of a furrow, were sacred. The gateways, though protected by the two-faced god Janus, did not share the same untouchable sacredness. Rykwert also considered the Roman military camp to be a diagrammic representation of the city of Rome (ibid.: 68), and camp construction was a ceremonial act. Although notionally arranged on a cardinal grid, the orientation of camps and forts was flexible and often dictated by the lie of the land.

For the Ancient Egyptians of the third and second millennia BC the social order was part of the cosmic order, described as *maat*. Within the recurring movements of the heavens and the Nile, the Egyptians lived their lives in an established and unchanging order. In the unusual landscape of the Nile valley the Egyptian cosmos was written into the natural topography and given explicit form in the pyramids and temples. It was a rigidly symmetrical conception with a vault of heaven above and an underworld or counterheaven beneath the earth. The cardinal directions were embodied in sacred architecture, with the sides of the pyramids aligned on each direction with great accuracy, often deviating only by tiny fractions of a degree (Edwards 1947: 208–9). The royal dead were buried on the west bank of the Nile, the direction of the dying sun. Left was east and right west, since the Egyptians were 'australized' (facing towards south) towards the source of the Nile, the bringer of fertility. The east was the place of the sun's rebirth; the funerary temples attached to the pyramids were located on their eastern sides. All of the pyramid tombs had entrances from the north side; their ramps supposedly inclined towards the pole star, around which circled the 'eternal' stars (Frankfort et al. 1946: 42–8). There is evidence for conflicting cosmologies within the official doctrines. For example, the people of north Egypt may have placed more emphasis on the east than on the south.

In Egyptian cosmology, in the beginning, out of the waters of chaos rose the primordial mound. This 'landscape of the first time' was modelled again and again in the architecture. The pyramids were re-creations of the mound, and all temples and shrines included slopes or steps advancing upwards towards their sacred centres. Each temple constituted a primeval mound of the 'first time'. The oldest place was considered to be Hermopolis, the centre of all ideas about the origin of the world. Lotus and papyrus were essential constituents of this unchanging 'first time' and were modelled in stone as columns and roof supports (Frankfort 1948b: 150–6). Temple designs were elaborated from relatively simple forms with a long axis, leading through a series of halls and courts to the focal point, the sanctuary containing the image of the god (Morenz 1960: 86–7). The architectural impact of these structures is profound. According to Frankfort, they 'express, with unanswerable finality, the ancient Egyptian's conviction that his universe was a world without change' (Frankfort 1948a: 156).

Moving closer to the present, the ideologies articulating medieval urban space have been explored to some extent in Redman's analysis of the fortified town of Qsar es Seghir in Morocco (Redman 1986). Here, a Muslim settlement was replaced by a Portuguese colony in AD 1458. Although the general layout remained unchanged, the Portuguese transformed the town. They emphasized public space, in the larger area devoted to streets and plazas, in the paving of public places, in the decor of public buildings, and in the decoration of doorways and windows. In contrast to Islamic houses, Portuguese interiors were poorly decorated, and had few sanitary facilities. Islamic houses centred on a courtyard and were relatively secluded, maintaining a clear boundary with the outside world, in contrast to the gradual 'privacy gradient' of Portuguese houses with their commercial facilities at their streetfronts. Such differences in seclusion reinforced different notions of community and gender interaction; the Islamic population were more communal, focused on the house and its activities, and centralized, whilst the Portuguese were more competitive, individualistic and less constraining on the social roles and domains of women. Redman's analysis is particularly interesting because he integrates the architectural evidence with other archaeological materials, such as tablewares, decoration, and personal artefacts (ibid.: 240–7).

One of the main goals of this volume is to demonstrate how architecture embodies and expresses certain principles of order and classification. As a constructed cultural space it is a defined context where people undertake particular activities at particular times. People move through its confines and do things at appropriate places. Hence, meaning is realized through social practices. Such contingency allows a redefinition of space without necessarily altering its physical properties. For the archaeologist, the reflexive nature of material culture, as revealed in the potential changes of spatial meaning within any given architectural form, is clearly problematic. However, we feel this does not represent an insurmountable obstacle and offer two short archaeological case studies which examine architecture and order in a social context.

ORCADIAN HOUSES IN THE BRITISH LATE NEOLITHIC[2]

The Orkney Isles lie off the most northern tip of the British mainland. The archaeological evidence which characterizes the Neolithic period of Orkney is the presence of a number of well-constructed stone buildings and monuments. These include houses often clustered in 'villages', passage graves, and henge monuments enclosing large stone circles. Perhaps the most extraordinary aspect of these constructions is the use of the local, easily laminated, sandstone slabs both to create extremely sophisticated masonry and as furniture and partitioning within the structures: hence the almost perfect survival of the most famous Neolithic settlement in Britain, Skara Brae.

The dwellings constitute the most remarkable architectural evidence as late Neolithic houses are virtually unknown in other areas of Britain. The Orcadian examples display a consistency of design which is maintained over several hundred years. The internal organization of stone furniture is a central square stone-built hearth, a rear shelving arrangement, known as a dresser, and two rectangular stone boxes, interpreted as box-beds, situated on either side of the hearth. The single entrance is positioned opposite the dresser thereby forming a cruciform pattern with the spatial organization of the house interior. These structural elements are present within all houses. In each case the internal organization of space defined by the cruciform arrangement of dresser/doorway: right-box/left-box is referenced to and around the central hearth. There is a striking homogeneity in the architecture of the late Neolithic house.

The central positioning of the hearth establishes a commanding focal point which, in the Northern Isles, appears to have been maintained over several millennia. In the inhospitable northern climate the fire, and by extension the fireplace, is central to the maintenance of life itself. Indeed, until recently in the Northern Isles one of the gravest acts of neglect within the home was to allow the fire to go out; many fires had reputedly been kept alight for over forty years. Such attitudes would probably have been as pervasive in the Neolithic period as they are today.

Fire, as a medium of transformation, is not restricted to producing heat and light; it also facilitates the change in food from raw to cooked and hardens clay into pottery. From this point of view it is easy to understand the consistent association of fire with supernatural and mythological qualities (e.g. Lévi-Strauss 1986). In many societies there is always an element of danger attached to fire and numerous sanctions surround its use. This extends both to ignition (e.g. Ingold 1986: 268–71) and the collection and disposal of ash (e.g. Moore 1986: 102–6). In attempting to assess the significance of the hearth in the Neolithic dwelling it may be suggested that its centrality transcended functional necessity, and that the fireplace embodied many disparate meanings as may be expected in such a dominant symbol.

The importance of the fireplace in the late Neolithic is reinforced by the evidence from the houses excavated at Barnhouse, Stenness, Mainland, where the careful laying out and assembly of the square stone hearth clearly constituted the primary act of house construction. Under these circumstances it is quite likely that construction rituals would have been centred on the hearth and the lighting of the first fire heavily sanctioned. Its alignment dictated the internal organization of the stone furniture and the orientation of the dwelling. Moreover, when houses were abandoned or demolished the hearth stones were frequently left in place.

Despite an apparent symmetry in the house interior, the entrance is frequently offset to the right. A closer examination of the stone furniture within the houses reveals that the right 'box-bed' is consistently larger than the left. This distinction is mirrored in the size of the ambry or keeping place positioned above each bed. How are these differences best understood?

The position of the doorway would appear to facilitate entry into the right side of the house. This interpretation is supported by the presence of a line of entrance slabs leading into the right side of House 7 (Figure 2.1) at the settlement of Skara Brae (Childe 1931), and by the entrance leading into the right side of House 2 at Barnhouse (Richards 1990a). Indeed, in both the above examples, strong architectural measures are introduced to ensure that on admittance the subject does not enter the left side of the house interior. Nowhere is this more clearly demonstrated than in the internal organization of House 2 at Barnhouse which is effectively a conjunction of two cruciform houses. This dual spatial arrangement is not restricted to buildings for the living but is also apparent within the 'houses for the dead' as at the passage grave at Quanterness. A clearer understanding of the spatial structure of House 2 at Barnhouse is provided by reconstructing the path of movement, which is strictly controlled by a combination of walling and partitioning (Figure 2.2). Here, access to the left area is denied until the subject has been directed to the far side of the house and there forced to turn left. This passage has entailed walking between two posts flanking a large slab, covering a pit containing a burial, which must be stepped over. On turning left the interior organization of House 2 becomes comprehensible since the view now presented is one of re-entry, from right of centre, into an inner area displaying the familiar cruciform architectural representation.

The consistent reproduction of right-hand entry may be related to wider social categories. For instance, on crossing the threshold into the Neolithic house, it would be the right-hand side of the internal spatial arrangement which would become visible, illuminated by light coming through the doorway. The left side would remain in semi-darkness. Thus, by design, the varying quality of light available to the interior highlights the path of movement of people entering the house. As will be shown later, these differences are part of a much broader symbolic system of classifications which includes light and darkness.

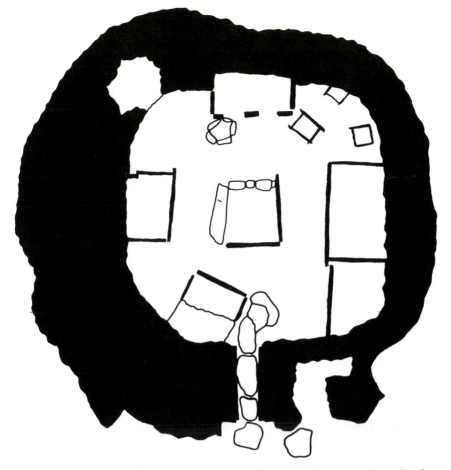

Figure 2.1 House 7 at Skara Brae showing the direction of access as shown by the entrance paving

How may we relate the nuances of entry to the difference in size of the stone furniture within the house? It will be noticed that the spatial balance of the house interior alters when someone enters into the right-hand area. Access therefore produces a spatial shift whereby the 'back' area of the house occupied by the dresser no longer constitutes the deepest space. By virtue of the appropriate path of movement inside the house, leading into the right-hand area, the deepest space is now situated in the left area of the house. The architectural elements of the Neolithic house may be essentially static but they are also the framework for a symbolic organization which reveals itself through human agency, in this example through the movement of the subject within the house interior. The spatial organization may be an

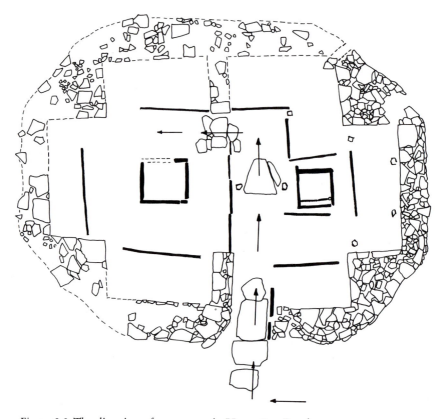

Figure 2.2 The direction of movement in House 2 at Barnhouse

ideal structure of order based on cosmological themes; human activity within the domestic space is directed by the architectural arrangements, but the architecture is itself a product of cosmology. Human action and environment form parts of a symbolic structure in which each affects and reflects the other. In certain social circumstances different aspects of this symbolic structure will be drawn on, thereby providing ontological status to everyday actions. The discrepancy in bed sizes may relate to distinctions of function, age, or gender within a left/right division of space which is realized only in specific social situations.

Analysis of the late Neolithic settlement of Barnhouse (Richards, in prep.) reveals that different practices occurred in different houses. The hearth, however, appears frequently to have been tended and cleaned out from the left, as revealed by spreads of charcoal and burnt material trodden into the floor. High levels of phosphate in close proximity to the hearth on the left-hand side are recognizable in some houses, suggesting areas of food preparation. Traditionally, in Orkney, it has been the woman's duty to tend the fire and prepare food on a daily basis, and whether or not we accept Childe's view that the disparity in box-bed size is attributable to gender, it seems likely that the left-hand area represented an inner domain associated with both domestic reproduction and women. This area would have been concealed in semi-darkness to anyone entering the house; their view of the interior would have been confined to the right side and rear dresser.

For certain family members, particularly women, everyday life in the house would have been constituted through a sequence of activities occurring either within the house or in the outside world. A series of tasks undertaken within spheres of temporality situated people at specific places. Each of these tasks was undertaken in the 'correct' place and through their employment spatial meaning was recreated. Hence, within a single temporal cycle such as a day, spatial meaning within the house and settlement would constantly have been redefined. The shift in activities from within the house to the settlement necessarily involved changes in the spheres of social discourse. Interestingly, it is possible to interpret the spatial organization of the late Neolithic settlements, such as Barnhouse, as a homology of the house, in which an open central area provided the context of fire and material transformation. Many tasks including pottery manufacture, bone tool production and secondary flint flaking were undertaken within this central area, mainly in its western confines. Again these activities may have been undertaken by women. As within the house, the symbolic definition of space was not static but contingent on different social practices and was therefore in a constant state of flux.

A good example of such redefinition within a house of similar spatial organization is the Blackhouse of the Scottish Western Isles. Indeed, it was to the Blackhouse that Childe (1931: 183; 1946: 32) turned for ethnographic parallels to the Orcadian late Neolithic houses. When the family was together in the Blackhouse, a frequent occurrence during the long dark nights of the northern Scottish winter, the left side of the house was associated with the woman and it was here that she prepared food and undertook the majority of her work. The right-hand side was the domain of the man and similarly the place where he attended to different tasks and activities. However, this left/right distinction was replaced by a back/front division on other social occasions, such as the invitation of a guest into the house. The status of the guest was defined in the position offered around the central fireplace, by its proximity to the most distinguished position directly behind the hearth and facing the entrance (Clarke and Sharples 1985: 70).

Having stressed the importance of the spatial organization of the house as a microcosm of the socially constructed world and the necessary links with wider spatial and temporal cycles, a broader understanding must be sought in terms of symbolic classifications. At this point, orientation and directionality may be introduced. It is suggested that the cruciform arrangement of the house relates to four Neolithic cardinal directions centred on the hearth.

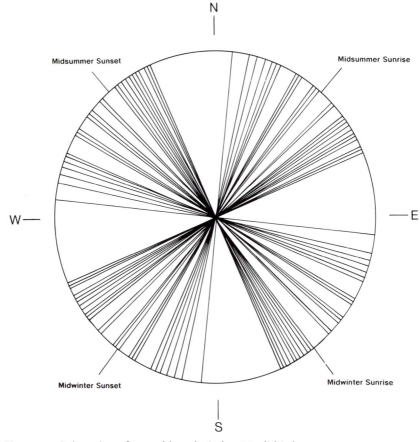

Figure 2.3 Orientation of central hearths in late Neolithic houses

An examination of the entrance orientation of houses at the villages of Barnhouse, Skara Brae and Rinyo reveals that 80 per cent lie on a north-west/south-east axis. This characteristic is also identifiable in the entrance orientation of Orcadian 'Maeshowe' passage graves. Returning to the houses, a larger sample number is obtained if the alignment of individual hearths is examined, since frequently the hearth remains *in situ* when the rest of the house is demolished or destroyed. Because of the square shape of the hearths, the orientations will always relate to the four elements within the house interior (dresser, door and two beds). It is clear that the hearth maintains a uniformity of orientation (Figure 2.3), and the significance of these directions becomes more apparent when midwinter and midsummer sunrise and sunset are considered. Here we recognize a fusion of space and time embodied within the architecture of the house. Each element in the cruciform organization is a spatial referent to the key points in the annual cycles which govern both the agricultural cycle and social practices.

The link between principles of order, as shown in architecture, and broader classifications, is clearly demonstrated within the passage grave of Maeshowe. Here a monument of the dead is oriented south-west, towards the setting midwinter sun which illuminates the interior of the tomb, marking the height of winter and the darkest day of the year. In the northern latitudes of Orkney there exists a marked contrast between the eighteen hours of sunshine at midsummer and eighteen hours of darkness at midwinter. An association between death and a westerly direction may appear unsurprising, and in the architecture of the passage grave we see the selection and emphasis of certain categories pertaining to the 'house' of the dead: south-west, midwinter, darkness, cold and death. Most tombs, however, have east-facing entrances. In contrast to Maeshowe, movement into the tomb is from east to west. In terms of the homology between house and tomb, the innermost recess corresponds to the left side of the house.

Just like human action, classifications are not static but only take on concrete expression in certain places at certain times. Thus, while the architecture of Maeshowe marks the depth of winter, the sun's illumination of the inside heralds the beginning of a new cycle of regeneration.

The categories of order inherent within the architecture of the late Neolithic house in Orkney formed part of wider symbolic classifications embracing many spheres of meaning. Such meanings could only be mobilized through social practices. Not only did the undertaking of different activities at particular places within the house draw on this symbolism, but also the religious or cosmological principles of order which underlay its organization provided an ontological status to those actions which inevitably involved authority and dominance. In the late Neolithic period of Orkney we can clearly recognize the reflexive nature and power of architecture.

THE ROUNDHOUSE IN LATER BRITISH PREHISTORY[3]

The second archaeological case study provides a different emphasis on architectural representation in examining the maintenance of a particular house form over a period of 1,200 years. The round house was the typical house form in Britain from the middle Bronze Age through to the late Iron Age. From the late Bronze Age onwards, entrances were oriented predominantly to the east (Figure 2.4) and more precisely to the direction of sunrise at the equinoxes and midwinter (Oswald 1991). This east–west structuring of space within houses and enclosures was also linked to classifications of men and women, domestic tasks and animal species (Parker Pearson, forthcoming). Despite these long-term structural continuities, architectural changes through time and context effected a subtle alteration in spatial organization and symbolic content.

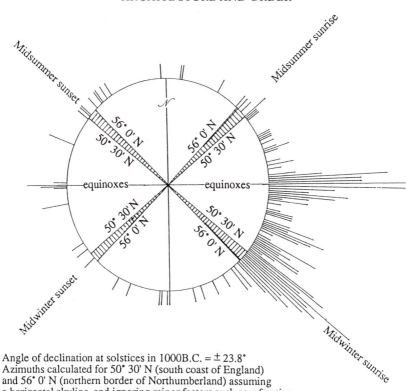

Angle of declination at solstices in 1000B.C. = ± 23.8°
Azimuths calculated for 50° 30' N (south coast of England)
and 56° 0' N (northern border of Northumberland) assuming
a horizontal skyline, and ignoring minor factors such as refraction

Figure 2.4 Round house doorway orientation in relation to cardinal solar directions
in Iron Age Britain (from Oswald 1991, by kind permission of the author)

In contrast to the Orkney study which emphasized the importance and permanence of the hearth, it is the entrance to the house during the first millennium BC which is most solidly marked, suggesting its status as a prime element in house form. The hearth will undoubtedly have held significance because of its central role in providing heat and cooked food. However, as Hill (forthcoming) has noted, it tends to be physically more ephemeral than the threshold. The position of an entrance dictates orientation and in the Iron Age houses it is frequently elaborated through the provision of a porch. Further emphasis on the threshold might be given by the placing of foundation deposits there. At the settlement of Haddenham the door posts were marked during construction by the deposition of sheep carcasses (C. Evans, pers. comm.; Boast and Evans 1986; Evans and Serjeantson 1988).

A number of houses demonstrate an axial symmetry between the doorway and the rear, thus emphasizing the east–west orientation (Guilbert 1982). To what extent this division was realized in practices within the house is unknown since the floors were generally kept clean. However, at

Longbridge Deverell Cow Down, where an early Iron Age house was destroyed by fire, the right (south) side contained large quantities of occupational debris while the left (north) side was clean and devoid of artefacts (Chadwick 1958). The dominance of the east–west axis extends beyond the confines of the dwelling. The vast majority of settlement enclosures have their entrance or entrances on an east–west alignment. Directionality will almost certainly be part of wider classifications which necessarily involve auspicious and inauspicious qualities. In this light it is interesting to note that when enclosures vary their entrance alignment away from the east–west to a north–south axis, they contain either no evidence of occupation (Bell 1977), or unusual pit deposits (Smith 1977; J.D. Hill, pers. comm.).

Evidence for variability in the use of round houses of the middle Bronze Age is restricted to a group of southern British settlements, comprising small clusters of houses at Blackpatch, Itford Hill and Thorny Down (Burstow and Holleyman 1957; Ellison 1978; 1987; Drewett 1982) which tend to be located on south-facing hillsides. The entrances of these houses are oriented to the south and south-south-east, in contrast to the houses of the late Bronze Age and Iron Age (Oswald 1991). Within these settlements certain houses are differentiated on the basis of internal features and material remains and these distinctions have been interpreted in terms of grain storage, food production and consumption (e.g. Barrett 1989). At Blackpatch the architectural and artefactual differences between houses have been tentatively interpreted as representing a division in labour and residence between men and women (Drewett 1982: 342).

In eastern England a series of late Bronze Age enclosed settlements have been discovered mainly in the Thames basin (Champion 1980), but also as far north as Yorkshire (Manby 1986). These settlements comprise a number of post-built round houses and exhibit a high precision of form in the circular geometry of the enclosure. Reference and orientation is provided through single or dual entrances on an east–west alignment. However, at Springfield Lyons, the apparent spatial balance created by the provision of two entrances is altered through the monumentality of the eastern gateway (Buckley and Hedges 1988). Access was also obtained through the less formal west entrance and possibly across several small causeways over the ditch (N. Brown, pers. comm.). The selection of the eastern gateway as the most prominent entrance suggests that this was deemed, in a formal sense, the correct line of approach and movement. Under these circumstances the use of a porch to enhance the central round house's eastern entrance creates a homology with the whole enclosure's organization.

As with the earlier settlements of the Middle Bronze Age, food production and consumption was spatially defined at Springfield Lyons. Food preparation and craft production occur in the south-west quadrant where a midden and smaller round house structure are situated. The central house has a series of pits in its western (inner) area, containing primary refuse of

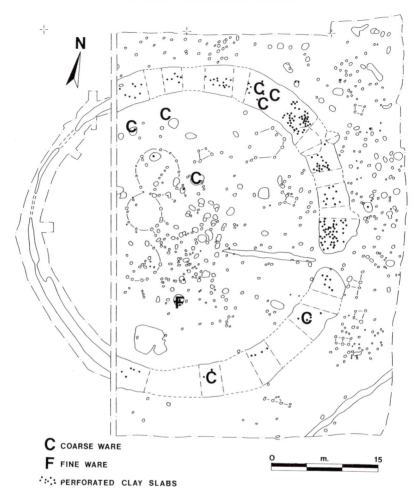

N

C COARSE WARE
F FINE WARE
: PERFORATED CLAY SLABS

0   m.   15

Figure 2.5 Plan of the North Ring, Mucking (after Bond and Jones 1988, redrawn by Colin Merrony)

fine-ware ceramics, suggesting that this was the context for food consumption.

Two circular late Bronze Age enclosures have been excavated nearby at Mucking, Essex. Little is known of the southern enclosure but the North Ring enclosure is well documented (Bond and Jones 1988). Like Springfield Lyons, this enclosure has opposed entrances with the main access at the east and an apparently minor entrance, which was later blocked, situated in the west (Figure 2.5). The interior of the enclosure, however, is structured quite differently from that at Springfield Lyons. A large wooden screen, running north–south, divides the enclosure into a clean and open front half and a

Figure 2.6 Reconstruction drawing of the North Ring enclosure in the late Bronze Age (by kind permission of Peter Dunn)

back area of pits, scoops and houses (Figure 2.6). The eastern half, clear of habitation, was traversed by a well-worn path from the main entrance to a gap in a large wooden screen. Beyond this monumental facade were three round houses; each house interior was similarly divided into an eastern and western area by a wooden screen. As at Springfield Lyons, the architecture of the enclosure forms a homology with the internal organization of the houses, where a front/back distinction was also enforced. Again, food preparation and consumption were spatially defined: the northern round house was associated with primary refuse from storage and cooking and the southern house with fine wares for serving food.

Different principles of classification are clearly expressed in the architecture of the late Bronze Age sites. However, certain daily activities are consistently differentiated within the enclosures. Middens and cooking areas are frequently at the 'back' or 'rear' and therefore conceptually 'out of sight'. Hence, anyone taking the correct path of movement, that is approaching the dwelling from the east, does not encounter refuse or cooking activities. If approach and presentation are important in formal occasions, it is interesting

51

to relate the temporal and spatial graduation inherent in the movement of the subject from east to west to other temporal cycles, such as the human life cycle or the passage of food through the human body. The consistent placing of the midden, a place of decay and transformation, in the west may enforce this conceptual scheme.

The maintenance of a basic spatial segregation of food storage, preparation and craft activities from the areas where food was consumed continued in the early Iron Age in the form of the two-house unit. This culinary division between round houses is found in the early Iron Age enclosure at Winnall Down (Fasham 1985). The kite-shaped enclosure contained some eight recognizable round-houses, not all contemporary. The excavators defined four activity areas: a living and weaving area, a second living unit perhaps with butchery and crop processing, an area of bone working and an area of houses and activities of unidentifiable nature (ibid.: 127–30). The enclosure was divided into northern and southern areas by an open space running from the west entrance to the north-east corner (Figure 2.7). The distribution of fine furrowed bowls shows two concentrations: one in the western ditch close to House E and a second on the east side associated with House K (ibid.: fig. 84f). The later fine ware – cordoned bowls – came from the open areas of the enclosure in the centre and north-east corner. The larger storage pits were grouped in two areas: in the north, adjacent to Houses F and G, and the south, adjacent to Houses I and J. The distribution of loom weights was also restricted to these two areas (ibid.: fig. 84d). Finally, the highest densities of animal bone fragments were recovered from the vicinity of Houses F, G, I, and J (ibid.: fig. 84a).

These examples exhibit patterns of spatial segregation for particular activities within a consistent dualistic structure. In the middle Iron Age in southern Britain this structure appears to have broken down and three important changes occurred. First, round houses increased in size and the differentiation of activities noted for the earlier periods took on a new definition. Second, some settlements were arranged as linear strings of houses although, as we will see, the tradition of enclosed settlement continued. Third, a more profound emphasis on settlement nucleation (Bradley 1984: 140) and external definition through enclosure, as demonstrated by the Wessex hillforts, seems to have negated the need for directional conformity of house entrances within the hillfort enclosures.

Hillfort boundaries at this time were now emphasized by elaborate defences (Bowden and McOmish 1987) and by deposits at the entranceways (Hill, forthcoming). The aggrandized house porches and exaggerated eaves-drip gullies around round houses (Boast and Evans 1986) also served to isolate and bound household units. The change toward enhanced 'enclosure' of both single round houses and hillforts may be linked to an emphasis on single units, with differentiation and variation of activities contained *internally*. For individual round houses, this may have been linked to changes in

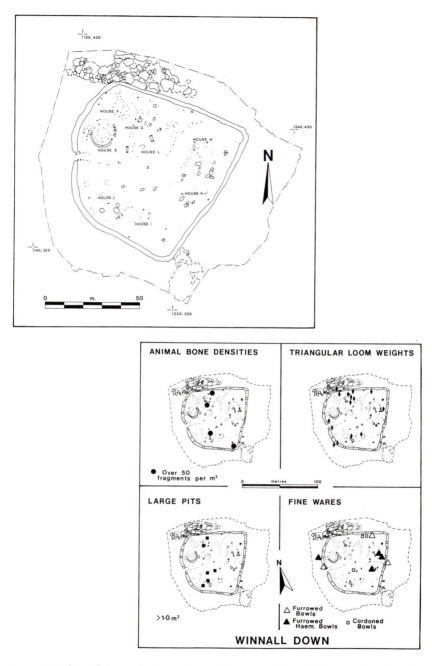

Figure 2.7 Plan of the early Iron Age enclosure at Winnall Down, showing the distributions of particular artefacts and features (after Fasham 1985, redrawn by Colin Merrony)

kinship (Barrett 1989). In the organization of hillforts, we may be witnessing changes in modes of political authority (Bradley 1984: 139–44). Within the hillforts, the eastern orientation of round house doors was replaced by an arrangement where most entrances faced towards the centre of the hillfort (Cunliffe 1984); the hillfort was now the referent, the *axis mundi*. At both levels, therefore, we can see changes in the classification of people, things and the world. This purposeful manipulation of cosmological principles brought concerns with 'place' and the localized control of space and people to the forefront. The transformation of space embodied in the construction of larger and more clearly defined round houses constituted a fundamental element in this process of change. The activities surrounding food preparation, craft production and consumption, which in the late Bronze Age and early Iron Age maintained spatial segregation, were now encapsulated within a single space (Hingley 1990: 128–35). Only the contexts of grain storage and middening remained outside the house. Space may have been concentrically ordered within the round house (Cunliffe 1978: 175; Hingley 1990), with the main household tasks being undertaken in the central 'public' area, defined in certain houses by an internal ring of timbers, and other activities, such as sleeping and food storage, located in the more 'private' outer area.

Amongst these changes, certain structuring principles remained unchanged. Special deposits of animal carcasses within settlements indicate that pig offerings were often restricted to the western halves of settlement areas. In contrast, cattle and sheep offerings were made in the eastern areas. Food offerings of meat were sometimes placed with the dead. In Wessex, pig bones were associated with the burial of women (and only those oriented to the north or west) whilst cattle bones were placed with the corpses of men. Such patterns were regional within Britain; in Yorkshire pig bones were placed with the corpses of both men and women, whereas cattle bones were never included as food for the dead (Parker Pearson, forthcoming).

ORIGINS AND EVOLUTIONS OF ARCHITECTURE

The idea of the first house ever built has enchanted artists, architects, philosophers and psychologists as well as archaeologists. There is a plethora of 'just so' myths of origins and development. Some of these narrative mythologies are worth examination since they have influenced the assumptions and thoughts of everyone concerned with the built environment and its changes.

According to Sigmund Freud, the first three acts of civilization were the manufacture of tools, the making of fire and the construction of a dwelling (cited in Wilson 1988: 180). For Freud the need for shelter, a womb substitute, was unquestioned and instinctual. As Wilson has indicated, the archaeological (and ethnographic) evidence suggests otherwise. From studies of gatherer-hunter groups such as the !Kung of the Kalahari desert or many of the groups of Australian Aborigines, it seems the requirement for a 'roof over our heads' is not a universal principle for the human species. The notion of the house as essential for basic economic needs (Clark 1952: 129) can also be dismissed on such evidence. For Raglan (1964) houses were originally neither shelters nor dwellings but temples. More recently, Highlands (1990: 55) has echoed this view that perhaps the most compelling reason for building is religious and has suggested that Girard's (1977) theory for the origin of sacrifice, deriving from an original murder, may also be applicable to the origins of building. From the studies we have looked at so far, none of these is likely to be true. Rapoport commented on the theory of religious origin as follows: 'It is one thing to say that the dwelling has symbolic and cosmological aspects . . . and another to say that it has been erected for ritual purposes and is neither shelter nor dwelling but a temple' (Rapoport 1969: 40). Part of the problem is undoubtedly the modern perception of clear distinctions between symbol and function, and religious and secular aspects of life.

The return to origins has been a regular theme of architectural theory over the last few centuries. Rykwert (1972: 190–2) has suggested that the primitive hut, situated in an idealized past, has become a paradigm of building, enshrined in ritual and myth. He interprets these returns to origin as a rethinking of customary practices and attempts to validate or renew everyday actions. For Le Corbusier, the 'primitive builder' operated by the light of instinct guided by reason, so that the builders' uncontaminated expression was in tune with the fundamental laws of creation (quoted in Rykwert 1972: 15–16). Much earlier the conception of the eighteenth-century philosopher Rousseau was of humankind living in a 'natural' condition before history, the family housed in its primitive hut (Rykwert 1972: 47).

For architects and other analysts of space there are other 'mythic' evolutionary schemes. Lefevbre (1991: 218) conceived of three great dialectical moments that traverse the world. The first moment is characterized by agriculture, time not separable from space nor form from content. Building consists of peasant dwellings, monuments and palaces, whilst labour distils the sacredness of elements from nature into religious and political edifices. It may be equated broadly with prehistory. The second moment, fixed in the historical era, involves the sundering of form from content and time from space, as space becomes an abstract entity. Abstractions and signs become elevated to ultimate truths. The accumulation of wealth and knowledge leads to production for exchange, money and capital. The third moment is the present system, the political space of capitalism.

A semiotic evolution is proposed by Broadbent (1980). His four stages of design types are:

1 Pragmatic: trial and error until a form emerges. This characterized

55

Palaeolithic settlements; 'the mammoth hunters' tent is a splendid example' (ibid.: 140).

2 Typologic or iconic: a fixed mental image of a building form shared by members of a culture (such as an igloo or tepee). By 'iconic' it is meant that an artefact reminds us of its object by some complex kinds of resemblance (such as a hot dog stand in the shape of a giant hot dog). This use of the term 'iconic' may be contrasted with the definition of *icon* as an image which carries a particularly heavy and conceptual weight (Horne 1986: 67), though this definition is also pertinent to the types of buildings envisaged.

3 Analogical: a structure which includes visual analogies with other structures or natural features. Just how this category can be separated from 'iconic' is not clear. For example, tepees are considered by the Sioux as analogous to the nests of birds and to the circular Power of the World that dominates Sioux life (Niehardt 1961: 198).

4 Canonic or geometric: the underpinning of design by abstract proportional systems, the use of canons of proportion. Broadbent sees canonical design as an Egyptian innovation. Again, we could suggest that concepts of abstract proportion may be found in a wide range of prehistoric societies.

Broadbent comes out firmly against the religious theory of architectural origins: 'It seems fairly certain then, that man's first impulses to build were purely utilitarian and that attempts to 'prove' his first buildings were symbolic are so much wishful thinking – which is not to deny in any way the importance of buildings as symbols once a capacity for abstract thought had developed' (Broadbent 1980: 136). He cites the pile of stones dating to 1.8 million years BP at Olduvai as an uninterpretable structure, and also the Upper Palaeolithic mammoth hunters' tents at Pushkari. Broadbent's argument appears to refute the possibility that the development of architecture and of abstract thought might be linked. We would argue that Mousterian cave shelters and burials do indicate simple demarcations of space and time by the Middle Palaeolithic (Botscharow 1989), and that the mammoth hunters' tents are not the pragmatic, trial-and-error structures that he thinks. The 15,000-year-old mammoth-bone dwellings on the Russian plain incorporate elements of repetition and symmetry in their design. Each structure also took over fifty person-days to build. This complexity of design and the large labour input suggest something beyond the utilitarian and that perhaps their building was a ritualized practice (Gladkih, Kornietz and Soffer 1984). These huts may be contrasted with the tents made without bone, built in the same period. The difference has been interpeted in terms of winter and summer camps but other distinctions (not necessarily mutually exclusive) such as sacred and profane might also be possible.

Broadbent's (1980: 12–14) evolutionary sequence is unworkable and we might turn to Eco's amalgamation of pragmatic, typologic and analogic in his story of a 'Stone Age man' sheltering in a cave. Having found his way in, the idea of a cave takes shape and he now recognizes the potential for shelter in other caves. This idea of 'cave' becomes a model or type, and thus an architectural code. This in turn generates an iconic code – the 'cave principle' becomes an object of communicative discourse. There is very little need for an elaborate chronological sequence in the relationship of these concepts. Nor do we need to formulate a Rousseauian split between 'natural' humans acting in a 'utilitarian' fashion and 'cultural' humans acting 'symbolically'.

Peter Wilson's book *The Domestication of the Human Species* (1988) sets out an intriguing evolutionary perspective on the cosmological symbolism of architecture. He identifies a stage of 'domesticated' life which began 15,000–5,000 years ago and is not yet fully complete. 'Domesticated' societies are those rural communities which inhabit hamlets, villages and small towns. They differ from societies with temporary dwellings (or no dwellings) and people who live in highly urban cultures and who work in factories and offices. Wilson contrasts the open and intimate life of gatherer-hunters, with their cosmologies of landscape, with the house cosmologies of simple farming communities. The former are typified by a social order founded on focus and the latter by one founded on boundary. The 'domesticates' inhabit an architectural environment imposed upon the natural world, as opposed to mental constructions utilizing the natural landscape (ibid.: 57–8). The house marks a major development in cosmological thinking. With settlement comes a proliferation of material culture; the house becomes the most powerful practical symbol available before the development of writing. It mediates and synthesizes the natural symbols of body and landscape, encoding, encapsulating and classifying the cosmos.

> People coming into the society, whether as strangers or particularly as children, have in their built surroundings a diagram of how the system works – their place in the household, their place in the village, their place in the territory. At the same time, they can perceive, graphically, how the individual, the various orders of groups, and the cosmos are linked and related. This is neither the only information available nor the only mode by which principles are represented; myths and rituals, and precedent present the same information and ideals in different forms. But in architecture and settlement plans a person's and a people's visual and material diagram of themselves is presented most systematically and, perhaps, most invariantly.
>
> (ibid.: 153)

Wilson's identification of this evolutionary stage which relates houses, architectural cosmology, formalized and reciprocal hospitality, exhibitions and spectacles centred on food, and tomb construction to actualize social power, is a persuasive one. We may compare it with other evolutionist schemes such as that proposed by Wilk and Netting (1984). They classify horticulturalists and other agriculturalist households as organized principally around production. In contrast, hunter-gatherer and industrial households function largely as distributive units (ibid.: 20).

ARCHITECTURE – TEXT, TIME AND TRANSCENDENCE

Yi-Fu Tuan (1977: 104) argued that non-literate societies may be relatively conservative but they have a greater awareness of their built environment. This awareness is engendered by their active participation in building, the frequency and repetition of building insubstantial structures, and the ceremonials and rituals that accompany acts of construction. In non-literate societies we might view architecture as the 'pre-text' for handing down traditions, rituals and cosmology. Tuan suggests that increasingly literate societies depend less on material objects and physical environment to embody values and meanings. Books not buildings instruct. He also considers that ambiguities of meaning, splintered and conflicting ideologies, and divergent opinions are also features of the modern world. When 'reading' architecture, the 'pre-modern' would have recourse to a consensus-based ideology (ibid.: 112–17).

Many of these points are open to debate. In urban society people are perhaps more aware, not less, of their built environment. The concerns with interior decoration, the many occupations involved with the building trade, and the complex and worrisome 'rites of passage' undergone when buying a house may all raise the level of awareness. Indeed, architectural appraisal is becoming an increasingly popular amateur pursuit in Britain. It is also highly unlikely that ancient societies were characterized by immutable single, dominant ideologies. There were conflicts of interest and ideological crises at many times in the past, when major social transformations occurred. With the advent of literacy, and the world religions which it underpinned, the universal beliefs of those religions may not have entailed the uniqueness of time, locality and place that localized cosmologies could embed so easily in their architecture. None the less, architectural buildings, such as churches, temples, mosques and major public buildings, still encode cosmologies. As we have seen, social practices and ideologies are very much alive, if implicit and non-discursive, in modern private house forms. We may no longer face east but we know where to look for the bathroom.

> In the ancient city the organization of space was a symbolic re-creation of a supposed cosmic order. It had an ideological purpose. Created space in the modern city has an equivalent ideological purpose. In part it reflects the prevailing ideology of the ruling groups and institutions in society. In part it is fashioned by the dynamics of market forces.
> (Harvey 1973: 310)

The embeddedness of ideology in architecture remains, merely its form has changed. Whereas pre-modern architecture and environments might readily incorporate transcendental systems of belief, the architecture of capitalism limits such elements to specifically 'religious' buildings. Even in a society where a third of the population believes in a supernatural world, contemporary Britons maintain a firmly pragmatic attitude to the built environment, and are mistrustful of new and challenging architectural styles. We may document the rise of the secular city over the last two millennia. Broadbent (1990: 11–27) has demonstrated that the principles behind the planning and development of the medieval city, both Christian and Moslem, were informal and social in contrast to earlier concerns with the symmetric geometry of the ancient sacred city. The 'renaissance' of symmetric geometry since the post-medieval period embodies a rather different search for order, involving 'universal' principles of aesthetics, the power of the nation-state, the rise of industry and mechanization, health and sanitation, and the effective control of people (Markus 1982). The requirements for transcendence are replaced by the worship of democracy, the market and the nation-state.

The ordering and experience of time have also changed. Pre-'domestic' societies are characterized as ahistorical, relying on myths of a past 'dream-time', a founding time beyond society and its origins. In contrast, 'domesti-cated' societies use oral history, geometry and diagrams to construct a cyclic, seasonal notion of time, existing alongside a conception of a progression from the time of the ancestors to the present (Wilson 1988: 154–5; Criado 1989). Time in the medieval world was linear and directional, the Christian story of salvation, and also cyclical, the practical passing of the seasons. By the eighteenth century the modern world view had formed, in which time is linear and historical (Tuan 1978: 10–11). Within such a system it is rare for buildings to be aligned on cardinal points or other astronomic markers. The orientation of the main street of Milton Keynes new town, begun in the 1960s, on the midsummer sunrise is something of a whimsical oddity within contemporary urban planning.

STUDYING CHANGE AND TRANSFORMATION

The circular arrangement of the huts around the men's house is so important a factor in their social and religious life that the Salesian missionaries . . . were quick to realize that the surest way to convert the Bororo was to make them abandon their village in favour of one with the houses set out in parallel rows.
(Lévi-Strauss [1955] 1973: 220–1; (see Figure 1.4, this volume)

There is a growing literature on the impact of western architecture on societies in the developing world. In many cases, the replacement of round houses by rectangular ones is linked to a prestige system with positive 'modern' values (Moore 1986: 191). Alternatively, rectangular buildings are incorporated into the traditional social organization (Hardie 1985). Archer's (1971) study of Nabdam compounds in northern Ghana shows that the 'modern' rectangular compounds provide a sharp definition of inside/outside, in contrast to the range of environments produced by the screens, walls and semi-enclosures of the traditional amorphous circular compounds. The rectangular compound was almost always empty while women seemed more able to identify with their traditional homes; Archer noted the almost exclusive use of rectangular forms for male rooms. In Botswana the adoption of modern housing has in many respects meant change for the worse among the poor and has shifted the responsibility for housing from the women's sphere to the men's, since building materials now have to be purchased (Larrson 1989). In other cases, local traditional house styles have not declined but instead have flourished while adapting to new circumstances, as Waterson (1989) noted in Indonesia. Rodman's (1985) study of house changes on Vanuatu shows that two opposed directions have been taken. The men's house is characterized by conservative and traditional styles, emphasizing the value of community and equivalence, while the residential houses have become increasingly modernized, using concrete and iron to bring a new sense of permanence, conspicious consumption and individual accomplishment. Western ways are associated with women while men view themselves as upholding the traditional values of the group. The meanings expressed by each type of building exist in relation to the other and in the contradictions expressed.

Rodman's research was framed within a general proposal about the status of dwellings within collectivistic and individualistic societies (Duncan 1981; 1985). James Duncan has argued that private houses are rarely objects of status display in collectivistic societies. Instead, they are containers of women, functional dwellings which reinforce group identity by their similarity and symbolism of corporate identity. In contrast the communal group house is more likely to be the object of architectural elaboration. In such societies social groups are closed, there is a shared value system, surplus is consumed by the collectivity, and the ideology includes notions of the incorporated and subordinated individual. Characteristic features are female pollution taboos, gender segregation within the house, gender separation inside and outside houses, and the presence of a men's house. Duncan contrasts this situation with individualistic societies where kinship ties are weakened, mobility (both spatial and social) is high, the individual's actions relatively unconstrained, and where fashions and competing value systems develop. While domestic life is more private, the residential house becomes more public. Identity, in terms of personal status, is affirmed through the residential house (and other objects) and it becomes a valued status object and source of conspicuous consumption in its own right.

A number of researchers see this polarity between collectivistic and

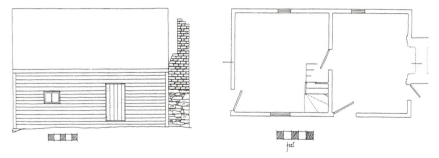

Figure 2.8 A Virginian house, exhibiting relatively little internal differentiation (after Glassie 1975, by kind permission of University of Tennessee Press)

individualistic as having an historical dimension. Glassie (1987; 1990) has identified a broad ideological and social transformation in the architecture of eighteenth- and nineteenth-century North America, which he links to similar changes, at different times, in Ireland, England, Denmark and Turkey. The open, non-symmetrical house with its large multifunctional spaces where entertainment and cooking happen together (Figure 2.8) is gradually replaced by closed and symmetrical forms (Figure 2.9). These employ barriers (porch, lobby, vestibule, hall) to restrict access to the centre, while the interior is divided up into small compartments, with separate rooms for cooking, entertainment and sleeping. Servants or women are removed from the house's sociable arena. A geometrically symmetrical mask is drawn across the house's facade so that the visitor cannot tell where people are within the house. Glassie considers this change to embody the replacement of an egalitarian and co-operative mode of work founded on sacred commandment by a hierarchical and competitive mode founded on secular law and rules of decorous behaviour. Similar changes in eating habits and accoutrements, in gravestone memorialization and in other forms of material culture may also be linked to this transformation (Deetz 1977).

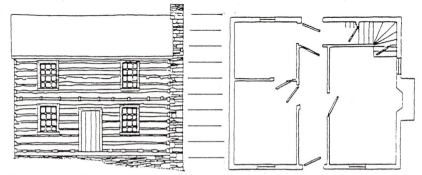

Figure 2.9 A Virginian house, exhibiting symmetrical and closed characteristics (after Glassie 1987, by kind permission of *Material Culture*)

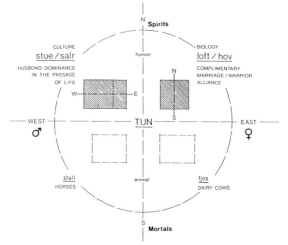

Figure 2.10 Nominal structural pattern of the Norwegian stue in the Middle Ages (after Doxtater 1990, by kind permission of Avebury Press)

Doxtater's (1990) study of changes in the symbolic space of Norwegian farming communities from the Viking period to after the Reformation illustrates structural continuity in architectural ideology throughout the Middle Ages. Up until the Viking period the organization of the Scandinavian long house had not changed substantially (other than increasing in size) since the beginning of the pre-Roman Iron Age (Parker Pearson 1984). Up to, and during, the Viking Age, houses were organized into hamlets and villages. Each house was aligned east–west and functioned as a household unit with its living area in the west end and the cattle byre on the east side. By the Viking period, some houses were aligned north–south as well as east–west. Norway became a Christian nation at the end of the Viking period, but the pagan cosmology embedded in the west–east aligned (and north–south) long houses continued despite the adoption of Christian theology (Figure 2.10), which at this stage was adapted to the existing circumstances. It was only in the sixteenth century that the internal organization of the domestic house changed to incorporate the religious ideology of Protestant Christianity (Figure 2.11). Despite major political and ideological transformations over two thousand years, the form of the house seems to have remained remarkably static. Original symbolism and meaning no doubt became modified over time but the absence of major structural changes implies a certain continuity of symbolic space, even if the beliefs associated with that cosmology had disappeared.

A rather different historical situation may be found in Indian prehistory. Miller's (1985) reappraisal of the Indus or Harappan cities (2600–2000 BC) shows how they were aligned on the cardinal points with a dominant north–south axis and divided into lower towns and associated citadels, an

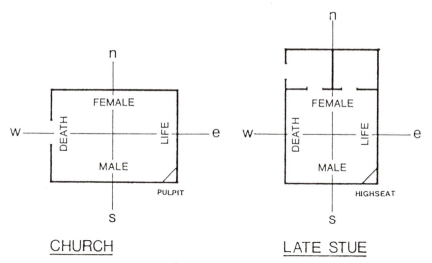

Figure 2.11 Eventual 'cosmic congruence' of Norwegian church and stue in the seventeenth and eighteenth centuries (after Doxtater 1990, by kind permission of Avebury Press)

organizational framework apparent in the smaller as well as the larger settlements. Miller rejects the traditional model of a redistributive elite of priest-kings and shows that there is no evidence for a 'middle class' of wealthy traders, as postulated by other researchers. He interprets the evidence as indicative of an order in the settlements that opposes the natural environment. There is also considerable standardization of the mundane in both buildings and artefacts. He suggests that Harappan society was authoritarian, non-ranked and puritanical, and considers the caste composition of contemporary Hindu society to be more of a polar opposite than a direct analogy. Over a considerable period the Indian subcontinent has seen a series of cycles, as the ideology of one period develops in reaction to that of the previous establishment. Miller speculates that Harappan 'puritanism' was replaced by a dialectically opposed Vedic Hinduism, itself replaced by Buddhist ideology, whilst modern Hinduism developed against the background of the dominance of Buddhism.

A provocative account of the 'domestication' of Near Eastern and European society from the seventh millennium BC onwards has identified the central importance of the house in changes from gathering to farming (Hodder 1990). Earlier cross-cultural investigations of house form had suggested that the change from rounded and circular houses to rectangular ones was due to the functional requirements of intensified production and individualized households resulting from village formation (Flannery 1972). Universal rule solutions such as this, however, do not explain particular historical contexts, nor do they account for exceptions. We may now perhaps see the need to understand such a transformation in ideological terms as well as 'economic' ones, as we have seen with the impact of 'modern' life styles on traditional societies.

Hodder defined three concepts which he thought were central to the European Neolithic: 'domus' (place and practice of nurture, control, symbolic elaboration and power relations focusing on the house); 'agrios' (field, outside, wild); and 'foris' (the doorway with the outside). During the Natufian period (11,000–9000 BC) in the Near East, the house as a production unit was put centre stage. The house as matter and concept was tied to the forces of social reproduction and articulated oppositions to the wild, the dangerous and the unsocial. As a structure it was elaborated through painting, paving and internal demarcation. The wild and dangerous were 'foregrounded' within the domus; death was 'domesticated' by burial of ancestors under the floors. Wild animals and wild plants were also brought into the domain of the domus, where they could be controlled and tamed. Collectivistic values were stressed over unsocial, individualistic behaviour. Social control was exercised through the medium of the control of the wild. The domus was now a metaphor for the domestication of society.

In south-east Europe by the fourth millennium BC the metaphor and mnemonic of domus as centre was shifting to the agrios as centre (Figure 2.11). Increased control of the external domain, particularly by men, was evident in the expansion of plough agriculture, use of secondary products, the appearances of symbols of hunting and of war, incipient social inequality, and burial of the dead away from the dwelling.

The houses of the Linear Pottery Culture in central Europe (fifth millennium BC) embody a new variation on the domus theme for Hodder. Their monumental size, deep interiors, linear grading of space and boundaries for houses and communal enclosures are linked as aspects of 'foris'. Instead of hearths, it is boundaries and entrances that are emphasized. Hodder interprets these developments as indicative of the creation of links and dependencies with neighbours and 'foreign' groups. After 4000 BC, we find a further transformation of the domus, in the long barrows and megalithic tombs of western Europe. These houses of the ancestors are monumental structures in contrast to the flimsy settlements of the living. Their construction and presence links relatively dispersed kin groups into large communities.

Whereas Wilson's (1988) approach to human 'domestication' has been global and totalizing, Hodder's has attempted to explore context and trajectories of change in some detail. Hodder's approach, which follows the work of Cauvin (1972), can be criticized for its structuralist assumptions as well as various inconsistencies in treatment of spatial frames across Europe (see Barrett this volume), but as archaeologists move beyond universal generalizations and identify rule paradigms for particular times and places (such as the focal importance of the house and its transformations in early farming

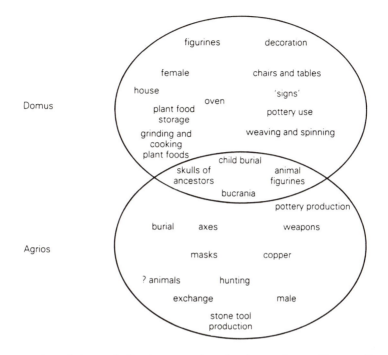

Figure 2.12 Associations of the domus and agrios in south-east Europe (from Hodder 1990, by kind permission of the author and Blackwells)

communities), so their attempts to mesh generalities and specific details are likely to improve.

This introduction has been very much focused on those cultures where highly organized cosmologies are articulated in spatial and architectural order. In part these manifestations of 'order' may relate to a historically bound rule paradigm of agricultural and city-state societies in certain relationships with the natural world. In part they may also be biased to the somewhat fastidious communities rather than the cosmological 'slobs', those who have no formal cosmology, or no concern with the physical manifestation of social and symbolic order. There are plenty of archaeological examples of settlements which exhibit no formal structuring along the lines of the principles we have elucidated. Of course, the difficulties of 'reading' archaeological remains in these terms should not be underestimated since the manifestation of such ideas may have been extremely subtle. Equally there are hundreds of ethnographies with no analysis of cosmology and architecture, either because those societies lacked such structures or because the anthropologists were uninterested in such matters. The variation through time of changing formality in applied cosmology is something that archaeologists can approach. Moreover, the transformations in guiding principles and rule paradigms may also be open to examination. The few archaeological studies which explore those transformations, some of which are outlined above, illustrate that such analyses are possible.

COSMOLOGICAL ORDER AND THE FUTURE

Today 'cosmology' is a field of study for physicists, a scientific quest for the origins and nature of the universe in terms too complex for most people to understand. Neither the scientific nor the spiritual concept of 'cosmology' has much bearing on people's everyday lives. The ideologies of control are essentially economic and territorial. The sense of communality and shared world view are profoundly fractured within a global culture where tensions of race, religion, gender, polity and economics have created deep rifts.

If there are lessons from the archaeological past, they are that profound cultural transformations have been relatively intermittent within long periods of gradual change. In these long-term scenarios there has been probably only slight modification of cosmology. Yet when the change has come, the transformation has been cataclysmic and almost total. Within the post-medieval world the search for novelty and concern with economic growth has become almost all consuming. Rates of change appear to be rapid. The rise of individualism and privatization (not just in late twentieth-century political economy) and the decline of communal systems of belief have also led to a new world order. The return of Christianity and Islam to fundamentals has brought a sense of order into many millions of people's lives, particularly where they felt it was lacking. The dominant ideology of economic and political utility is increasingly undermined by recourse to transcendental experiences and beliefs. After the apparent demise of religion and superstition in the wake of science's progress, we face a potential return, on a global scale, to medieval ideologies and cosmologies.

The population displacements and atrocities of the twentieth century have increased people's concerns with rootedness, paradoxically because of their very uprootedness. As the concept of home becomes even more firmly fixed to house and political territory, so the gulf increases between the possessors and the dispossessed. As one element seeks to retreat further into its cultural shell, elaborating domestic interiors and securing boundaries with the outside, the other either rejects, or is forced to give up, the domestic way of life for a more mobile and homeless quest. The increase in spontaneous shelter in and around the cities of the world (Rapoport 1988) is perhaps the most serious manifestation of this tension.

We undoubtedly have the capacity to transform our world. With the collapse of communism and the rise of the environmental movement an optimistic view of the end of ideology was briefly mooted. Yet social inequalities and ethnic intolerance seem as great as ever before. The architectural legacy of the hierarchical past, from the royal states of the last five hundred years to the 'international' styles of recent years, constrains institutional transformation. Class hierarchies are continuously reproduced through the structure of domestic housing. International styles destroy concepts of place and local community.

Whilst many admire the cosmological coherence of various traditional societies, these systems aid the replication of often repressive power relations. In other cases they provide a forum for resistance to political repression imposed by governments and outside groups. We may find such ideas odd or quaint in the post-modern world, yet contexts of uprootedness, alienation and environmental degradation are most likely to lead to the formulation and reformulation of applied cosmologies.

NOTES

1 Some notable studies include the Pueblo of the south-west of North America (Saile 1977; Fritz 1987; Doxtater 1991), the Aztec and Maya of Mesoamerica (Coe 1965; Fuson 1969; Ingham 1971; Marcus 1973; Pollard 1991; Sarro 1991; Stone 1992), the Inka and Wanka (Hastorf 1991; Farrington 1992), southern African Iron Age kraals (van Waarden 1989), the central European Mesolithic (Handsman 1991), early farmers of the Near East (Watkins 1990), the Neolithic and Copper Age in the Balkans (Chapman 1991b; Tringham 1991), Mycenean Greek sanctuaries (van Leuven 1978), the villas of Roman Britain (Scott 1990; Hingley 1990), German medieval cathedrals (Hause 1992), English medieval churches (Graves 1989) and monasteries (Gilchrist 1988; 1989), the palace societies of medieval India (Fritz 1987; Fritz and Michell 1987), and the ancient city states of China, South-East Asia (Wheatley 1971), India (Miller 1985), and Rome (Rykwert 1976).
2 For a broader discussion of architecture and cosmology in late Neolithic Orkney see Richards 1990b; 1991; in press.
3 A more detailed examination of the relationship between changing social practices and the spatial organization of houses and settlements, from the late Bronze Age through to the late Iron Age, is provided in Parker Pearson, forthcoming; Hill, forthcoming; and Hingley 1990.

BIBLIOGRAPHY

Archer, I. (1971) 'Nabdam compounds, northern Ghana', in P. Oliver (ed.), *Shelter in Africa*, London: Barrie & Jenkins.
Barrett, J.C. (1989) 'Food, gender and metal: questions of social reproduction', in M.L. Stig Sørenson and R. Thomas (eds), *The Bronze Age – Iron Age Transition in Europe: Aspects of Continuity and Change c. 1200 to 500 BC*, Oxford: BAR Int. Series S483.
Bell, M. (1977) 'Excavations at Bishopstone', *Sussex Archaeological Collections* 115: 1–299.
Boast, R. (1987) 'Rites of passage: topological and formal representation', *Environment and Planning B: Planning and Design* 14: 451–66.
Boast, R. and Evans, C. (1986) 'The transformation of space: two examples from British prehistory', *Archaeological Review from Cambridge* 5: 193–205.
Bond, D. and Jones, M. (1988) *Excavation at the North Ring, Mucking, Essex*, East Anglian Archaeology 43.
Botscharow, L.J. (1989) 'Sites as texts: an exploration of Mousterian traces', in I.

Hodder (ed.), *The Meanings of Things: Material Culture and Symbolic Expression*, London: Unwin Hyman.

Bourdier, J.P. and Alsayyad, N. (eds) (1989) *Dwellings, Settlements and Tradition:Cross-cultural Perspectives*, Lanham, Maryland: University Press of America.

Bowden, M. and McOmish, D. (1987) 'The required barrier', *Scottish Archaeological Review* 4(2): 76–84.

Bradley, R. (1984) *The Social Foundations of Prehistoric Britain: Themes and Variations in the Archaeology of Power*, London: Longman.

Broadbent, G. (1980) 'The deep structures of architecture', in G. Broadbent, R. Bunt and C. Jencks (eds), *Signs, Symbols and Architecture*, Wiley: Chichester.

——(1990) *Emerging Concepts in Urban Space Design*, London: Van Nostrand Reinhold.

Buckley, D.G. and Hedges, J.D. *The Bronze Age and Saxon Settlement at Springfield Lyons, Essex: an Interim Report*, Essex County Council Archaeology Section Occasional Paper 5.

Burstow, G.P. and Holleyman, G.A. (1957) 'Late Bronze Age settlement on Itford Hill', *Proceedings of the Prehistoric Society* 23: 167–212.

Cauvin, J. (1972) *Religions Néolithiques de Syro-Palestine du IXème au VIIème millénaire*, Lyons: Gean Maisonneuve.

Chadwick, S. (1958) 'Early Iron Age enclosures on Longbridge Deverill Cow Down, Wiltshire', in S.S. Frere (ed.), *Problems of the Iron Age in Southern Britain*, London: University of London, Institute of Archaeology.

Champion, T. (1980) 'Settlement and environment in later Bronze Age Kent', in J.C. Barrett and R.J. Bradley (eds)., *Settlement and Society in the British Later Bronze Age*, Oxford: BAR 83.

Chang, K.C. (1983) *Art, Myth and Ritual: the Path to Political Authority in Ancient China*, Cambridge, Mass.: Harvard University Press.

Chapman, J. (1991a) 'The creation of social arenas in the Neolithic and Copper Age of SE Europe: the case of Varna', in P. Garwood, D. Jennings, R. Skeates and J. Toms (eds), *Sacred and Profane: Proceedings of a Conference on Archaeology, Ritual and Religion, Oxford 1989*, Oxford University Committee for Archaeology.

——(1991b) 'The early Balkan village', in O. Grøn, E. Engelstad and I. Lindblom (eds), *Social Space: Human Spatial Behaviour in Dwellings and Settlements*, Odense: Odense University Press.

Childe, V.G. (1931) *Skara Brae: a Pictish Village in Orkney*, London: Kegan Paul, Trench, Trubner & Co.

——(1946) *Scotland before the Scots*, London: Methuen.

Clark, J.G.D. (1952) *Prehistoric Europe: the Economic Basis*, London: Methuen.

Clarke, D.V. and Sharples, N. (1985) 'Settlements and subsistence in the third millennium BC', in A.C. Renfrew (ed.), *Prehistory of Orkney*, 1st edn, Edinburgh: Edinburgh University Press.

Coe, M. (1965) 'A model of ancient community structure in the Maya lowlands', *Southwestern Journal of Anthropology* 21: 97–113.

Criado, F. (1989) 'We the post-megalithic people . . .', in I. Hodder (ed.), *The Meanings of Things: Material Culture and Symbolic Expression*, London: Unwin Hyman.

Cunliffe, B.W. (1978) *Iron Age Communities in Britain*, 2nd edn, London: Routledge & Kegan Paul.

——(1984) *Danebury: An Iron Age Hillfort in Hampshire. Volume 1. The Excavations 1969–1978: the Site*, London: Council for British Archaeology Research Report 52.

Deetz, J. (1977) *In Small Things Forgotten: the Archaeology of Early American Life*, New York: Anchor Press.

Doxtater, D. (1990) 'Socio-political change and symbolic space in Norwegian farm culture after the Reformation', in M. Turan (ed.), *Vernacular Architecture: Paradigms of Environmental Response*, Aldershot: Avebury Press.

——(1991) 'Reflections of the Anasazi cosmos', in O. Grøn, E. Engelstad and I. Lindblom (eds), *Social Space: Human Spatial Behaviour in Dwellings and Settlements*, Odense: Odense University Press.

Drewett, P. (1982) 'Later Bronze Age downland economy and excavations at Blackpatch, East Sussex', *Proceedings of the Prehistoric Society* 48: 321–409.

Duncan, J.S. (1981) 'From container of women to status symbol: the impact of social structure on the meaning of the house', in J.S. Duncan, (ed.), *Housing and Identity: Cross-cultural Perspectives*, London: Croom Helm.

——(1985) 'The house as symbol of social structure: notes on the language of objects among collectivistic groups', in I. Altman and C.M. Werner (eds), *Home Environments. Human Behavior and Environment: Advances in Theory and Research. Vol. 8*, New York: Plenum.

Eco, U. (1980) 'Functional and sign: the semiotics of architecture', in G. Broadbent, R. Bunt and C. Jencks (eds), *Signs, Symbols and Architecture*, Wiley: Chichester.

Edwards, I.E.S. (1947) *The Pyramids of Egypt*, West Drayton: Penguin.

Ellison, A. (1978) 'The Bronze Age of Sussex', in P.L. Drewett (ed.), *Archaeology in Sussex to AD 1500*, London: Council for British Archaeology Research Report 29.

——(1987) 'The Bronze Age settlement at Thorney Down: pots, post-holes and patterning', *Proceedings of the Prehistoric Society* 53: 385–92.

Evans, C. and Serjeantson, D. (1988) 'The backwater economy of a fen-edge community in the Iron Age: the Upper Delphs, Haddenham', *Antiquity* 62: 360–70.

Fairclough, G. (1992) 'Meaningful constructions – spatial and functional analysis of medieval buildings', *Antiquity* 66: 348–66.

Farrington, I.S. (1992) 'Ritual geography, settlement patterns and the characterization of the provinces of the Inka heartland', *World Archaeology* 23: 368–85.

Fasham, P.J. (1985) *The Prehistoric Settlement at Winnall Down, Winchester*, Hampshire Field Club and Archaeology Society Monograph 5.

Flannery, K. (1972) 'The origins of the village as a settlement type in Mesoamerica and the Near East: a comparative study', in P.J. Ucko, R. Tringham and G.W. Dimbleby (eds), *Man, Settlement and Urbanism*, London: Duckworth.

Frankfort, H. (1948a) *Ancient Egyptian Religion: an Interpretation*, New York: Harper & Row.

——(1948b) *Kingship and the Gods: a Study of Ancient Near Eastern Religion as the Integration of Society and Nature*, Chicago: University of Chicago Press.

Frankfort, H., Frankfort, H.A., Wilson, J.A., Jacobsen, T. and Irwin, W.A. (1946) *The Intellectual Adventure of Ancient Man: an Essay on Speculative Thought in the Ancient Near East*, Chicago: University of Chicago Press.

Fritz, J.M. (1987) 'Chaco Canyon and Vijayanagara: proposing spatial meaning in two societies', in D.W. Ingersoll and G. Bronitsky (eds), *Mirror and Metaphor: Material and Social Constructions of Reality*, Lanham, Maryland: University Press of America.

Fritz, J.M. and Michell, G. (1987) 'Interpreting the plan of a medieval Hindu capital, Vijayanagara', *World Archaeology* 19: 105–29.

Fuson, R. (1969) 'The orientation of Maya ceremonial centres', *Annals of the Association of American Geographers* 59: 494–511.

Gilchrist, R. (1988) 'The spatial archaeology of gender domains: a case study of English medieval nunneries', *Archaeological Review from Cambridge* 7: 21–8.

——(1989) 'Community and self: perceptions and use of space in medieval monasteries', *Scottish Archaeological Review* 6: 55–64.

Girard, R. (1977) *Violence and the sacred*, trans. P. Gregory, Baltimore: Johns Hopkins University Press.

Gladkih, M.I., Kornietz, N.L. and Soffer, O. (1984) 'Mammoth-bone dwellings on the Russian plain', *Scientific American* 251(5): 136–43.

Glassie, H. (1975) *Folk Housing in Middle Virginia*, Knoxville: University of Tennessee Press.

——(1987) 'Vernacular architecture and society', in D.W. Ingersoll and G. Bronitsky (eds), *Mirror and Metaphor: Material and Social Constructions of Reality*, Lanham, Maryland: University Press of America.

——(1990) 'Vernacular architecture and society', in M. Turan (ed.), *Vernacular Architecture: Paradigms of Environmental Response*, Aldershot: Avebury Press.

Graves, C.P. (1989) 'Social space in the English medieval parish church', *Economy and Society* 18: 297–322.

Grøn, O. (1991) 'A method for reconstruction of social structure in prehistoric societies and examples of practical application', in O. Grøn, E. Engelstad and I. Lindblom (eds), *Social Space: Human Spatial Behaviour in Dwellings and Settlements*, Odense: Odense University Press.

Guilbert, G. (1982) 'Post-ring symmetry in roundhouses at Moel y Gaer and some other sites in prehistoric Britain', in P.J. Drury (ed.), *Structural Reconstruction*, Oxford: BAR 110.

Handsman, R.G. (1991) 'Whose art was found at Lepenski Vir? Gender relations and power in archaeology', in J. Gero and M. Conkey (eds), *Engendering Archaeology: Women and Prehistory*, Oxford: Blackwell.

Hardie, G.J. (1985) 'Continuity and change in the Tswana's house and settlement form', in I. Altman and C.M. Werner (eds), *Home Environments. Human Behavior and Environment: Advances in Theory and Research Vol. 8*, New York: Plenum.

Harvey, D. (1973) *Social Justice and the City*, London: Edward Arnold.

Hastorf, C.A. (1991) 'Gender, space, and food in prehistory', in J. Gero and M. Conkey (eds), *Engendering Archaeology: Women and Prehistory*, Oxford: Blackwell.

Hause, M.T. (1992) 'A place in sacred history: coronation ritual and architecture in Ottonian Mainz', *Journal of Ritual Studies* 6: 133–57.

Highlands, D. (1990) 'What's indigenous? An essay on building', in M. Turan (ed.), *Vernacular Architecture: Paradigms of Environmental Response*, Aldershot: Avebury.

Hill, J.D. (forthcoming) 'Hillforts and the Iron Age of Wessex', in T. Champion and J. Collis (eds), *The British Iron Age: Recent Trends*, Sheffield: Collis Publications.

Hingley, R. (1990) 'Public and private space: domestic organization and gender relations among Iron Age and Romano-British households', in R. Samson (ed.), *The Social Archaeology of Houses*, Edinburgh: Edinburgh University Press.

Hodder, I. (1984) 'Burials, houses, women and men in the European Neolithic', in D. Miller and C. Tilley (eds), *Ideology, Power and Prehistory*, Cambridge: Cambridge University Press.

——(1990) *The Domestication of Europe: Structure and Contingency in Neolithic Societies*, Oxford: Blackwell.

Hopkins, M.R. (1987) 'Network analysis of the plans of some Teotihuacan apartment compounds', *Environment and Planning B: Planning and Design* 14: 387–406.

Horne, D. (1986) *The Public Culture: the Triumph of Industrialism*, London: Pluto.

Ingham, J. (1971) 'Time and space in ancient Mexico: the symbolic dimensions of clanship', *Man* 6: 615–29.

Ingold, T. (1986) *The Appropriation of Nature*, Manchester: Manchester University Press.

Johnson, M. (1986) 'Assumptions and interpretations in the study of the Great Rebuilding', *Archaeological Review from Cambridge* 5: 141–53.

Larsson, A. (1989) 'Traditional versus modern housing in Botswana – an analysis from the user's perspective', in J.P. Bourdier and N. Alsayyad (eds), *Dwellings,*

Settlements and Tradition: Cross-cultural Perspectives, Lanham, Maryland: University Press of America.

Lefebvre, H. (1991) *The Production of Space*, trans. D. Nicholson-Smith, Oxford: Blackwell.

Lévi-Strauss, C. [1955] (1973) *Tristes tropiques*, Paris: Librairie Plon, trans. J. & D. Weightman, London: Jonathan Cape.

——(1986) *The Raw and the Cooked*, Harmondsworth: Penguin.

Manby, T. (1986) *Thwing: Excavation and Field Archaeology in East Yorkshire*, unpublished interim report.

Marcus, J. (1973) 'Territorial organization of the Lowland Classic Maya', *Science* 180 (4089): 911–16.

Markus, T.A. (1982) 'Introduction', in T.A. Markus (ed.), *Order in Space and Society: Architectural Form and its Context in the Scottish Enlightenment*, Edinburgh: Mainstream.

Miller, D. (1985) 'Ideology and the Harappan civilization', *Journal of Anthropological Archaeology* 4: 34–71.

Moore, H.L. (1986) *Space, Text and Gender: an Anthropological Study of the Marakwet of Kenya*, Cambridge: Cambridge University Press.

Morenz, S. (1960) *Egyptian Religion*, London: Methuen.

Niehardt, J.G. (1961) *Black Elk Speaks: being the Life Story of a Holy Man of the Oglala Sioux*, London: Abacus.

Oswald, A. (1991) 'A doorway in the past: roundhouse entrance orientation and its significance in Iron Age Britain', unpublished BA dissertation, Dept of Archaeology, University of Cambridge.

Parker Pearson, M. (1984) 'Economic and ideological change: cyclical growth in the pre-state societies of Jutland', in D. Miller and C. Tilley (eds), *Ideology, Power and Prehistory*, Cambridge: Cambridge University Press.

——(forthcoming) 'Food, fertility and front doors in the first millennium BC', in T. Champion and J.R. Collis (eds), *The British Iron Age: Recent Trends*, Sheffield: Collis Publications.

Pollard, H.P. (1991) 'The construction of ideology in the emergence of the prehispanic Tarascan state', *Ancient Mesoamerica* 2: 167–79.

Raglan, A. (1964) *The Temple and the House*, London: Routledge & Kegan Paul.

Rapoport, A. (1969) *House Form and Culture*, Englewood Cliffs: Prentice-Hall.

——(1988) 'Spontaneous settlements as vernacular design', in C.V. Patton (ed.), *Spontaneous Shelter: International Perspectives and Prospects*, Philadelphia: Temple University Press.

Redman, C.L. (1986) *Qsar es-Seghir: an Archaeological View of Medieval Life*, New York: Academic Press.

Renfrew, A.C. (1979) *Investigations in Orkney*, Society of Antiquaries of London Research Committee Report 38, London: Thames and Hudson.

Richards, C. (1990a) 'The Neolithic settlement complex at Barnhouse Farm, Stenness, Orkney', in A.C. Renfrew (ed.), *The Prehistory of Orkney*, 2nd edn, Edinburgh: Edinburgh University Press.

——(1990b) 'The late Neolithic house in Orkney', in R. Samson (ed.), *The Social Archaeology of Houses*, Edinburgh: Edinburgh University Press.

——(1991) 'Skara Brae: revisiting a Neolithic village in Orkney', in W.S. Hanson and E.A. Slater (eds), *Scottish Archaeology: New Perceptions*, Aberdeen: Aberdeen University Press.

——(forthcoming) 'Monumental choreography: architecture and spatial representation in late Neolithic Orkney', in C. Tilley (ed.), *Interpretative Archaeology*, London: Berg Publications.

——(in prep.) *The Evolution of a Late Neolithic Monumental Landscape: Excavations at Barnhouse and Maeshowe, Stenness, Orkney.*

Rodman, M.C. (1985) 'Contemporary custom: redefining domestic space in Longana, Vanuatu', *Ethnology* 24: 269–79.

Rykwert, J. (1972) *On Adam's House in Paradise: the Idea of the Primitive Hut in Architectural History*, New York: Museum of Modern Art.

——(1976) *The Idea of a Town: the Anthropology of Urban Form in Rome, Italy and the Ancient World*, London: Faber.

Saile, D.G. (1977) '"Architecture" in prehispanic Pueblo archaeology: examples from Chaco Canyon, New Mexico', *World Archaeology* 9: 157–73.

Sarro, P.J. (1991) 'The role of architectural sculpture in ritual space at Teotihuacan, Mexico', *Ancient Mesoamerica* 2: 249–62.

Scott, E. (1990) 'Winged-corridor villas and the social construction of space', in R. Samson (ed.), *The Social Archaeology of Houses*, Edinburgh: Edinburgh University Press.

Seamon, D. (1980) 'Body-subject, time-space routines, and place-ballets', in A. Buttimer and D. Seamon (eds), *The Human Experience of Space and Place*, London: Croom Helm.

Smith, K. (1977) 'The excavation of Winklebury Camp, Basingstoke, Hampshire', *Proceedings of the Prehistoric Society* 43: 43–130.

Stone, A. (1992) 'From ritual in the landscape to capture in the urban center: the recreation of ritual environments in Mesoamerica', *Journal of Ritual Studies* 6: 109–32.

Tringham, R.E. (1991) 'Households with faces: the challenge of gender in prehistoric architectural remains', in J. Gero and M. Conkey (eds), *Engendering Archaeology: Women and Prehistory*, Oxford: Blackwell.

Tuan, Y.F. (1977) *Space and Place: the Perspective of Experience*, London: Edward Arnold.

——(1978) 'Space, time, place: a humanistic frame', in T. Carlstein, D. Parkes and N. Thrift (eds), *Making Sense of Time. Timing Space and Spacing Time, Volume 1*, London: Edward Arnold.

van Leuven, J.C. (1978) 'The mainland tradition of sanctuaries in prehistoric Greece', *World Archaeology* 10: 139–48.

van Waarden, C. (1989) 'The granaries of Vumba: structural interpretation of a Khami period commoner site', *Journal of Anthropological Archaeology* 8: 131–57.

Waterson, R. (1989) 'Migration, tradition and change in some vernacular architecture of Indonesia', in J.P. Bourdier and N. Alsayyad (eds), *Dwellings, Settlements and Tradition: Cross-cultural Perspectives*, Lanham, Maryland: University Press of America.

Watkins, T. (1990) 'The origins of house and home?', *World Archaeology* 21: 336–47.

Wheatley, P. (1971) *The Pivot of the Four Quarters: A Preliminary Enquiry into the Origins and Character of the Ancient Chinese City*, Edinburg: Edinburgh University Press.

Wilk, R.R. and Netting, R. McC. (1984) 'Households: changing forms and functions', in R. Netting, R. Wilk and E. Arnould (eds), *Households: Comparative and Historical Studies of the Domestic Group*, Berkeley: University of California Press.

Wilson, P.J. (1988) *The Domestication of the Human Species*, New Haven: Yale University Press

3

ARCHITECTURE AND MEANING: THE EXAMPLE OF NEOLITHIC HOUSES AND TOMBS

Ian Hodder

It is often claimed that archaeologists and anthropologists need to build a theory of material culture. This claim now seems suspect to me because it assumes that 'material culture' constitutes a category about which 'a theory' can be built. It is not at all obvious that screwdrivers, paper clips, a landscape, a tower block, flags and a Rembrandt painting have very much in common or that they have more in common with each other than they do with writing (which is also a material product but which is usually considered in the context of 'language'). It remains to be demonstrated convincingly that all the different types of material have something in common so that a unified category can be described (for attempts to do this see Gould and Schiffer 1981; Hodder 1982; Shanks and Tilley 1987).

Minimally, we might begin by distinguishing material culture which has primarily emotional effect (as in a teddy bear or child's favourite blanket) or aesthetic effect (as in the Rembrandt), from that which signifies in a way similar to language (such as a national flag) and from that which has meaning largely through its utilitarian use (such as a hammer or nail). Certainly all material culture has both use and meaning, style and function, and perhaps all material culture has all four types of meaning (emotional, aesthetic, semiotic and experiential) to some degree. But I do want to argue that at least degrees of referential and experiential emphasis can be distinguished. Put differently, some material culture is primarily representational, as in the case of a national flag or passport, while other material culture may not be intended to signify very much at all. Indeed, it has recently been argued that the semiotic nature of material culture has been overstressed and that practical knowledge differs fundamentally from linguistic knowledge (Bloch 1991; Byers 1991; Hodder 1992). For example, while language is linear and abstract, material culture practice is organized into packets of highly contextualized knowledge. The meanings of many types of material culture are grounded in physical constraints and in the materiality of existence. Thus

73

while hair-style might be fairly arbitrary and semiotic, the meaning of a major monument is tied up with the material conditions of its production – not everyone can build a pyramid. Similarly, the meaning of an axe is embedded in the practical skills of production and use.

Of course all material culture has more than utilitarian, functional meaning. Yet the referential nature of material culture often seems overstated. Sometimes objects just 'are'. Particularly in the early stages of the introduction of new styles of dwelling or pottery, the referential or metaphoric component of meaning may be high. The referential meanings may initially be self-consciously stressed. But through time material meanings often become self-evident – an object comes to mean in its own right, in terms of people's experience of its use. Thus not only different objects but also the same or similar objects through time may be more or less referential, more or less experiential.

Another reason why a general unified theory of material culture should be regarded with some scepticism is that some characteristics of material culture also hold for language. For example, material culture can be described as active rather than passive. However, the same can be said of language. The study of sociolinguistics demonstrates the link between language and society. But this is not a passive link. Language does not simply reflect social group – it also forms the group. It is not simply that an individual who holds power says the right thing, but that power can only be wielded if framed within the right language – power is also obtained actively by saying the right thing.

In much the same way, material culture is active in that the right clothes correctly worn are the necessary condition for the wielding of power. Some material objects confer power. Material culture does not passively reflect society but is actively manipulated to construct society. Byers (1991) has developed an action-constitutive approach to material culture and especially to monuments. He shows that there are few speech acts which do not depend for their significance on an appropriate material setting. The right words spoken and the right actions carried out in the wrong place often lose much of their significance and social power. Monuments and places thus actively constitute society.

But here we return to differences between different types of material culture. Dress and monuments have different potential for constituting society in different ways. Items of decorative clothing may be active in ways similar to language, giving authority and power to individuals or to individual utterances. But monuments and architecture can act in different ways. Their size and physical nature mean that they can be active in a direct, bodily way – direct control over people, their access, movement and interaction in architectural space. Architecture embeds certain specific meanings in society through the control of people and their encounters with the world around them.

So I want to make two points about tombs and houses in the European Neolithic. The first is that their referential or metaphoric nature varied through time. They 'meant' in different ways through time. Second, they played an active role as monuments in the construction of society.

THE TOMBS MEAN HOUSES

I wish to explore these ideas while embellishing the long-recognized idea that the linear Neolithic tombs of north-west Europe 'mean' houses (for references see Hodder 1990). In other words, we can start with the notion that the tombs represent houses. Since, on the whole, the linear houses are confined to the late fifth and early and middle fourth millennia BC in central Europe, while the tombs are more clearly associated with the later fourth and early third millennia BC in northern and western Europe, we need to demonstrate spatial and temporal contiguity between houses and tombs in order for the diffusion process to be admitted as feasible. In fact, in both Poland and northern France there is evidence of continuity in time in the mid-fourth millennium BC (Hodder 1990; Sherratt 1990). In France, sites such as Les Fouaillages and Passy indicate chronological and cultural links between tomb-builders and the loess-based long houses (ibid.).

The argument that the tombs represent houses is based on a number of formal similarities between earthen long barrows and Danubian long houses. I have outlined these in some detail (Hodder 1984; 1990) and only wish to summarize them here. Many of the long mounds have rectangular or trapezoidal shapes, with similar length/breadth ratios to the long houses. Midgley (1985) argues specifically for Kujavia that the tombs and houses have similar ranges of lengths and widths. She also argues that both have very similar asymmetrical trapezoidal plans with one long wall slightly concave. Another general similarity is that the trapezoidal forms of tombs and houses tend to have the entrance at the broader of the two ends. The long axes of the tombs and houses are normally aligned north-west to south-east, with the entrance or broader end facing the south-east. The entrances in both types of monument are often marked off, elaborated or emphasized in various ways. There are also internal subdivisions of space along both the linear and transverse axes. In particular it has recently become clear from excavations of houses in Czechoslovakia and Poland that the central axis of the house often divides it into two linear halves, with pits or high phosphate readings on one side of the house only (Czerniak 1980; Jaromír Beneš, pers. comm.). Such evidence recalls the frequent division of the long earthen mounds into two sides, with different types of soil being dumped on either side (Ashbee et al. 1979) or different types of artefact being found (Weber 1983). A final similarity noted by Midgley (1985) is that the tombs and houses are clustered into groups in the landscape in similar ways.

As has already become clear, some of the closest similarities between houses and tombs occur in areas such as northern Poland where the transition to tombs seems most likely to have taken place first. This early representational nature of the tombs forms part of a more general conclusion made by Sherratt (1990). He argues that despite much regional variation in the sequences of construction of different types of tomb, there seems to be a general trend in the tombs in many areas. The earliest forms of burial are often long trapezoidal mounds of earth and timber. Round forms then become more frequent and the chambers increase in size. Despite much overlap, co-existence and revivalism, Sherratt claims an overall regularity. Thus the link between houses and tombs is supported by the indication that the earliest tombs are often the most similar to the houses.

Sherratt also adopts an idea that originates with Montelius that some elements of megalithic design, such as round mounds and chambers, may result from an indigenous contribution, contrasting with the long mounds and long houses. The round and chambered tombs are more common in areas which had had dense Mesolithic settlement. They are seen as reflecting native house types or concepts of space. Various forms of fusion or incorporation of the central European long form and the Mesolithic Atlantic round form also occur.

For example, in northern and western France, passage graves were particularly characteristic of areas where relatively dense Mesolithic settlement can be inferred, especially on the coasts. The basic design, of a round chamber in a round mound, may be a reference to indigenous house types. But the grouping of passage graves in a trapezoidal mound (as at Barnenez) shows some accommodation with the long mound model.

Equally, in northern Europe the megalithic forms found in strongly Mesolithic areas are especially dolmens. Round mounds too are found in dense Mesolithic areas in Denmark, on the eastern coasts, whereas the first unchambered long mounds occur in Jutland in an inland area associated with Volling pottery.

Overall, then, Sherratt describes a spatial polarity between the intrusive monumentalized long house tomb and alternative megalithic forms which developed in Mesolithic areas in reaction to the incoming forms. How are we to explain the shift from long houses to long tombs in the Neolithic of north-west Europe? Both Sherratt (1990) and I (Hodder 1990) argue that the shift is related to the pattern of dispersed settlement in north-west Europe. The LBK house helped to form an important productive and social unit. The domus in central Europe was based on joint construction of a monumental form and on the control of movement through its increasingly important entrance (ibid.). But settlement begins to disperse in many areas in central Europe in the late fourth millennium BC. The spread of the Neolithic into north-west Europe is part of this process of settlement dispersal. Houses are less easy to discern in the earlier Neolithic of north-west Europe. A new economic regime based on the plough and secondary animal products is soon adopted. In this less stable, more varied system, houses and villages could not provide a long-term community focus. Daily settlement practices did not form the basis of long-term social structures. The latter were, however, set up in the practices of death and the veneration of ancestors. It was the tomb, especially as it began to be used over many generations, which could become the 'home' of dispersed local units. The tomb created continuity and stability in the face of the death and dispersal of community members.

TOMBS, THE ANCESTORS AND SETTLEMENT DIRT

I wish to turn to another aspect of the information about Neolithic tombs which supports the link made between tombs and houses but which also allows the argument to be taken further. Many tombs are built on top of houses or settlements. In Britain, Hazleton North (Saville 1990) and Haddenham (Hodder and Shand 1988) are built on late Mesolithic or earlier Neolithic settlement. The Kujavian long barrows are sometimes located on the sites of earlier TRB settlements, and there are many examples in western Pomerania, Mecklenburg, Lower Saxony and Denmark of barrows being located directly upon earlier settlements (for example, at Sarnowo, Gaj, Wollschow, Tosterglope, Stengade and Barkaer – Midgley 1985; Madsen 1979).

Such associations could simply result from the placing of tombs in cleared abandoned areas. Even if this is the case, the practices create links to earlier settlements and houses. But at times the link between tombs and earlier buildings is so precise as to suggest a more intentional and more complex association. Several earthen long barrows in northern Europe have traces of timber buildings which are not burial chambers themselves. However, the question remains of their chronological and functional links to the burial rituals. Did the buildings occur as settlement houses before burial, were they put up just before burial as part of the burial ritual, or are they contemporary or later than the burial? Related questions concern the 'occupation' material that is associated with some of these buildings. Is this domestic refuse, and if so was it reused in burial rituals, or is it the by-product of ritual activities?

At one of the Sarnowo barrows in Poland, a small rectangular building is stratigraphically later than the grave although its location directly over the grave suggests the placement was not accidental (Midgley 1985). In most other cases, the buildings are contemporary with or earlier than the graves. In another case at Sarnowo the central grave was dug into the possible floor of a building, although this could have been a ritual building. Graves 1 and 4 at Obalki were dug into previous 'settlement' material. At Gaj, traces of earlier settlement have been found beneath the mound, but the building

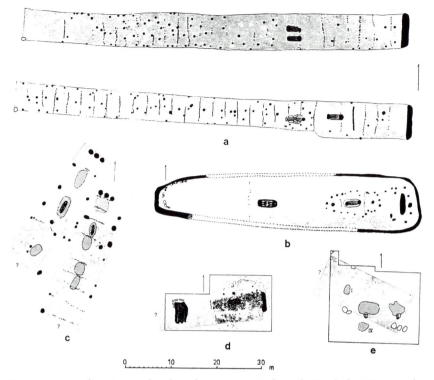

Figure 3.1 Scandinavian earthen long barrows: a) Barkaer, b) Bygholm Nørremark, c) Østergård, d) Rustrup, e) Tolstrup (from Madsen 1979, by kind permission of the Prehistoric Society)

associated with the grave has an interior which is very 'clean' and was either cleaned out or had never been occupied.

At Bygholm Nørremark, the barrow covers three possible houses. The central building containing the grave is the largest, being oval and 12 m by 6 m. There are four central posts in a line, with the two central ones having the grave between them (Figure 3.1). The building was probably already in place when the grave was inserted (Midgley 1985).

But it is to the 'occupational' material associated with these buildings and with the mounds and graves that we need to turn in order to attempt to discern their function. Unfortunately there has been no detailed comparative work, describing the assemblages in relation to undoubted settlement sites. In Britain at Haddenham (Hodder and Shand 1988) the late Mesolithic material in the mound has a high ratio of by-products to implements, indicating settlement activity, but here the temporal link between settlement and tomb cannot be argued to be immediate. At Hazleton North (Saville 1990) the central axis of the trapezoidal stone mound is placed directly over a

Neolithic 'midden' which is described as containing 'domestic' material in view of the wide range of flint, pottery, quernstone fragments, faunal and botanical remains including burnt hazelnut shells. The flint material included a high proportion of waste products. Remains of a hearth and post structure were also found. The radiocarbon evidence places this pre-cairn activity immediately before construction of the cairn, although there was probably a phase of cultivation between the midden and the cairn. Reviewing the evidence from this and other Cotswold-Severn sites and from adjacent regions, Saville comments 'these hints suggest that the phenomenon of tomb construction over areas of previous occupation is a recurrent one' (ibid.: 254).

In the Mecklenburg barrows, older excavation reports refer to substantial amounts of charcoal, ashes, burnt and unburnt bones, animal bone and pottery sherds, often mixed together. Under some Kujavian barrows there is mention of layers of charcoal called 'hearth middens', a term which captures both the widespread evidence of burning (to which I will return below) and the occupational nature of the deposits. For example, at the Lesniczowka complex, layers of between 15 and 30 cm in thickness have been found at three barrows. In some cases the material covers the graves and may indicate the burning of a building after the insertion of a grave. The edges of the midden material in one case are well defined, indicating a rectangular building and the material consists of pottery, flint tools, bone needles, burnt and unburnt animal bones, shells, a copper ring, burnt clay and charcoal. At Obalki, in addition to the midden material there was a 'hearth' which was attributed by the excavator to an earlier, pre-barrow phase. Overall the evidence is far from conclusive, but Midgley cautiously suggests 'that some of the timber building remains do represent earlier settlement structures and that the barrows were placed in their locations precisely with a view to incorporating earlier house structures into the overall ritual' (Midgley 1985: 161).

As has already been noted, the cultural material associated with long tomb graves in Denmark might be taken to derive from former habitation sites. In ten out of the twenty-nine tombs discussed by Madsen (1979) such deposits are present. Once again it would have been helpful if detailed study had compared the material in such deposits with material from settlement contexts unassociated with burial mounds. In the absence of such comparative analyses evaluation of the function of the midden material is difficult. The deposits often contain pottery, flint and hearth material or ash layers. At Østergård and Rimsø, the material clustered round the graves (ibid.). A similar clustering was found at Tolstrup, and the material here has been described as possibly domestic on the basis of the types of pottery recovered and the high frequency of flint (Madsen 1975).

Given the location of some tombs on earlier settlement sites it seems possible that some of the buildings and midden layers associated with the graves represent houses or habitation. The notion that tombs represent houses would thus be strengthened as would the emphasis on continuity and fixity over the long term. But whatever the nature of the pre-grave buildings, whether domestic or ritual or some combination of the two, the association of midden material with death ritual may be of wider significance. One way or another, the midden material is the result of discard or burning and destruction and collapse or decay. This is the context which is constructed or used for the body to disintegrate in and for the flesh to decay.

The mounding of earth over settlements and perhaps houses gives the 'dead' sites a continued presence in the landscape. The deceased too are referred to by the mounding procedure, so that they become ancestors. A continuity is created between past and present in the face of death, decay and destruction. The continuity of the local group is established in the practices of creating the 'home' of the ancestors. The rituals of death and decay are played upon in order to establish the long-term continuity of the domus. It is this aspect of the domus to which I now wish to turn more specifically, by looking at the abandonment practices of houses and tombs across Neolithic Europe. In all cases the problem being dealt with in prehistory was how to create continuity out of discontinuity.

REPRODUCING THE DOMUS

The domus is a set of ideas and practices which focus on the house. The very fabric and practices of the house created Neolithic society because they involved bonds, dependencies and boundaries between people. The domestic social unit was constructed in the practices of the house. My domus hypothesis is that the members of small-scale social units were defined as those that built the house together and took part in its maintenance and rituals. These social units had duration because they 'owned' or had jointly invested in the house.

Continuity through periods longer than the life of an individual house appears to have been dealt with in south-east Europe by constructing new houses directly over old. Such a pattern of replacement is found at Lepenski Vir, in the late sixth and early fifth millennia BC, associated with a hunter-gatherer-fisher economy. While some degree of displacement is evident, most of the houses are above earlier houses (Srejovic 1972). Tringham (1991) argues that houses are built directly over each other generally in the earlier Neolithic of south-east Europe. Such a pattern certainly continues into the fourth millennium BC. For example, Bailey (1990) has discussed the continuity of houses at tell sites in north-east Bulgaria. Radiocarbon evidence suggests that Ovcarovo was occupied for at least 570 years. The site has thirteen habitation horizons with perhaps only one major hiatus. Continuity through time is represented not only by the redecoration of houses (one house had forty-seven layers of painted clay) but also by the superpositioning

Figure 3.2 Reconstruction of a Linearbandkeramik long house being built (by kind permission of Peter Dunn)

of houses. Some phases show more evidence of houses being rebuilt from earlier phases and Bailey indicates that low numbers of house continuities are offset by high numbers of 'tectomorphs' – house models (ibid.: 42). So continuity of the domus at Ovcarovo is established either by rebuilding houses on older houses or, perhaps, by making symbolic equivalents of earlier houses.

Tringham (1991), however, argues that through time in the Neolithic of south-east Europe there is increasing evidence of partial or small-scale displacement of houses to immediately adjacent plots. This may seem odd given that through time settlements become more permanent and complex. This new practice might relate to a still greater sensitivity to issues of abandonment, inheritance and continuity. By the fourth millennium BC Tringham suggests that abandoned houses are universally burnt in south-east Europe. Such burning has traditionally been interpreted in terms of site-wide catastrophes of an accidental or violent nature. But, at Opovo, the lack of evidence of burning in the areas between houses suggests that the houses burned in separate fires (ibid.). At some points at Opovo these fires reached temperatures of over 1000°C which are regarded as very high for accidental fires of wattle-and-daub houses and suggest some deliberate fueling and tending. Perhaps such destruction of a house by burning was 'a deliberate act carried out at the death of the household head as a symbolic end of the household cycle' (ibid.: 123).

This whole emphasis on closure and continuity in the late fifth and fourth millennia BC in south-east Europe may also account for the high quantities of artefacts left on house floors. Such artefacts include whole pots, found broken *in situ* as well as ritual vessels and figurines. Even if some of the fires which destroyed the houses were accidental and some of the abandonment violent, it is remarkable that so much material was left in the houses. An alternative hypothesis is that material associated with the houses was respected as symbolically charged. Leaving the artefacts in the house during and after its destruction 'closed off' the past in order to allow renewal and continuity. Through time, as already noted, new houses respected the old by avoiding them.

This tactic of avoidance reaches its clearest expression in the LBK settlements of central Europe in the late fifth and early fourth millennia BC. One of the major problems in corroborating the stylistic ceramic sequences stratigraphically at these sites has been that there is little overlap between houses. Despite often dense concentrations of house plans such as at Sittard, Geleen and Elsloo, the houses themselves studiously avoid each other. Such a pattern is also found at extensively excavated sites such as Bylany and the Aldenhoven Plateau. Only at the later Lengyel villages such as Brzesc Kujawski does overlap occur, although even here the separate development of individual houses can sometimes be observed. Occupation horizons have not survived in LBK and later Danubian houses, so we have no evidence of whether artefacts were left in abandoned houses or whether there was widespread burning of individual houses. But the avoidance of earlier houses is distinctive. Since LBK and later settlements often endured several centuries, the location and remains of earlier houses must have been visible or known over the long term. Luning (1982) suggests that later buildings were built near earlier, socially related buildings in small settlement cells. Small cells of old and new buildings thus formed the evidence of the continuity of the domestic group over time.

Overall, then, the evidence from houses suggests that one of the main concerns of the domus in south-east and central Europe was continuity and renewal in the face of the death of household members and the abandonment of houses. Death and abandonment practices differed through place and time, varying from superpositioning to burning and leaving artefacts in houses to making models of houses. But it is perhaps possible to argue for an increasing concern with continuity over time as production intensified, investment in production with delayed returns increased, and as the inheritance of rights and properties became more contested (for a general account of this process see Hodder 1990). A greater concern with continuity is seen in the increased avoidance of earlier houses and the increased evidence for burning and the ritual abandonment of artefacts in houses in south-east Europe.

In many ways the tombs of north-west Europe continue the same emphases on continuity and abandonment rituals. Certainly many of the tombs were used over several generations and were constructed to allow repeated access. The very notion of a chambered wooden or stone tomb with entrance or passage creates the possibility of continued use, and the use of large stones or large slabs of wood (Hodder and Shand 1988) ensures long-term durability. In those areas and at those sites where there is evidence of ritual sorting, defleshing and recirculation of human bones in the tombs, continuity is again established over death and finality.

But there are also specific abandonment procedures at the tombs which recall the house rituals in central and south-east Europe. Artefacts are often placed in or at the front of the tombs. The evidence for the blocking or closure of tombs is widespread. But there is also widely found specific evidence of burning. In Scandinavia, wooden facades of tombs are frequently fired and megalithic graves also show evidence of fire (Madsen 1979). Many of the burial 'houses' mentioned above in Poland are associated with burnt layers which sometimes overlie the grave and must therefore be associated with the closure and mounding over of the tomb (Midgley 1985). The burning of tombs is apparent in Britain, particularly in the Yorkshire 'crematoria' (Manby 1970). At Haddenham, the dismantling of the wooden mortuary building was followed by a controlled burning and a mounding of soil (Hodder and Shand 1988). Also at this stage pots were deposited at the front of the tomb in an earth bank which closed the entranceway to the tomb.

Both houses and tombs, then, are concerned with continuity and both have similar rituals to deal with the end of use, to close off. But the tombs also introduce new ways of creating renewal in the face of discontinuity or death. Tarlow (1990) has discussed the evidence of plough marks under barrows. As the debate between Rowley-Conwy (1987) and Kristiansen (1990) has shown, it is not clear how many of these are ritual. Some may simply be traces of earlier fields on which barrows were situated. But in at least one case, Lundehøj, the marks were made after the burial chamber was constructed and are definitely ritual. Tarlow (1990) draws together the widespread ethnographic evidence for the use in small-scale societies of an agricultural metaphor to deal with death and continuity. The dead are often planted or ploughed in some way in order to make the crops grow.

The widespread evidence for the closure, blockage, dismantling or burning of tombs parallels the evidence from the houses of central and south-east Europe of a major concern with abandonment procedures. As the tomb- or house-using group moved to a new location or for other reasons had to abandon the 'home' of the tomb or house, the continuity or transformation of the group was ensured in the conduct of appropriate closure and regeneration rituals. The monuments thus not only provided a focus for the daily activities of the group, but they also acted to reproduce the group over the long term. After abandonment, the house or tomb came to 'stand for', refer to or represent the long-term ancestry of the group.

CONCLUSION

The house or house tomb is a 'home' which acts as an objectification of the relationships between those most closely connected to the domestic unit of production. For even a relatively small tomb such as Hazleton North, Saville (1990: 242) estimates that construction would have needed either a small group of five or six adults working for five or more years, or a larger group working for a shorter period. The use of the houses and tombs and their continued presence in the landscape also provided a fixed point for long-term economic dependencies. The continuity and reproduction of the domus may also have been related socially to the need to define rights, inheritance, property. Such common rights and investments are held by the 'tomb- or house-using group'. In other words the primary social units are constructed actively through the domus – actively in the sense that the groups are formed through participation in house and tomb.

The active nature of the monuments is particularly clear with regard to the tombs. In a dispersed economic and settlement system, property and inheritance rights may be categorized and defined primarily by reference to those who participate in the activities surrounding the tomb. There may be very little else which holds the group together. Without village or long-term settlement organization, even participation in agricultural labour and exchange may be defined in terms of the tomb-using group. In such a case, society and economy are indeed actively constructed in the events associated with the tomb.

But the way in which the tombs could act probably changed through time as they became more or less representational. Initially the tombs acted to create social units by referring to the stable house. As already noted, Sherratt suggests that the earlier tombs are more like houses. This point has also been made by Midgley (1985: 159), who suggests that in Kujavia the wooden buildings associated with graves appear to belong to the earlier phase of the earthen long barrow tradition. But we cannot assume that through the following centuries and even millennia of tomb construction in north-west Europe people gave the tombs meaning by reference to houses. Even if the tombs were called 'houses' of the ancestors and were built on house or settlement sites, they presumably came to have meaning in their own right as associated with a specific set of activities. Those who dug the soil together, who carried the stone or timbers to make the chambers, who carried in the dead, moving aside earlier remains of their ancestors, who gave gifts, who burned, mounded over and closed the tomb, in their joint activities developed a common tradition. For them the tomb acted less through reference and more through direct experience. Stability and continuity of rights and inheritance were constructed through a common ritual experience. But after the tombs had been closed off, they often came to act as reference points on the landscape (e.g. Barrett, Bradley and Green 1991), now being meaningful less through direct experience and more through reference to the past. Thus the meaning of tomb material culture may have shifted through time from referential to experiential to referential again.

BIBLIOGRAPHY

Ashbee, P., Smith, I.F. and Evans, J.G. (1979) 'Excavation of three long barrows near Avebury, Wiltshire', *Proceedings of the Prehistoric Society* 45: 207–300.

Bailey, D. (1990) 'The living house: signifying continuity', In R. Samson (ed.), *The Social Archaeology of Houses*, Edinburgh: Edinburgh University Press.

Barrett, J., Bradley, R. and Green, M. (1991) *Landscape, Monuments and Society*, Cambridge: Cambridge University Press.

Bloch, M. (1991) 'Language, anthropology and cognitive science', *Man* 26: 183–98.

Byers, A.M. (1991) 'Structure, meaning, action and things: the duality of material culture mediation', *Journal for the Theory of Social Behaviour* 21: 1–26.

Czerniak, L. (1980) *The Development of the Late Band Pottery Culture in Kujawy*, Poznan: Adam Mickiewicz University Press.

Gould, R. and Schiffer, M. (1981) *Modern Material Culture – The Archaeology of Us*, New York: Academic Press.

Hodder, I. (1982) *The Present Past*, London: Batsford.

——(1984) 'Burials, houses, women and men in the European Neolithic', in D. Miller and C. Tilley (eds), *Ideology, Power and Prehistory*, Cambridge: Cambridge University Press.

——(1990) *The Domestication of Europe*, Oxford: Blackwell.

——(1992) *Theory and Practice in Archaeology*, London: Routledge.

Hodder, I. and Shand, P. (1988) 'The Haddenham long barrow: an interim statement', *Antiquity* 62: 349–53.

Kristiansen, K. (1990) 'Ard marks under barrows: a response to Peter Rowley-Conwy', *Antiquity* 64: 322–7.

Luning, J. (1982) 'Research in the Bandkeramik settlement of the Aldenhover Platte in the Rhineland', *Analecta Praehistoria Leidensia* 15: 1–30.

Madsen, T. (1975) 'Early Neolithic structures at Tolstrup near Logstor', *Kuml* 1973/4: 149–54.

——(1979) 'Earthen long barrows and timber structures: aspects of the early Neolithic mortuary practice in Denmark', *Proceedings of the Prehistoric Society* 45: 301–20.

Manby, T.G. (1970) 'Long barrows of northern England; structural and dating evidence', *Scottish Archaeological Forum* 2: 1–28.

Midgley, M. (1985) *The Origin and Function of the Earthern Long Barrows of Northern Europe*, Oxford: BAR Int. Series S259.

Rowley-Conwy, P. (1987) 'The interpretation of ard marks', *Antiquity* 61: 263–6.

Saville, A. (1990) *Hazleton North*, English Heritage Archaeological Report no. 13.

Shanks, M. and Tilley, C. (1987) *Archaeology and Social Theory*, Cambridge: Polity Press.

Sherratt, A. (1990) 'The genesis of megaliths', *World Archaeology* 22: 147–67.

Srejovic, D. (1972) *Europe's First Monumental Sculpture*, London: Thames and Hudson.

Tarlow, S. (1990) 'Metaphors and Neolithic–Bronze Age Burial Mounds', unpublished M.Phil. dissertation, Dept of Archaeology, University of Cambridge.

Tringham, R. (1991) 'Households with faces: the challenge of gender in prehistoric architectural remains', in J. Gero and M. Conkey (eds), *Engendering Archaeology*, Oxford: Blackwell.

Weber, A. (1983) *Studies in the Burial Ritual of the Lupawa Group of Funnel Beaker Culture*, Poznan: Adam Mickiewicz University Press.

4

DEFINING DOMESTIC SPACE IN THE BRONZE AGE OF SOUTHERN BRITAIN

John C. Barrett

THE ARCHAEOLOGICAL RECORD

Archaeologists take the object of their study to be the material residues of the human past. These residues appear to derive from, and to thus represent a record of, a number of complex and extinct processes. As a consequence it appears that archaeologists must identify those extinct processes if they are to explain how the record was formed. I will define this as the *representational* model of archaeology. In this model the material residues stand in for the absent processes which the archaeologist seeks to 'uncover' or to 'construct' to establish an image of the past.

The archaeological record is patterned, and most archaeologists seem to agree on how they describe that patterning. Indeed, these descriptions are often regarded as the factual basis of archaeology. For example, the identification of settlement sites, or what constitutes domestic architecture in the form of walls, entrances, spaces and fittings, are all regarded as relatively unproblematic issues of observation, as is the identification of the various categories of artefact recovered from these sites. A great deal of methodological effort has been invested to increase the resolution by which these mute data-sets may be described and compared. More contentious, however, are the interpretations which link these descriptions of contemporary phenomena to an archaeological construction of a past. Whilst archaeology has therefore witnessed a developing consensus regarding the sampling strategies employed in fieldwork and excavation, an increasing divergence has occurred in views concerning the processes which we might select as having caused the observable variablities of the record. There are also strong disagreements as to how these different views may be validated with reference to the available data (see for example Shanks and Tilley 1989 with the comments published alongside that paper).

I will begin by outlining an argument against the representational model of archaeological evidence. This model treats historical research as a problem of cause and effect, linking the past (as cause) to its present-day record. I will then attempt to develop this argument by considering some recent approaches towards the definition of 'domestic architecure' in British later prehistory.

As I have already suggested, we are in possession of substantial bodies of data which represent refinements in our understanding of the structural details, depositional patterning and environmental contexts as they relate to settlement archaeology. Different cross-cultural generalizations have been used to explain the formation of these data, including questions of settlement location, architectural organization, the distribution of activity areas within settlements, and the development of settlement patterns through time. These explanations place either a greater or a lesser emphasis upon technical or environmental determinants, issues of social organization, and the symbolic values which were maintained by the spatial organization of tasks or depositional activities. Susan Kent (1990: 2) comments that many of these processes are discussed in 'notoriously vague' terms, but her examination of the variability of domestic architecture inevitably returns her to the assertion stated by McGuire and Schiffer that when we ask why certain structures have a specific form, we are asking about design process: 'In particular, we must identify the general causal factors (and their interrelationships) that influence the decision leading to the design of particular structures' (quoted in Kent 1990: 127). The selection of these particular 'causal factors' relating to design decisions represents a shift in explanation, away from environmental and technological determinants towards an understanding of the social and symbolic use of space as expressed through the 'design process'. Underlying this shift is the desire to incorporate a knowledgeable human agency into the historical process.

These newly established concerns with human agency have not won universal acceptance. One reason for this is that they appear to raise a substantial methodological challenge; if archaeology has now arrived at a position, long developed in anthropology, away from a geographical or technological determinism and towards accepting the social and symbolic value of the house, where the house may even be taken as encoding a model of the society itself, then we are left with the problem of how we might recover the culturally specific meanings carried by this code.

> If I know nothing of a culture and am placed in its architectural remains, the walls will tell me nothing. I cannot learn symbolic meaning from the house remains alone.
>
> (Donley-Reid 1990: 115)

It would appear that the very absence of that which we hope to use to explain the record – the reasons why people acted in one way and not another to build in a certain form – must operate to set severe limits on the nature of archaeological interpretation.

I would suggest that efforts simply to explain the formation of the archaeological record – and thus to answer such questions as 'why did these settlements take this particular form?' – are misplaced. Certainly we must have some understanding of the mechanical formation processes of the materials which we study, but to move beyond this and to seek reasons why certain forms of material culture were created will always lead to the adoption of functionalist explanations where ancient societies are represented as administrative systems organizing their own functional integration or transformation (for a critique of the 'administrative' model of society see Bauman 1992). Let us consider what is involved if we abandon the traditional questions concerning the causes of certain material conditions, and consider instead their possible consequences. People reproduce the conditions of their own lives through their ability to interpret and thus to understand the conditions which they inhabit. This places the analytical emphasis upon a 'recursive' role for material culture. We move away from trying to understand people as the authors of some original, authentic meaning which they inscribed upon material culture, and towards an understanding of people who acted capably because of their ability to understand and to monitor – in other words to read and interpret – the material conditions which they occupied.

It is therefore not enough to say that material culture is meaningfully constituted; material culture in itself means nothing until it is situated within a regime of interpretation. This has important implications for archaeology. If we retain a cause-effect relationship between 'the past' and its modern-day 'record' we will burden ourselves with the view that past human agency was responsible for creating (as an author) the meanings which were then seemingly transmitted by that record into our present-day world. That meaning then appears to be objectified by the archaeological attempt to understand what those others meant by creating particular forms of material pattern. This objectification raises the false hope that the past is the location for an original, intended and true meaning. I would reject this position, and not for the kind of methodological reasons given by Donley-Reid (namely that we need the authors to be present so that they may explain to us what the material meant). I would reject it because no interpretation or reading is ever possible without the active involvement of the reader, and no absolute grounding exists for us to assess our own readings of the material against some spurious original and transcendental meaning. Archaeological practice involves the committed engagement of the archaeologists themselves in the struggle to understand the material residues. This interpretative practice encounters fragments of the material conditions which others once also sought to understand. That we are responsible for making interpretative statements which cannot arise independently of us is not a 'problem' which challenges the objectivity of our work, rather it exposes the way material culture is open to multiple and contested readings. History is written as we attempt to come to terms with other ways of knowing and other ways of reading. There has never been a single or uncontested meaning of the material which we choose to study, instead there have been contested readings and social strategies which have attempted to limit the possible ranges of those interpretations. It is this struggle to know the world in certain ways, and to act upon the implications of those understandings, which lies at the heart of historical and cultural dynamics.

Archaeological evidence need not be seen as the 'record' of various 'meaningful statements' which originated in the past. Instead it may be viewed as the residual remains of a widely diverse range of materialities. These materialities were inhabited and interpreted in the light of assumptions and prejudices about the nature of the world. The validity of those assumptions was experienced and monitored through practice, an empirical evaluation carried forward by bodily and sensory dispositions as well as discursively. As archaeologists, we might enquire into how these different materialities could be known, the practices through which those knowledges were realized and monitored, and the consequences of those practices.

INTERPRETATIVE ARCHAEOLOGY

Life is lived sequentially, as a movement from one place and experience to another. Memory and expectation enable people to understand and to act effectively as they enter each new region of daily practice. Time-geography has shown how an individual's biography can be described as a sequence of regionalized encounters, the routines of life are movements from one region to another (for example see the papers in Gregory and Urry 1985). What distinguishes between different cultural and social experiences is not simply the differences in material conditions but also the way those conditions are understood and linked together, in other words the way prior experiences and understandings are carried forward and reworked within given materialities. It is as if each new experience was predictable upon the expectation that the world is ordered and thus conformed with the understanding of that order. Cosmologies are not simply intellectual schemes by which the world may be described, they are revealed empirically when carried forward in practice, and such practice works upon, and thus transforms, its material conditions. Sahlins (1985) refers to practice as being a 'gamble' played out in nature because it is always possible that the world will not conform to expectation.

Routine or institutional activities are often described in terms of their repetitive, cyclical or timeless quality. These routines seemingly embody, and endlessly rework, certain cultural values and it was these values which structuralist anthropology, among other traditions, sought to identify. However, to describe these values as timeless (for example in the way cosmological schemes are often described) is to forget that they are re-worked in practices which occupy a trajectory in time–space. In other words, for the practitioner the sequential and situated practices by which institutions are maintained have a beginning and an end, a direction and an order of priorities. This is the fundamental point of departure which Bourdieu (1977; 1990) established in his critique of structuralism.

I would like to explore this issue in a little more detail with reference to Ian Hodder's recent (1990) work on the European Neolithic. In this book Hodder suggests that domestication arose through the establishment of a set of cultural values where the hearth and the house (the domus) stood in opposition to an external world (the agrios). Domestication involved bringing the resources of the agrios into the domus. There are two ways in which such argument might be developed. One is to trace the manifestation of the domus/agrios duality through the various historical and cultural systems which make up the European Neolithic, and this type of analysis does form a substantial part of Hodder's study. The second line of development is rather different. Implicit in Hodder's argument is not simply the idea of the domus/agrios duality but also its practical creation out of a sense of direction, of primacy and of dominance. Domestication involved 'the need to control "the wild" by *bringing it within* the control of "the domus"' (ibid.: 39, my italic). From this perspective we touch upon the situated experiences and the practical contingencies whereby the house came to be known to obtain 'its dramatic force from the exclusion, control and domination of the wild, the outside (. . . agrios)' (ibid.: 45). Practice thus reproduces an order (such as the cultural duality of domus/agrios), but the one should not be confused with the other. Now it is not only the unintentional outcome of those practices which concerns us (such as the making of The Neolithic or some similar abstraction): we must also consider how the world was known in a certain way through the temporal and spatial practices which sustained that knowledge and its dominant metaphorical associations. Although this challenge is present in much of Hodder's study, it is one which remains largely unanswered.

Architecture will mean little if we only view it in terms of the allocation and the ordering of space, or of the activities which may have occupied those spaces. Inhabited architecture facilitates the orientation of the body's movement, it directs progress from one place to another, it enables activities to be assigned to particular places, it orientates and focuses the attention of the practitioners. Architecture is therefore used in the structuring of time–space, and the various settings and the activities which they may contain represent the consumption of time, as does the path of movement linking these settings. Clearly the allocation of activities within the spaces demarcated by the architecture may vary, and different sequences of movement may be chosen between these activities, forming what Rapoport (1990) terms 'activity systems'. These linkages are directional and the primacy given to one place by following one path of movement is a definition of temporal order. The human body thus works through a series of strategies, guided by memory and expectation, which inscribes architecture with meaning. Architecture operates as a technology to order time–space, enabling activities to be regionalized and linked sequentially, thus establishing priorities and chains of metaphorical association. Donley-Reid (1990) is correct: the walls mean nothing, their significance emerges as containers of situated practices. The building does not therefore encode some original meaning which the archaeologist should seek to uncover; rather it was, and it remains, a site open to signification, to be occupied and understood through practice (cf. Olsen 1990).

Although archaeologists agree on their identification of 'domestic architecture' and its description in terms of its walls, entrances, fittings, and also in terms of its functions, none of this in fact represents historical analysis. Domestic architecture is fixed at the intersection of a number of interpretive regimes which extend beyond the settlement. Sometimes the house may form the 'principle locus for the objectification of generative schemes' (Bourdieu 1977: 89), at other times the house may be read by reference to a primary order which is found within a much wider landscape. Historical questions concern the operation and the consequences of these interpretative regimes.

REDEFINING DOMESTIC SPACE

During the second millennium BC the landscape of much of southern Britain began to undergo a transformation in terms of its physical organization. Field systems, paddocks, trackways, as well as various forms of more substantial boundaries including 'cross-ridge dykes', 'ranch boundaries' and 'reaves' are variously attested on many of the uplands, as well as in some lowland areas, by the beginning of the first millennium BC. This evidence for an increasing division of the landscape is still best known from the chalk downland of central southern England where it has long been taken as indicative of an 'agricultural revolution' (Curwen 1938; Childe 1947). Despite quite extensive fieldwork, it is not possible to trace this history of land division much earlier than the middle of the second millennium. From the late fifth to the early second millennium, monuments which marked places of ancestral veneration, communal gatherings, ceremonial display and burial seem to have been among the main points of reference by which the landscape, and a person's place in that landscape, could be defined. From the second millennium onwards these monuments remained, but they did so in a landscape which was increasingly enclosed and in which many of the settlements were also surrounded by fences or earthworks. The evidence from the chalk downland indicates that some settlements were initially enclosed by relatively insubstantial banks and palisades, but by the first millennium more substantial earthworks were being constructed (Barrett, Bradley and Green 1991). I want to consider the implications of these changes in the form of the landscape, and in the place of settlements within those landscapes, and to suggest that these changes arose out of a shift in the interpretive strategies by which people were able to fix themselves within certain 'imagined communities'.

People may lay claim to belonging to a community whose well-being is served by their own actions. Anderson (1983) has described some aspects of modern-day nationalism in terms of 'imagined communities' and Bauman has written of imagined communities which exist 'solely through their manifestations: through occasional spectacular outbursts of togetherness . . . – sudden materializations of the idea' (Bauman 1992: xix). By linking the biography of the agent to that of things, places and times (cf. Kopytoff 1986), the 'imagined co-presence' of others who may be geographically distant or dead (or yet to be born) may be evoked (Urry 1991: 170). I wish to apply this to the way the agents may bind themselves to certain regions of time–space as a way of situating their own lives within the biographies of these larger communities.

Ingold has argued that tenure is about

> the ways in which a resource locale is worked or bound into the biography of the subject or into the developmental trajectory of those groups, domestic or otherwise, of which he is a member.
>
> (Ingold 1986: 137)

Tenure, as a means of situating the subject's control, or the control of the community to which that subject belongs, over resources can be considered as operating either on *places, paths*, or over *areas of ground surface* according to Ingold. I would suggest that the British Neolithic represents a continuity in tenurial claims over path and place, tenurial systems which will also have characterized earlier gatherer-hunter communities (Barrett 1993). The non-megalithic and megalithic long mounds and the causewayed enclosures did not lie at the centres of areas of land surface, but were instead places at the ends and at the beginnings of paths. These were the intersections of paths; places of meeting and departure which may have been part of a wider and seasonal cycle of movement. Such places reaffirmed the permanence of the community which included the ancestors themselves, indeed it may have been the ancestors who provided the metaphor for that permanence. The enclosures and long mounds were therefore more likely to have been the expression of a traditional reading of the landscape, which extended back over centuries, than to have represented some 'rethinking' of the world in terms of a Neolithic.

This argument has immediate implications for the nature of Neolithic agriculture, not only in southern Britain but also more widely in western Europe. We could envisage these earlier agricultural practices operating in terms of 'long-fallow' systems (Boserup 1965). Regeneration of vegetation on the cultivation plots would have been expected during periods of fallow, and access to such plots could have been claimed from the rights of member-ship to the general community. Long-fallow cultivation would have required little investment in terms of agricultural technology, with culti-vation more generally by spade and hoe than by plough. Major subdivisions of the landscape would not have been attempted, and access to cultivable land was secured as part of the mosaic of resources over which the commu-nity exercised its rights. Biographical continuity was therefore dependent upon the continuity of the community of whom the ancestors were the only permanent members. The living could not expect, indeed it was unnecessary, to establish an individual or household-based long-term claim upon an area of cultivation.

The manifestation of the ritualized community, among whom the living were transient members, may have been expressed most eloquently in the great ceremonial landscapes of the late Neolithic in southern Britain and Brittany. Here formal avenues and pathways linked one place to another, the significance of each place being realized by the arrival of the celebrants and the execution of the ritual and ceremony. It was in these rituals that metaphysical forces of spirits and ancestors were presenced among the living (Barrett 1993). By inhabiting these places the image of the larger community was thus evoked through a 'spectacular expression of togetherness'. However, by the end of the third millennium another form of biographical narrative and a different form of togetherness was being established. Most recent work on the early single-grave burial rites of southern Britain has questioned those interpretations which see them as indicating an emergent social ranking (Barrett 1990 and 1993; Garwood 1991; Mizoguchi 1993). The selection of the place for the grave and its marking, and the placing of subsequent burials either in or alongside earlier graves, must have involved the mourners in a narrative exploration of lineal relationships between the dead and into which they, the living, were also drawn. The importance of the single-grave tradition was not so much that the dead were now situated at particular places in the landscape, but by being fixed in this way the cemetery mapped relationships between the dead which reached out to incorporate the living. New biographies emerged. More specific lines of inheritance were given voice, and with them a more complex identity for the agent was established in terms of status and obligations. The weight of the past could now bear down to fix those lives as a moment of being in the directional flow of time (Barrett 1993).

These new biographical narratives contributed to the fragmentation of the earlier imaginary communities and the establishment of a new type of tenurial claim, namely that over areas of ground surface. This form of tenure can be equated with systems of short-fallow agriculture, demanding more intensive land-use with a higher level of technological input and in which crops were removed with a greater frequency, even to the extent of multi-cropping (Boserup 1965). These systems would demand a different organization of labour, a greater investment in technology, particularly a greater emphasis upon plough agriculture, and a routine intervention to maintain the land resources and the fertility of the soil (cf. Goody 1976). Such long-term investments were made in the ways particular areas of land were maintained from one year to the next, an investment which bound the reproduction of a smaller, perhaps residentially based community to that particular area.

The contrast is hopefully clear. The earlier biographical systems created an agent who belonged to a wide and open community, the continuity of which was fixed by the ancestral presence. Long-fallow systems represented the expectation that resources, such as land and co-operative labour, arose from the alliances maintained with that wider community. From the end of the second millennium these communities fragmented, as did the landscape itself. No longer was that landscape simply a constellation of sacred sites linked by paths of access, it was now overlain by enclosed surfaces, tracts of intensively cultivated and grazed land. A new form of biography created agents who belonged to smaller and differently situated communities. The continuity of these communities was reproduced through the tenurial rights claimed to land. These areas of land were worked more intensively, implying a labour force which was local and in more regular contact. The joint investment was also in land worked from one generation to the next; the agent inherited rights of which some at least were now spatially bound. It is not surprising that the settlement and house should have become the locus for enacting some of the dominant metaphorical associations by which the community's own continuity could be expressed.

From the end of the second millennium the locus of the settlement was increasingly defined through the interpretative schemes by which the agents were able to read of their own existences and of the communities with which they identified. The expressions of togetherness may now have been more routinely expressed through the cycles of agricultural labour (cf. Barrett 1989), and from about 1100 BC some settlements were enclosed and some were occasionally the focus for small-scale votive deposits (Barrett, Bradley and Green 1991: 225). The life history of the settlement itself may have expressed the genealogy of human existence. Settlements clearly grew – Ellison (1978) has demonstrated the shifting location of the settlement at Itford Hill and the multiple fence lines recorded at Black Patch (Figure 4.1) would indicate the eastward addition of buildings here. These circular buildings were placed on terraces at the back of small embanked and fenced enclosures, the fence lines defining small yards immediately outside each building (Drewett 1982). To enter one of these houses was perhaps to enter into the presence of those who stood at a particular genealogical relationship to the continuity of the community.

The monumental architecture of British later prehistory is predominantly domestic, and if the house and the settlement eventually replaced the

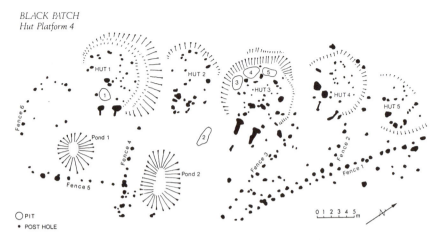

Figure 4.1 Settlement plan at Black Patch 'Hut Platform 4', Sussex (from Drewett 1982, by kind permission of the Prehistoric Society)

cemetery as the physical manifestation of biographical continuity, this may find archaeological expression in the complex longevity of our later prehistoric settlements. It is through such interpretive strategies that we may begin to grasp the significance of the domestic architecture of the late Bronze Age and Iron Age, over and above its simple characterization in terms of architectural style or the formal arrangement of space.

NOTE

I am grateful to the editors for their patience, to Colin Richards for his guidance during the writing of this paper, to Lorraine McEwan for preparing the illustration and to Lesley McFadyen for discussing approaches to the materiality of the past.

BIBLIOGRAPHY

Anderson, B. (1983) *Imagined Communities: Reflections on the Origins and Spread of Nationalism*, London: Verso.

Barrett, J.C. (1989) 'Food, gender and metal: questions of social reproduction', in M.L. Stig Sorensen and R. Thomas (eds), *The Bronze Age – Iron Age Transition in Europe: Aspects of Continuity and Change c. 1200 to 500 BC*, Oxford: BAR Int. Series 483:304–20.

——(1990) 'The monumentality of death: the character of early Bronze Age mortuary mounds in southern Britain', *World Archaeology* 22: 178–89.

——(1993) *Fragments from Antiquity: An Archaeology of Social Life in Britain c. 2900–1200 BC*, Oxford: Blackwell.

Barrett, J.C., Bradley, R. and Green, M. (1991) *Landscape, Monuments and Society: The Prehistory of Cranborne Chase*, Cambridge: Cambridge University Press.

Bauman, Z. (1992) *Intimations of Postmodernity*, London: Routledge.

Boserup, E. (1965) *The Conditions of Agricultural Growth*, London: Allen & Unwin.

Bourdieu, P. (1977) *Outline of a Theory of Practice*, Cambridge: Cambridge University Press.

——(1990) *The Logic of Practice*, Cambridge: Polity Press.

Childe, V.G. (1947) *Prehistoric Communities of the British Isles*, London: Chambers.

Curwen, E.C. (1938) 'The early development of agriculture in Britain', *Proceedings of the Prehistoric Society* 4: 27–51.

Donley-Reid, L. (1990) 'A structuring structure: the Swahili house', in S. Kent (ed.), *Domestic Architecture and the Use of Space: An Interdisciplinary Cross-cultural Study*, Cambridge: Cambridge University Press.

Drewett, P. (1982) 'Later Bronze Age downland economy and excavations at Black Patch, East Sussex', *Proceedings of the Prehistoric Society* 48: 321–400.

Ellison, A. (1978) 'The Bronze Age of Sussex', in P.L. Drewett (ed.), *Archaeology in Sussex to AD 1500*, London: Council for British Archaeology Research Report 29: 30–7.

Garwood, P. (1991) 'Ritual, tradition and the reconstitution of society', in P. Garwood, D. Jennings, R. Skeates and J. Toms (eds), *Sacred and Profane, Proceedings of a Conference on Archaeology, Ritual and Religion, Oxford 1989*, Oxford: Oxford University Committee for Archaeology.

Goody, J. (1976) *Production and Reproduction: A Comparative Study of the Domestic Domain*, Cambridge: Cambridge University Press.

Gregory, D. and Urry, J. (eds) (1985) *Social Relations and Spatial Structures*, London: Macmillan.

Hodder, I. (1990) *The Domestication of Europe*, Oxford: Blackwell.

Ingold, T. (1986) *The Appropriation of Nature: Essays on Human Ecology and Social Relations*, Manchester: Manchester University Press.

Kent, S. (ed.) (1990) *Domestic Architecture and the Use of Space: An Interdisciplinary Cross-cultural Study*, Cambridge: Cambridge University Press.

Kopytoff, I. (1986) 'The cultural biography of things: commoditization as process', in A. Appadurai (ed.), *The Social Life of Things: Commodities in Cultural Perspective*, Cambridge: Cambridge University Press.

Mizoguchi, K. (1993) 'A historiography of a linear barrow cemetery: a structurationist's point of view', *Archaeological Review from Cambridge* 11.

Olsen, B. (1990) 'Roland Barthes: from sign to text', in C. Tilley (ed.), *Reading Material Culture*, Oxford: Blackwell.

Rapoport, A. (1990) 'Systems of activities and systems of settings', in S. Kent (ed.), *Domestic Architecture and the Use of Space: An Interdisciplinary Cross-cultural Study*, Cambridge: Cambridge University Press.

Sahlins, M. (1985) *Islands of History*, London: Tavistock Publications.

Shanks, M. and Tilley, C. (1989) 'Archaeology into the 1990s', *Norwegian Archaeological Review* 22: 1–12.

Urry, J. (1991) 'Time and space in Giddens' social theory', in C.G.A. Bryant and D. Jary (eds), *Giddens' Theory of Structuration; A Critical Appreciation*, London: Routledge.

5

SEPARATION OR SECLUSION? TOWARDS AN ARCHAEOLOGICAL APPROACH TO INVESTIGATING WOMEN IN THE GREEK HOUSEHOLD IN THE FIFTH TO THIRD CENTURIES BC

Lisa Nevett

The title of this paper is intended to encapsulate one of the main questions that has recently been asked about women in Greek society, and one which is eminently suited to investigation using archaeological data: to what extent were the women of this period confined to specific parts of the household, and was any such practice simply a matter of convenience based on the need to supervise household chores, or was it, as suggested by some commentators (for example, Walker 1983: 81–2) a rigorously enforced cultural requirement for social respectability? The aim of this paper is to build upon previous work that has examined the archaeological material, through the use of an ethnographic parallel. Such a device can obviously not re-create in every respect the society of ancient Greece. Nevertheless, it may help us to break away from some of the constraints imposed by the fragmentary nature of much of our evidence, allowing us to build a more coherent picture of the way in which different factors within a society may interrelate, and the possible consequences of one particular form of social organization in terms of both the household organization and adjustments that are made in other spheres of life. Thus, the parallel used here is intended to suggest possibilities rather than to set up a rigid model that can simply be transplanted into the ancient context.

BACKGROUND: THE CLASSICAL CONTEXT

The specific question of the position of women within the household is of broad significance in terms of Classical studies in general, not only because of the insights it provides into the lives of the women of the time, but also because of its wider implications with respect to social relations within and between individual households, which form a background for our under-standing of the literature and for historical research. The relatively large number of extant texts from the period have been used by many past scholars as a basis for arguing that women were to a large degree secluded from public life, and kept within the bounds of the household compound (Just 1989: 106). It has usually been assumed that the women of a household were given their own area (called the *gunaikon* or *gunaikonitis*) in the upper storey of the house. It is clear, though, that in terms of the number of references, the evidence for such a form of gender separation is extremely limited indeed (Jameson 1990a: 171). Whether this corresponds to a scarcity of the phenomenon itself, or whether it is due to biases in the literature that has come down to us is unclear; however, there is a more widespread trend which consists of an underlying opposition between male and female areas of the house, which are used as similes where two contrasting opposites are being described, and this continues from the fifth century down to the first century and beyond.

Together with the fact that only a small number of sources deal with seclusion *per se*, there are also limitations built into such sources (Just 1975: 153), and the problems that these cause have often been overlooked. Most of the authors whose works are preserved were male; this means that they provide evidence only from a male view-point, and that at best we will be getting only a partial picture of society, especially if it is correct to argue for a high degree of seclusion. A second problem is that the authors of these literary works seem usually to have been from wealthy backgrounds. (Euripides, for example, is mocked by Aristophanes because his mother is supposed to have been a vegetable seller [*Thesmophoriazusae* 387], which implies that this was not the usual background for an author.) The result of these biases is that only a limited section of the total economic and social range within the population is likely to be represented in the written sources. A further source of potential bias is geographical: a high proportion of the literary works together with a number of the relevant inscriptions that survive today come from Athens. However, during the period in question the Greek world stretched over a broad area, and was composed of a number of independent polities with different systems of government. If we are to believe the sources relating to Sparta, which is the other major city for which we have evidence, these different communities encompass a range of accepted norms of social behaviour.

As well as biases due to the authors, difficulties are also caused by the media which we have available as sources of information: there is a relative paucity of descriptive accounts relating both to women in general, and to their role in the home in particular. This is partly a function of the types of writing that were carried out at this time; in particular there is a lack of descriptive fiction, and one of the main sources that is available, drama, is hard to interpret in terms of the lives of real women of the period (Pomeroy 1975: 58–9). Cultural factors are also relevant here, since the woman's main activity seems to have taken place in the domestic context, which was considered a private domain and therefore rarely discussed in public or, by extension, in literature. All these factors have combined to obscure varia-bility in the types of social role that must have been played by women, and to produce an impression of homogeneity across the Greek world and throughout the different social strata.

Thus, although from the written sources the impression is that some degree of spatial separation was practised, we cannot continue to ignore the implications of the limitations in the available sources, especially in view of the fact that even amongst those literary sources, 'there is a significant body of evidence which will not square with a picture of rigorous physical confinement' (Just 1989: 106). As is shown below, this variety of conflicting impressions is not confined to the literature alone, but is also present in the archaeological material.

One likely explanation for this contradictory picture is that over a period of time the consequence of a stress upon use of the written sources has been a tendency to create a normative view. A major problem that has dogged past research into female life in antiquity, and one to which the title of this paper might seem to succumb, is the use of one overarching category of 'women'. Previous research has tended to be directed at the investigation of the female as a single category, in structural opposition to that of the male, and this tendency is now coming under criticism (see, for example, Arrigoni 1985: xii; Blok 1987: 6; Versnel 1987: 60). The result is that stress has been given to the homogeneity of members of the category 'female' because of their shared quality of 'femaleness', and the substantial amount of underly-ing variability has been ignored. Only recently has a more sophisticated approach been taken in which the term 'woman' has begun to be unpacked, and the possible range of social identities involved have been isolated and subjected to separate investigation.[1] The extent to which these approaches can hope to succeed is, however, limited by the sources themselves, and as indicated above, it is likely that there are whole sections of the population that are simply not represented in the literary evidence, so nothing can be learned about them through literature.

Archaeological material offers an obvious alternative to texts, in that although there are biases in the types of material that have survived, if excavation is thorough and systematic, these biases should cross-cut those introduced in the literary evidence: in geographical terms, although Athens is the city most strongly represented in the literature, the archaeological evidence is, to say the least, patchy, owing to the growth of the modern city. In fact, some of the most informative archaeological material comes from areas of the Greek world scarcely known from the literary sources. Furthermore, if excavation is carried out using a strategy that will provide a representative sample of a site, even the poorest elements of its population should be documented in the archaeological record. Such material offers an opportunity to look directly at the domestic context and at the results of activities themselves, rather than through a cultural filter.

Although in comparison to the amount of public architecture that has been excavated, relatively little attention has been paid to domestic assemblages, there is enough excavated material to allow preliminary investigation of this question. None the less, the fact that the evidence most frequently available is the house plan (Figure 5.1), often with little or no detail as to the distribution of finds within the house, means that enquiry must be based largely on house-layout. Two scholars have recently examined the question of seclusion, using such evidence, and come to conflicting conclusions (Walker 1983; Jameson 1990a; 1990b). My examination of the way in which seclusion may have worked in practice will build upon the progress made by these investigations and reconcile or account for some of the differences of opinion.

Walker (1983) adopts the position of Flacelier (1965: 55) and others, relying on those texts that seem to indicate seclusion of women within the house. She reasons that any such seclusion should be visible in the organization of space within the Greek household, and therefore detectable in the archaeological remains of Greek houses. She then undertakes a brief survey of four examples of houses, three from Greece at the period in question, and an ethnographic parallel from Kano in Nigeria. In brief descriptions of these, various characteristics of each plan, such as spatial separation of different rooms and the staggering of entrances, are pointed out as characteristic of a desire for isolating various parts of the house. Different areas of the individual structures are designated as male and female, and the house plans are divided accordingly (although no account is taken of possible upper storeys). It seems reasonable to assume that, for practical reasons, any form of female seclusion may be detectable in the archaeological record (*pace* Jameson 1990a: 172), although there are fundamental weaknesses in the approach taken. The main difficulty lies in the fact that instead of looking at the archaeological material itself for evidence of seclusion, the consideration of the archaeology is only secondary to a foregone assumption of seclusion. A second problem is that there is no discussion of the degree or nature of the seclusion practised in any of the areas interpreted as 'female', although the possibility for such a discussion is present in the inclusion of the ethnographic comparison, and such a question must surely arise out of the Kano example itself, since two of the rooms designated for male use can only be

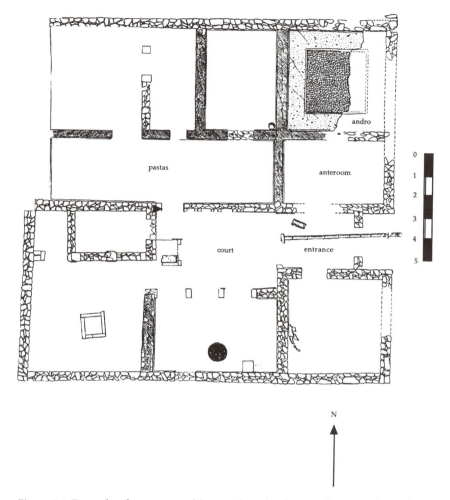

Figure 5.1 Example of an excavated house plan: the 'house of many colours' from Olynthos (after Robinson 1946)

approached through so-called 'female' areas. Indeed, the aim of including the Kano example is obscure: there is no systematic analysis of the organiz-ation of the houses, nor are there generalized conclusions drawn from the comparison. The potential of using such an analogy is explored further below.

Jameson's comments on seclusion arise from a wider-ranging consider-ation of public versus private space as a whole, and as such represent shorter treatments of the subject. In stating that 'important as the distinction between male and female areas was, it did not affect directly the actual planning and building of houses' (Jameson 1990a: 172), the position he adopts is in direct conflict with that of Walker, and (as noted above) given the archaeological evidence that we do have from the period, it seems unwarrantedly pessimistic. One of the most characteristic features of many of the excavated houses of this period is the men's dining room (called the *andron* or *andronitis*). From the literary and iconographic evidence, this room has been identified as the location for male parties, at which respectable women were not to be seen, and thus the room has been seen as a counter to the *gunaikon*. In the archaeological record the *andron* has reasonably been identified on architectural grounds: the couches seem to have been ranged around the walls and cement pavements have been found on which they are assumed to have been located. Furthermore, such an arrangement is likely to be responsible for the atypically asymmetrical position for the doors of these rooms. Lastly, these two features often also correspond with decorated mosaic floors and plaster walls.

Sites from the late Classical and Hellenistic period often provide such examples of the *andron* or *andronitis* (the many instances include houses from Olynthos, Halieis, Eretria and Delos). Aside, however, from Walker's somewhat unconvincing designations, a true example of the *gunaikonitis* has yet to be found. It is a fact that the lack of upper storeys for investigation is a handicap in a situation where literary evidence has often been used to suggest that a female area existed in an upper storey, but even where houses have been assumed by the excavators to have been single-storey constructions, no *gunaikonitis* has yet been convincingly identified. It may be that investigations of this problem have foundered because there has been no systematic attempt to establish the material correlates which would allow us to identify such a room in the archaeological record. An alternative explanation is that there was no specialized female area and that what we are seeing is a true pattern of asymmetry. Through a careful examination of the archaeological material, it should be possible to distinguish between these two possibilities, but what is badly needed is enough detailed evidence on the distribution of finds within a large number of houses to enable a statistically valid analysis of room-function to be carried out.[2] In view of the current absence of such data, the remainder of this chapter aims to investigate the feasibility of an asymmetrical pattern of organization, by looking at a better-documented and more recent analogy. This will clarify the manner in which spatial organization within the household may be linked with patterns of social relations and will also illustrate some of the complexities that can be involved in such relationships, in a context in which these have in the past tended to be deduced from textual evidence or ignored altogether.

ETHNOGRAPHIC COMPARISON: THE ORGANIZATION
OF DOMESTIC SPACE IN ISLAMIC SOCIETY

Bearing in mind the recent stress that has been placed on using analogies that are suited to the archaeological case in question (Wylie 1985), comparative material must be chosen carefully: it is less important that the cultures being compared are related in terms of a shared heritage (for instance using modern Greece as a simile for ancient Greece) than that they are alike in dimensions relevant to the topic under examination. Some explanation is therefore required of the ways in which the example used here, traditional Islamic society in the city of Tunis, northern Africa, offers a relevant parallel for ancient Greece.

The status of women in both Islamic and ancient Greek societies is open to a variety of interpretations, ranging from accusations of severe repression to protective paternalism,[3] and one is left with the suspicion that in trying to distinguish between these alternatives purely in terms of our own cultural expectations, we are probably trying to ask the wrong kind of question (Just 1975: 155). What is of more importance here, though, is that underlying these similar ranges of opinion is the fact that the women of both these societies seem to have had very comparable roles and rights, which perhaps betrays a similar attitude to women as a group within each society.

In legal terms, the woman of Classical Athens (which is the principal region of Greece for which we have adequate evidence) seems by and large to have lived her life as a minor, passing from the care of her father or guardian to that of her husband, in a system of patrilocal residence (Garner 1987: 84; Sealey 1990: 36). Although she could own property, business would have been transacted on her behalf by her closest male relative, and even in the case of a woman petitioning for divorce, which she was allowed to do, it was usual for her father or brother to represent her in court (Harrison 1971: 84). In the same way the Muslim woman is under the protection of a male relative, also within the context of a system of patrilocal residence (Minces 1982: 66). The Koran provides for her welfare, allowing her to inherit some property (although only half of that to which her male counterpart is entitled). It also enjoins a man to take only a single wife if he cannot treat several wives equally, and regulates divorce.

Both in ancient Greece and in Islamic societies the woman is provided with a dowry and she has the right to keep it if she is divorced by her husband.[4] This gives some degree of insurance against the break-up of a marriage, and also acts as a disincentive to the husband to end the marriage without due cause, since the household will then lose some of its assets to the female, who will take them with her back to her own family.

Thus in both societies the woman is very much separated from public life and closeted within the family, which it is her responsibility to nurture in return for the protection of her husband or other male relative.

THE ORGANIZATION OF ISLAMIC HOUSES

It is time now to turn to the material culture, and examine the way in which attitudes to women affect the spatial organization of the house. The idea of female segregation in the Muslim world is to keep the sexually mature woman away from possible contact with sexually mature, non-related men. Woman is traditionally seen as a sexual temptation to man, and one from which he must be protected. Thus the practice is often represented not as demonstrating woman's inferiority to man, but as showing man's need for control over her (ibid: xvi). Physical segregation is one way of achieving this (Mernissi 1975: 4), and there is also a set of elaborate fictive marriage customs allowing strangers to become relatives and therefore out of bounds for sexual liaisons which also permits female contact with men who are not blood relatives, for instance male servants (Khatib-Chahidi 1981).

There is obviously considerable variability within the Muslim world, and it is impossible to take all of this into consideration in such a brief account; indeed, it is not the aim here to be comprehensive,[5] but simply to examine the concrete manner in which segregation of women in social terms may affect the organization of domestic space. For these reasons, discussion will centre on one particular example.

One of the most widespread house forms in the Islamic world is the courtyard house, comparable to that found in many areas of ancient Greece. The benefits of such an arrangement in terms of climatic control have frequently been outlined (see, for example, Badawy 1958: 122; Al-Azzawi 1969: 92). Well-documented examples of this type of house are found in the north African city of Tunis (Revault 1967; 1971).[6] Here the house is entered through a series of lobbies, which are often richly decorated and have benches arranged along the walls (for an example of this type of house, see Figure 5.2). These rooms serve as a location for the master of the house to meet with outsiders for entertainment and the discussion of business. In the larger houses a side-room off the lobby is also provided for this purpose. A different entrance leads to a suite of guest rooms either in an upper storey of the house, or in a separate wing.

Within the house the rooms are arranged around one, or sometimes two courts, which are bordered by galleries. The ranges around the family court include the main living room (off which lead bed- and couch-niches) which is used by the master of the house, together with storage rooms. In a few instances rooms are mentioned as being for specific use by women. Where these are present they are most frequently located upstairs, and have no distinguishing characteristics in terms of architecture or furnishing. In the larger houses where there is a second court, this is where the kitchen and service rooms are located and where the servants live and work.

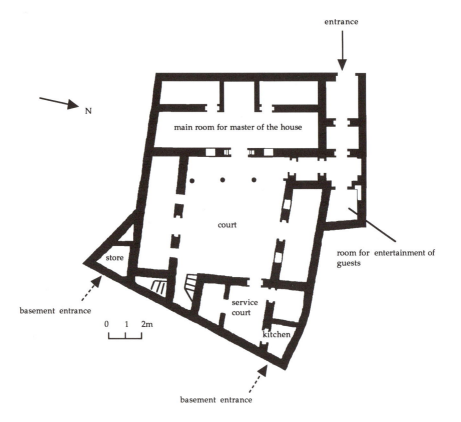

Figure 5.2 Example of an Islamic house from Tunis: Dar Romdane Bey (after Revault 1967)

Two features of the organization of these houses are striking: the first is the extent to which they are constructed so as to exclude the possibility of outsiders entering the domestic areas, through the provision of the lobby areas and of separate guest quarters. The second is the extent to which individual areas exist within the house for the different household members, from the master through to the servants. Social organization is therefore both reflected in and shaped through the organization of space within the house. In particular the desire for privacy from the outside world operates to prevent contact between the women of the house and strange men. The main links with the outside world take place either through the master of the house in the outer area, or (in wealthier houses) through the servants, for whom separate access is also provided. In no case is it necessary for any outsider to enter the main part of the house, and the entrances are arranged so as to prevent casual social, or even visual contact.

In this instance, then, the desire to keep women away from unrelated men is not translated directly into a provision of male and female rooms within the house, but a more complex pattern emerges. Rather than confining women to particular regions of the house, a more practical solution is to provide facilities for any strangers such that they need not enter the main living areas of the house at all, leaving the women relatively free to move about within the limits of their homes. Thus the characteristic feature of the separation of male and female in this context is not the provision of female quarters where the woman is shut away, but on the contrary the creation of male areas, where the men can do business without contact with the interior of the house. In this way the desire to separate women from contact with unrelated males is transformed into a need for privacy for the household as a whole.

Support for the assumption that these patterns are indeed the result of a desire for the isolation of the household from external contact comes from textual sources which are roughly contemporary with the construction of the earliest houses examined from Tunis, and which emphasize the importance of privacy from neighbouring houses, and these are available in summary form for the English reader (see Hakim 1986). A whole complex of laws restricts the right of one household to engage in activities whose effects might be detrimental to the neighbours. Residents are able to object to interference from adjoining households in the form of offensive smells and vibration as well as noise. The highest number of rules, however, governs the arrangements that must be made to avoid neighbours overlooking each other, thus ensuring visual privacy. These include structural measures such as the building of parapets to block views, the placement of doorways so that they are not opposite each other, and the construction of windows, which must be over a given height above floor level (ibid.: 33ff.). Such rules provide for the seclusion of the whole house, rather than distinguishing selected parts such as the family rooms, the court or the women's areas.

CONCLUSION: AN ASSESSMENT OF THE POSSIBILITY OF AN ASYMMETRICAL PATTERN OF SPATIAL ORGANIZATION

On the basis of the evidence currently available, there is nothing to suggest that some form of asymmetrical spatial organization could not have existed in the Greek house. Most of the known houses from this period are constructed on an inward-looking plan, with the rooms grouped around a courtyard which is usually shaded by colonnades on one or more sides. This arrangement has often been interpreted as a response to environmental conditions, providing a shaded, outdoor space in which household activities can be carried out (see, for example, Jameson 1990b: 97), and this (as noted above in connection with the occurrence of the courtyard house in the Islamic world) is probably part of the explanation for this feature. It is also reasonable, though, to suggest that other factors must be involved: although such an arrangement does provide one solution to the problem of achieving a comfortable working environment in a warm climate, modern-day traditional architecture shows that there are a variety of others, including a complete reversal of the courtyard model, which is to say, a veranda house, where shade is provided by colonnades around the outside of the house, which also function as traps for any cool breezes. In addition, although in some areas of the Greek world heat must have been a problem for much of the year (such as Doura Europos, to take an extreme example), there are others where its effects would have been more limited (for instance Macedonia), yet where the houses follow the same pattern of construction. Thus, climate is unlikely to be the only reason for this form of organization or to account for the widespread occurrence of such a house form across the Greek world.

It seems possible, then, that the use of the courtyard house can be explained as a product both of environmental conditions and of social requirements. There is some evidence to suggest a concern for privacy which may have played a role in determining the inward-looking structure. Although the walls have rarely been preserved to sufficient height to reveal the windows, where these have been found, they seem to have been located high enough to prevent passers-by from seeing into the house,[7] so that an important feature of such an arrangement is that it presents a blank exterior to the passer-by in the street, thus keeping the household environment very much separate from strangers.

Despite the desire to exclude unwanted observation from the outside world, literary sources suggest that Greek society was far from being inhospitable. Indeed, the tradition seems to have been quite the reverse, that it was the responsibility of the householder to offer food and shelter to those from beyond as well as within the family circle. It is this fact which is likely to be responsible for the presence of the *andron*, which provided a *locus* for the fulfilment of such obligations (see Figure 5.3). If we focus on this aspect of the *andron*, namely its function as a reception area, rather than on its male associations, we have an explanation for the way in which an asymmetrical arrangement may have come about. It is possible that the term *gunaikon* refers to the remainder of the house aside from the *andron*, in the sense that in these other areas the women of the house are present, although they are in no sense specifically dedicated to female use. In practical social terms such a form of organization makes more sense than positing a space specifically reserved for women, since it would make for more efficient organization and communication between different members of the household. It also fits better with the picture we have of women's social status, as possibly not

Figure 5.3 A mythical dining scene from a Greek vase (after Thonges-Stringaris 1965)

meriting a space of their own, and with iconographic sources, which not infrequently show women within the house in the presence of men.

The claim of Walker and others that the *andron* is spatially separated from the remainder of the house is one which has been challenged by Jameson (1990b: 100) on reasonable grounds. Like the other rooms of the house, it is usually approached through the courtyard, either directly or via an ante-room, without any necessity for (or even possibility of) passing through any other rooms in the house. Any contact between the women of the house and visiting males, which might occur in the central courtyard area, could have been avoided by scheduling of activity.[8]

In a sense, then, Jameson is correct to argue that attempts to divide house plans into *gunaikonitis* and *andronitis* are 'arbitrary' (ibid.: 104), but this is only part of the story. It is possible to argue that the presence of a specific male area of the house may be read not as part of a balanced pattern of

109

male–female opposition, but as an indication of something far more subtle and complex, involving the segregation of women not from men as a whole, but from men from outside their families. Thus a gender distinction is combined with a contrast between family and outsider (which is also a strong theme in the Greek literary tradition), and causes an asymmetry in the material, and therefore also in the archaeological record.

NOTES

Since this Chapter was written, a paper has appeared by David Small which would have deserved consideration as it consists of a discussion of the likely archaeological correlates of various types of female seclusion, including Islamic practices (Small, D. (1991) 'Initial study of the structure of women's seclusion in archaeological past', in D. Walde and N. Willows (eds) *The Archaeology of Gender: Proceedings of the 22nd Annual Chacmool Conference*, Calgary: Archaeological Society of the University of Calgary: 336–42.

1 For instance Bremmer (1985; 1987) on old women, Sinclair Holderman (1985) on the specific functions of priestesses, and Sourvinou-Inwood (1988) on the variety of social roles assumed by females of different ages and the ways in which these are incorporated into cult practice. Walker (1983: 81) also points out the likely differences between women in households with contrasting levels of wealth, as does Pomeroy (1975: 60).

2 Even at Olynthos, which has the largest number of excavated houses and relatively detailed information on finds and their spatial distribution, comparison with the amount of material from other sites suggests that much information is missing, so attempts to discern patterns in spatial layout and usage are disappointing (Nevett 1992).

3 For a discussion of the alternative views of the Classical world see Pomeroy (1975: 59–60) who concludes that such differing opinions are largely due to the sources used. For alternative views of the Muslim woman compare the recent works of female scholars such as Minces (1982: 108), who accuses Islam of being 'grossly unfavorable to women', with the less extreme opinion of Islamic customs of Mernissi (1975: xvi).

4 For Islam see Minces (1982: 69). In the case of Athens elaborate laws were enacted to provide for the splitting of the household or *oikos* in order for the dowry to be returned to the wife: see, for example, Wolff (1943: 64).

5 For an alternative, though less architecturally comparable treatment of spatial organization in an Islamic context, see Donley (1982) and Donley-Reid (1990).

6 The choice of historical examples here is deliberate, since these will not have been so open to influence by modern, western modes of behaviour.

7 For instance the fourth-century stone houses at Ammotopos (Hammond 1953: 138). For a more detailed description of an excavated house at the site, see Dakaris (1986).

8 Such a strategy, also with the aim of restricting male–female interaction, has been observed in the Islamic world today: see Akbar (1982: 174)

BIBLIOGRAPHY

Akbar, J.A. (1982) 'Courtyard houses: a case-study from Riyadh, Saudi Arabia', in I. Serageldin and S. El-Sadek (eds), *The Arab City*, Medina: Arab Urban Development Institute.

Al-Azzawi, S.H. (1969) 'Oriental houses in Iraq', in P. Oliver (ed.) *Shelter and*

Society, London: Barrie & Jenkins.

Arrigoni, G. (1985) 'Le donne dei "margini" e le donne "speciali" ', in G. Arrigoni (ed.) *Le Donne in Grecia*, Rome: Laterza.

Badawy, A. (1958) 'Architectural provision against the heat in the Orient', *Journal of Near Eastern Studies* 17: 122–8

Blok, J. (1987) 'Sexual asymmetry: a historiographical essay', in J. Blok and P. Mason (eds), *Sexual Asymmetry*, Amsterdam: Gieben.

Bremmer, J.N. (1985) 'La donna anziana: liberta e indipendenza', in G. Arrigoni (ed.), *Le Donne in Grecia*, Rome: Laterza.

——(1987) 'The old women of ancient Greece', in J. Blok and P. Mason (eds), *Sexual Asymmetry*, Amsterdam: Gieben.

Dakaris S. (1986) 'Το Οϱϱαον: το σπιτι στην αϱχαια Ηπειϱο', *Αϱχαιολογικη Εφεημεϱις*, 1986: 108–.

Donley, L.W. (1982) 'House power: Swahili space and symbolic markers', in I. Hodder (ed.), *Symbolic and Structural Archaeology*, Cambridge: Cambridge University Press.

Donley-Reid, L.W. (1990) 'The structuring structure: the Swahili house', in S. Kent (ed.), *Domestic Architecture and the Use of Space*, Cambridge, Cambridge University Press.

Flacelier, R. (1965) *Daily Life in Greece in the Time of Pericles*, London: Weidenfeld & Nicolson.

Garner, R. (1987) *Law and Society in Classical Athens*, London: Croom Helm.

Hakim, B.S. (1986) *Arabic-Islamic Cities: Building and Planning Principles*, London and New York: Kegan Paul International.

Hammond, N.G.L. (1953) 'Hellenic houses at Ammotopos in Epirus', *Annual of the British School at Athens* 48: 135–40

Harrison, A.R.W. (1971) *The Law of Athens: Part III: Procedure*, Oxford: Clarendon.

Jameson, M. (1990a) 'Private space and the Greek city', in O. Murray and S. Price (eds), *The Greek City from Homer to Alexander*, Oxford: Clarendon.

——(1990b) 'Domestic space in the Greek city-state', in S. Kent (ed.), *Domestic Architecture and the Use of Space*, Cambridge: Cambridge University Press.

Just, R. (1975) 'Conceptions of women in Classical Athens', *Journal of the Anthropological Society of Oxford* 6(3): 153–70

——(1989) *Women in Athenian Law and Life*, London: Routledge.

Khatib-Chahidi, J. (1981) 'Sexual prohibitions, shared space and fictive marriages in Shi'ite Iran', in S. Ardener (ed.), *Women and Space: Ground Rules and Social Maps*, London: Croom Helm.

Mernissi, F. (1975) *Beyond the Veil: Male–Female Dynamics in a Modern Muslim Society*, New York: Schenkman.

Minces, J. (1982) *The House of Obedience: Women in Arab Society*, London: Zed Press.

Nevett, L. (1992) 'Variation in the Form and Use of Domestic Space in the Greek World in the Classical and Hellenistic Periods', unpublished Ph.D. thesis, University of Cambridge.

Pomeroy, S.B. (1975) *Goddesses, Whores, Wives and Slaves*, New York: Schocken.

Revault, J. (1967) *Palais et Demeures de Tunis (18e et 19e siècles)*, Paris: Editions du Centre National de Recherche Scientifique.

——(1971) *Palais et Demeures de Tunis (16e et 17e siècles)*, Paris: Editions du Centre National de Recherche Scientifique.

Robinson, D.M. (1946) *Excavations at Olynthos 12: Domestic and Public Architecture*, Baltimore: Johns Hopkins Press.

111

Sealey, R. (1990) *Women and Law in Classical Greece*, Chapel Hill: University of North Carolina Press.

Sinclair Holderman, E. (1985) 'Le sacerdotesse. Requisiti, funzioni, poteri', in G. Arrigoni (ed.), *Le Donne in Grecia*, Rome: Laterza.

Sourvinou-Inwood, C. (1988) *Studies in Girls' Transitions*, Athens: Kardamitsa.

Thonges-Stringaris, R.N. (1965) 'Das Griechische Totenmahl', *Mitteilungen des Deutschen Archaologischen Instituts Athenische Abteilung* 80: 1–99.

Versnel, H.S. (1987) 'Wife and helpmate: women of ancient Athens in anthropological perspective', in J. Blok and P. Mason (eds), *Sexual Asymmetry*, Amsterdam: Gieben.

Walker, S. (1983) 'Women and housing in Classical Greece', in A. Cameron and A. Khurt (eds), *Images of Women in Classical Antiquity*, London: Croom Helm.

Wolff, H.J. (1943) 'Marriage law and family organization in ancient Athens', *Traditio* 1: 43–95

Wylie, A. (1985) 'The reaction against analogy', in M. Schiffer (ed.), *Advances in Archaeological Method and Theory. Volume 8*, New York: Academic Press.

6

THE SPATIALITY OF THE ROMAN DOMESTIC SETTING: AN INTERPRETATION OF SYMBOLIC CONTENT

Clive Knights

The undiscoverable house where this lava flower blows, where storms and exhausting bliss are born, when will my search for it cease?[1]

Some of the finest examples of Roman domestic architecture that persist in modern times have been found beneath the volcanic debris of the Vesuvian eruption of the year AD 79. Entombed by natural disaster, a segment of first century AD Roman culture has been remarkably preserved in its embodied form, and in a manner which has the potential to provide an enhanced insight into the Roman understanding of the human situation. The extant remains of Pompeii and Herculaneum, in particular, exhibit not only an architectural articulation of space, as understood in our modern sense, but also a degree of pictorial articulation which confounds any attempts at categorization in terms of genre or style that has become the norm in art historical circles. Indeed, the four well-known Pompeian styles of wall painting are just such an attempt at classification which serves to lead the spectator towards preconceptions imposed upon, rather than revealed within, those works. To talk of architecture and to talk of painting in separation is currently a common misdemeanour, and one which is wholly inappropriate in the context of the discussion of symbolic representation and, as I hope to elucidate, in the context of the Roman domestic setting. The onus is on us to interpret rather than to classify – to throw ourselves into the depth of the situation as it is presented by the reality of the Pompeian house as a phenomenon. Our access to its nature and its significance as the result of human creative activity, as a product of 'poiesis', rests upon the conservation of the physiognomy of the spatial setting and its current availability for experience. To engage oneself bodily, as it were, in the situational paradigm that we call the Pompeian house is not to attempt a simulation of what it must have been like, in the literal sense, to be a middle-class Roman in the early Empire; but rather, it is to participate in a mode of dealing with being

113

in the world. Authentic understanding, whether of Roman art or of art made yesterday, is never a matter of historical reconstruction, fact upon fact, event after event, piecing together information; it is a matter of revelation by interpretation.

Above and beyond the distinguishing idiosyncrasies of a first century AD imperial subject and a twentieth-century democratic citizen a profound identity presides. The possibility of an encounter with the meaning of the Pompeian house is guaranteed by the persistent condition of being mortal, on the earth, beneath the sky, in the face of unknowingness (Heidegger 1971). The symbolic representations that human beings make for themselves, as embodied in works of poiesis, become the residual evidence of participation in a common field: the cosmos. Through religion, philosophy, politics, art and social conduct a common direction was engendered by Roman culture. The underlying momentum of this imperial intent was a desire to produce the ultimate symbol of cosmic order: the Empire. It is imperative to keep this guiding notion in mind throughout all dealings with particular aspects of Roman culture so that particularities do not cloud the issue of participation. The explicit nature of, for instance, a certain arrangement of public buildings around a square, a certain arrangement of painted figures in a fresco, or a certain arrangement of mythic events in a Virgilian poem, is nothing but the thematization of an implicit predicament: the condition of humanity's inescapable involvement with the cosmic order of things, its ineluctable situatedness.[2]

The Pompeian house, then, is an embodiment of Roman culture; it is a conglomeration of symbols arranged in a way that testifies to a sense of belonging. Its symbolic organization is rooted with a great degree of complexity to its wider field of reference, the city, which in its turn is rooted to *its* wider field of reference, the Empire, and on to the cosmos. This is not to suggest a series of isolated entities linked by some all-embracing, determinable formulation. The integral rootedness of each mode of embodiment (house, city, empire, if we choose – artificially – to distinguish them) arises from a common urge to address the cosmic order through every avenue of representational possibility. The Pompeian house is not an object amongst others, moulded, smoothed and polished in perfect isolation like some jewel of Roman artistic achievement that we can slip beneath the lens of an analytical microscope. It is the manifestation of a way of being; it is a paradigm of a human way of acting in the face of the ominous insurmountability of the world. Every aspect of the Pompeian house in some way contributes to an immanentization of this transcendent condition. For the sake of common understanding it articulates, expounds and bears witness to the cosmic themes dominating the cultural field in which it participates as an expressive medium. Essentially, to discuss the house is to discuss, indirectly, the cosmos; and it is this discourse, this cosmology, that makes it and any other study of artistic production exhilarating and meaningful. By focusing on any one aspect of the house one finds oneself being drawn into an arena of digression whereby following the paths indicated one is led, in fact, not digressively, but ingressively to a core of significance which imbues each and every aspect with its unique and unchallengeable place in the symbolic network that we call the Pompeian house.

To refrain from imposing validity upon the house in accordance with the criterion of objectivity is to remain open to its reality as a setting for the events of human existence. The Pompeian house, like all aspects of Roman architectural reality, is to do with the elaboration of 'participation' and 'passage'. It is about being involved in a 'movement-through', whereby the mundane kinetic understanding of movement is, here, an analogical representation of a spiritual movement, that is, the force of divine activity which, in itself, is analogical in the face of the cosmic 'given'. The notions of divinity and spirituality as manifest in the whole gamut of deities that saturate Roman culture are the first line of defence, so to speak, in the face of transcendence. The naming of the gods and the simultaneous apportioning out of responsibility for the workings of the cosmos (for example, the seasons, the movement of the stars, the passing of night and day, etc.) is the first act of 'relief' for humanity from overbearing unknowingness. These gods are perceived as active; they are busy bringing about storms, floods, earthquakes, the destruction of crops, the promotion of war, and so on. Of course, they are also active in preventing these events so long as they receive due recognition and generosity from human beings. In a sense, the creation of the gods is the primal poetic act of humanity – engendering divine personalities whose behaviour is based on the model of cosmic order but whose manifestation is based on the analogy of human action. As such, humanity's involvement in the acts of the gods and the perpetration of its own conduct ensures a contributory role in the general cosmic process:

> The cosmos . . . is neither the external world of objects given to a subject of cognition, nor is it the world that has been created by a world transcendent God. Rather, it is the whole, *to pan*, of an earth below and a heaven above – of celestial bodies and their movements; of seasonal changes; of fertility rhythms in plant and animal life; of human life, birth and death; and above all . . . it is a cosmos full of gods.
>
> (Voegelin 1974: 68)

Here, Voegelin alludes to the essential intracosmic 'one-in-anotherness' that binds all differential aspects of an experienced reality to a unified cosmic ground:

> The intracosmic areas of reality, one may say, provide one another with analogies of being whose cosmological validity derives from the experience of an underlying, intangible *embracingness*, from a something

that can supply existence, consubstantiality and order to all areas of reality even though it does not belong as an existent thing to any one of these areas. The cosmos is not a thing among others; it is the background of reality against which all existent things exist; it has reality in the mode of non-existence. Hence, the cosmological play with mutual analogies can not come to rest on a firm basis out-side itself; it can do no more than make a particular area of reality transparent for the mystery of existence over the abyss of non-existence.

(ibid.: 68)

In this sense, every aspect of Roman culture is involved in making 'reality transparent for the mystery of existence'. Religion and art overlap in such a way that the distinction becomes purposeless; gods and men participate together in a mutual setting where the action of each is directed towards the attainment of a common understanding, the revelation of cosmic truth. The site of this mutual participation becomes etched out onto the surface of the earth; materiality falls in around activity as it passes through. The passage of being across the face of the terrestrial landscape installs permanent disfigure-ments; these are the tracks of activity, the response of the material earth to the flux of divine presence as it makes itself known via the motivation of human action towards the cosmic horizon. Voegelin calls the notion of a site for participation the 'perspective of the habitat' (ibid.: 202), Heidegger (1971: 157) calls it the 'dimension of dwelling'.[3] In either case it is to do with carving out a niche in the spatio-temporal domain of reality from which to gaze upon an horizon beyond, like a belvedere perched on the very edge of the 'here and now', built for the reconnaissance of the 'everywhere and always'. But this is not to imply a fixed and static viewpoint, for the construction of the belvedere is relentless.

In order to understand fully the unrelenting manner in which Roman life directed itself towards the revelation of cosmic truth it is necessary to glance at the sources of philosophical understanding which were absorbed and appropriated implicitly from influential Hellenistic models. In particular, the infusion of Stoic ideas concerning the predominance of natural order and its compatibility with reason (logos) were instrumental in providing a cohesive philosophical explanation with which to identify the cohesive pragmatic reality of Roman life. The essence of Stoicism lay in its monistic understanding of world order: that reality is corporeal and comprises, in its most fundamental form, a fiery breath which animates all things – 'pneuma'.[4] Following Aristotle, they assumed that all things are in a state of perpetual change, thus nominating pneuma as the driving force inhabiting the body of the world, distributing reasonableness, and operating from within the differentiated, though cohesive, aspects of nature (inorganic things, plants, animals and humans). The apparent clarity of a conception of cosmic order directed by, and subject to, a 'universal reason' was impeded, however, by the difficulty of securing a meaningful life within this order. It was a question of determinism that was to fuel Stoic discussion for centuries because of its problematic ethical implications. If all things and all events, even those instigated by human impulses, are subsumed beneath the umbrella of a greater unity for which all the differentiated happenings are merely contributory, then a notion of all-pervasive Fate or Destiny comes to light with such an overbearing predominance that it makes the delimitation of good and evil, and of ethical action, altogether meaningless. But for the Stoics, human beings were rational animals in that in acting out their lives according to nature they were at liberty to promote the cause of nature by the character of their own actions, by virtue of the fact that human reason was perceived as a portion, 'imperfect but perfectible' (Long 1974: 168), of universal reason. In humans 'reason supervenes as the craftsman of impulse' (Laertius quoted by Long 1974: 186). To act rationally is to act according to, and in harmony with, the natural order of things and, thus, it is to do justice to the spark of pneumatic universality that has been placed under human guardianship:

> Unlike all other natural beings, man alone is endowed by Nature with the capacity to understand cosmic events and to promote the rationality of Nature by his own efforts. But equally, he is the only natural being who has the capacity to act in a manner which fails to accord with the will of Nature. These antithetical capacities are what make man a moral agent, that is, someone of whose conduct and character 'good' and 'bad' can be said.
>
> (Long 1974: 182)[5]

To adhere to the pretext of natural reason is the sign of the virtuous human being. Virtue adheres to action, not to projected goals or results; it is a continuous and pressing concern. Under its guidance the idiosyncrasies of human existence, such as poverty, wealth, disease, health, life, death, become indifferent. Through the agency of a universal reasonableness (virtue) human beings can attain a condition of equality amongst each other that manifests in a communal goodness and happiness:

> All men are interrelated, all have the same origin and destiny, all stand under the same law and are citizens of one state, members of one body. All men have as men a claim to our good will.
>
> (Zeller 1980: 225)[6]

In the Roman context, the adoption and development of this understanding was greatly pursued in the writings of Cicero, for example his formulation of virtue into the concept of 'duty'. But the strength of community and of belonging that was procured throughout the formative years of the Empire, and sustained for much of its duration (indeed, to a great extent the cause of the Empire's prolongation), is indebted largely to the Stoic dimension of Hellenistic thought.

The insights of Polybius, the Greek historian living in Rome during the mid-second century BC, display the characteristics of a Rome which had assumed for itself the divine mission of inculcating the ultimate manifestation of cosmic unity on earth. Roman imperial expansion, by conquest, across the face of the physical globe was the pragmatic answer to the pull of cosmic order that dispersed its fiery breath throughout the inhabited world. The community of mankind struggled to find its analogy in the completeness of worldly possession, the 'ecumene'. The annexation of the extent of the physical world had its paradigmatic counterpart in the extent of Roman jurisdiction, which was itself the paradigmatic counterpart to the extent of divine presence that required to be acknowledged:

> Jupiter, when he looks from his height over the whole earth, has nothing which he can behold but that which is under Roman sway.

> To other nations, land has been allotted with some fixed limits; the extent of the Roman City and of the earth is the same.
>
> (Ovid *Fasti* 1887 trans.: 9, 77)

It is in such a context that 'participation' and 'passage' impress their relevance upon the discussion of any aspect of Roman culture. Participation in the imperial scheme is participation in humanity, in divinity and in the cosmic. All are collapsed and fused into the immediacy of pragmatic, virtuous action (praxis). But it is a journey, in that it is a condition of moving forever on into continued participation. As such it is a passage towards an horizon, a route marked by the milestones that are laid down as we pass, markers not signifying distance still to travel or distance having been but simply bearing witness to the perpetuity of the voyage. The nature of the destination is not known; the milestones cannot tell us where we are headed, only that we are on our way.

In the Roman context the notions of participation and passage become concrete throughout every level of poetic production, from the most embodied to the most articulated. The first has its manifestation in such ritualistic activities as 'inauguration' and the setting down of settlements. The augur, in his contemplation of the order of the sky (the movement of the sun, the movement of portentous birds, etc.) and the lay of the land (the delimitation of the landscape by locating natural phenomena such as trees, hills, rivers, healthy animals, etc.) sets the boundaries of the proposed site in strict collaboration with a given order. The inscription of the templum, the installation of the mundus, the lighting of the initial hearth, and the cutting of the first furrow (with the lifting of the plough at points of threshold) all illustrate in a very concrete way the importance of participation in activities not entirely under human control (Rykwert 1976).

The second has its manifestation, for example, in Virgil's *Aeneid*, and at many levels too. From the intricacies of the plot, such as Aeneas's departure from Troy, his departure from Carthage, or his journey in and out of the underworld, the message of his ordeals reveals itself slowly through encounters which suggest participation in a greater scheme of things (Figure 6.1). It may well be Aeneas who has to 'go through' all the trials and tribulations, just as it is the augur who has to 'go through' the inauguration ritual, but it is not the intention of either to remain as isolated events in individualized existences, for they serve as a symbolic reference towards more fundamental issues. They each in their own way bring to light, from the realm of darkness, a cosmology, an attitude towards the cosmos, a thematization of the cosmos that it is our lot, as humans, never to exceed, only to reiterate. These levels of articulation and embodiment span the breadth of Roman artistic production in which we find the Pompeian house. It is the habitat of gods and humans, the material extension of their actions and their gestures as they grapple with the world.

A brief descriptive synopsis of the formal organization of the Pompeian house is necessary in order to introduce a familiarity upon which to locate succeeding discussion. Vitruvius provides such a description in a cold and detached manner which does little to convey the nature of spatiality and significance. Even the most cursory glance through a Pompeian ruin could persuade the most disinterested spectator that there seems to be a great deal Vitruvius is not telling us. Speculation as to why his account is so barren often hinges on the fact that the representational content of the house was so familiar and so infused in everyday Roman life that to explicate such details would be, for Vitruvius, stating the obvious. Proportion, geometry and construction, on the other hand, being more specialized artisanal skills, were perhaps more specifically architectural and less immediately obvious, and therefore more appropriate to the context of his books. Reiteration of Vitruvius, here, is unnecessary. Similarly, the typological ground plan devised by Mau (1899), for instance, presents the organizational skeleton of what is an abundantly fleshy being (Figure 6.2).

The succession of spaces – vestibule, fauces, atrium, tablinum, peristyle – betrays an alignment in plan which is a general feature throughout the house type. Formal rigidity, however, is secondary, as many examples indicate – in particular those houses on irregular plots and homes which have been extended at various times. No two houses are the same and yet all evidence would suggest a level of identity arrived at through subtleties which transcend the scope of mere formal repetition, and imply a strong sense of interpretative flexibility.

The street facade of the house is often a simple vertical planar surface with minimal articulation – maybe a small number of openings correspond to minor service rooms, or in a great many cases tabernae line the streets limiting the street facade of the house to its entrance (Figure 6.3). In any case, we find the focus of elaboration clustered about the entrance recess, the

Figure 6.1 'Crossing': thematic study from the Roman House Series by Clive Knights

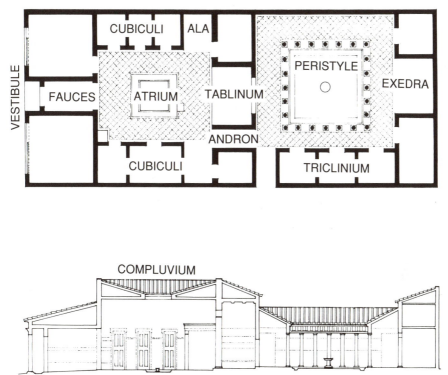

Figure 6.2 Pompeian house: typical plan and section (drawn by L. Foster)

vestibule. Little ambiguity accompanies the experience of this primary aspect of the house: the threshold to the scenario of the household, the initial penetrative event. Eliade expounds the spiritual significance of 'threshold' in the context of his discussion of the symbolism of the centre and construction rites. All acts of construction, he suggests, whether of towns or of houses, every act of carving out a dwelling is simultaneously an imitation of the creation of the world and the establishment of its 'centre':

> Every dwelling, by the paradox of consecration of space and by the rite of its construction, is transformed into a 'centre'. Thus, all houses – like all temples, palaces and cities – stand in the self-same place, the centre of the universe.
>
> (Eliade 1958: 379)

It is the very nature of the transcendent significance of each that makes this multiplicity of centres acceptable, and every act of passage across a threshold

Figure 6.3 Elaboration of a doorway on the street facade

meaningful. The establishment of the city boundaries and the sacredness of the pomoerium reinforce this notion.

Passing through the large double doors into the fauces presents the participant with a preludial experience of the depth of the domestic setting. Layered beyond in receding spatial progression are the series of punctured screens, openings, doorways, columnal screens, wells of light and shade, which signify a reciprocal limitation and extension of space, and penetrative possibilities (Figure 6.4). Essentially, what is encountered is a reciprocity between bounded and unbounded spatiality, a boundedness which detains and releases simultaneously by the exercise of creative interpretation. The primary spatial ground comes to us in terms of these territories, with their enclosing walls and soffit, their doorways and columnal screens; but they are at the same time both the creation of an interior closedness and the structuring components of an outward opening onto a metaphorical domain. They are the more persistent, physical attributes of an overall symbolic disclosure of meaning.

Around the enclosing walls of the fauces the pictorial extension of spatiality commences, complementing the directional pull of the dominant axis. In other words, a spatial dimension opens up laterally around the participant which is at odds with the dimension of physical manoeuvrability, denying it predominance whilst offsetting its significance, inviting realignment. This notion is difficult to comprehend with a modern understanding of spatiality. If we can not physically move into a space we are inclined to conclude that it is not spatial; in the restricted, architectural sense of the term, space is a void that we move around in freely. However, physically to move across the earth 'merely displays spatial and temporal implications in a more striking way' (Merleau-Ponty 1962: 275).[7] Movement has no monopoly over being, it is merely one mode of becoming.

Moving into the atrium space, like a domestic 'forum', with a centralized compluviate opening in the roof enclosure, echoed on the floor plane by the impluvium, we encounter a pool of light, a pool of water and a circumambulatory space surrounded on the two lateral sides by the punctured walls to the adjacent ancillary chambers (which include storerooms and bedrooms: cubiculi), and to the front by the emphasized opening to the tablinum. Often the centrality of the impluvium–compluvium arrangement in the atrium is enhanced by a peripheral row of columns. The main room in the house, the tablinum, is like a study, but used to serve as the master bedroom. It extends the penetrative direction towards the peristyle garden, providing a fundamental link between atrium and peristyle which is elaborated by the articulation of the grand opening from atrium to tablinum and the more subdued, often occular, opening from tablinum to peristyle. The most important side chamber, opening onto the atrium or peristyle, is the triclinium: the dining room. Associated with the whole ceremony of feasting and receiving guests,

Figure 6.4 Entering the House of the Silver Wedding

'the triclinium was where the master of the house showed who and what he was' (Aries and Duby 1987: 365).

The pictorial decoration of atrium, tablinum, peristyle, triclinium and other rooms (the number and location of which vary greatly from house to house) is always extensive and integral to the experience of spatiality within the house. It is their content and their placing in conjunction with the placing of partitions, screens, openings, volumes, sculptures and artefacts that exhibits the structured paradigm of the domestic situation – the inter-woven fabric of household activity and symbolic representation, of the mundane and the mythic.

The orthogonality of the Pompeian house appears to derive from the setting down of the cardinal directions of the settlement – the cardo and decumanus, from which the general street pattern takes its orientation. In this way the primordiality of the templum is reiterated in every street intersection and in the perpendicularity between the alignment of the street and the main alignment of each house. From this the order of orthogonality is distributed further by resounding across the domestic site, filling it up with rectangular rooms and enclosures regardless of the site's regularity, or lack of it. The consistency is not foolproof, as many examples show, but it is too predominant not to be intentional. So, from an intention to 'set the order of the sky in a particular place' (Rykwert 1976: 6), the ritual movement of the augur's lituus initiates an imitative reverberation throughout the struc-ture of the city, simultaneously imposing alignment whilst permitting communion.

The vestibule with its tall double entrance doors has been described above as the articulation of the initial penetrative event, and its significance has more avenues of interpretation open to it than immediately evident. To begin with, Ovid makes the etymological connection of vestibule with Vesta, the goddess of the hearth and the eternal fire, and he mentions that the hearth once stood in the porch of the houses, 'Oh Vesta, thou who dost inhabit the foremost place' (Ovid *Fasti* 1887 trans.: 224). Indeed, but how much more evocative is the association of her virginal qualities, her absti-nence from violation, her penetrative resistance and the respect it gains her when considered in relation to the main entrance of the private dwelling of a Roman citizen (Figure 6.5).[8] However, this may be a secondary consider-ation in the light of the true pre-eminence of the sacred fire and the hearth of the household with its fundamental relationship to the Lares, Manes and Genii of the family. In any event, the significance of the vestibule rests on the fact that it is the primary figuration of threshold, of passage from one domain to another, as a breach in the boundary; it is symbolically the 'place of doors'. In this case it manifests a passage from urban life to domestic life, but its recurrence as a theme throughout the house and in all Roman architecture imbues it with a primacy which can not be overlooked:

Figure 6.5 Entering the House of the Vettii

Every gate has two fronts, one on either side, of which the one looks out upon the people, but the other looks inward upon the household shrine; and as the gate-keeper among you mortals, sitting near the threshold of the front of the building, sees both the goings out and the comings in, so do I, the door-keeper of the vestibule of heaven, at the same time look forth upon the regions of the east and the west.

(ibid.: 12)[9]

Thus speaks the voice of double-faced Janus in the opening book of Ovid's *Fasti*, on January, the opening of the new year, and there credited with the transformation of the primordial chaos into the four elements – air, fire, water, and earth, the opening of the universe. The temple of Janus, about which little is known, is believed to have been one of the most ancient and consisted of a passage between two parallel walls with arched gates at either end. Symbolically, the opening and closing of these gates marked the commencement of periods of war and peace. Later manifestations in the form of dedicatory arches reveal just how important an explicit sense of passage with its material embodiment became. The ceremonial opening of the doors of the house by the janitorial servant at dawn, the opening of each day, initiated the recurrent dialogue of patron and client, the 'salutatio' (Figure 6.6).

The theme continues in Virgil's *Aeneid* (1956 trans.: 147–74). For Aeneas the acts of crossing and entering become a synonymous and persistent engagement. A multiplicity of thresholds besiege his every move, and culminate in the flurry of gates and doors that signify his passage through the underworld: the gates of Cumae's golden temple of Apollo; the vast cavern in the Euboean Rock with its, 'hundred tremendous orifices'; the mighty 'double-doors' that open onto Pluto's infernal kingdom; the 'Entrance Hall in the very jaws of Hades'; the 'gigantic gate with columns of solid adamant' through which Aeneas glimpses the horrors of Hell, and the corresponding 'archway' opposite that gives access to the Fortunate Woods, the joyful domain of Elysium. The climax of Aeneas's subterranean journey, having traversed the seething marsh of Styx and reached the banks of the Lethe, is the speech of his dead father Anchises (who, incidentally, was delivered to safety when Aeneas carried him out through the gates of burning Troy), whose prophesy describes the opening of the 'golden centuries' of an emerging empire under the auspices of Augustus.

In relation to the domestic setting, Aeneas's passage from overworld to underworld symbolizes the most important aspect of Roman household tradition, upon which are layered corresponding facets of civic tradition. In particular, it is Aeneas's desire to seek the advice of his dead father as a mythical event that represents the tradition of the ritual appeasement of the Lares, the shades of the dead ancestors of the resident family.[10] It has been noted above that the veneration of the Lares coincides with that of the sacred

Figure 6.6 'Entering': thematic study

fire and the hearth. The embodiment of these deities was often combined within a small aedicular structure situated in the atrium or sometimes in the peristyle (Figure 6.7). The sacred fire itself was embodied by continually burning coals since 'neither Vesta nor fire has any likeness' (Ovid *Fasti* 1887 trans.: 224), and the shades of the dead were represented by small statuettes. Daily offerings of salt, wine, cakes or incense were made and on special days of the year such as the Caristia,[11] or on the occasion of new births, family celebrations were conducted, centred on the 'lararium', and often involving more substantial sacrificial offerings. Again Virgil addresses the tradition in the *Aeneid*:

> In formal libation he poured onto the earth two bowls of unwatered wine, two of fresh milk, and two of hallowed blood. Then he scattered some bright flowers and said: 'Father, my Father Sanctified, hail to you once again. Hail, ashes now; since it was for this only that I saved you. Hail. Father's spirit, spectre, shadow; hail. It was not granted to me to have you at my side as I quested for Italy's boundaries where fate has given us lands . . .' He had just finished when a gigantic snake crept, slippery, from the base of the mound, trailing seven huge loops, and seven arching coils, encircling the tomb in kindly embrace, and sliding over the altars. . . . The snake crept with all his long trailing length between the bowls and smooth vessels. Last, he tasted the fare; and harmlessly moved back to the base of the tomb.
>
> (Virgil *Aeneid* 1956 trans.: 121–2)

The tradition of the snake as a symbol of the underworld, of fertility and of regeneration is a long and well-established one, especially in partnership with the moon and its lunar rhythms (Eliade 1958: 167–9; Figure 6.8). By the shedding of its skin and its habitational inclinations towards the earth and caves it obtains a mythical power of great influence, as another mythical event indicates:

> Augustus's mother, Atia, with certain married women friends, once attended a solemn midnight service at the Temple of Apollo, where she had her litter set down, and presently fell asleep as the others also did. Suddenly a serpent glided up, entered her, and then glided away again . . . the birth of Augustus nine months later suggested a divine paternity.
>
> (Suetonius *Twelve Caesars* 1957 trans.: 101)

So, the lararium provides the Roman household with a spiritual focus, a centre of gravity, so to speak, which is the symbolic embodiment of a profound threshold onto the underworld, the world beyond life, the realm of the dead (Figure 6.9). By its presence the passage from the living to the dead is kept ajar, just wide enough to push through offerings to the other side, but just too narrow to pass through without the right credentials such

Figure 6.7 Atrium and lararium of the House of Menander

Figure 6.8 Lararium of the House of the Vettii

Figure 6.9 'Offering': thematic study

as a golden bough or the relinquishment of one's body. This pre-eminent spiritual threshold has its place amongst a plethora of worldly imitations which are hampered in their transcendent achievements by the friction of the excess baggage of our body against the resistance of the earth. For the Roman, the spatiality of the terrestrial earth beneath the sky is the habitat for a community of gods and men, a brotherhood of beings acting virtuously. The transcendent power of virtue draws their actions forth, giving direction to pragmatic activity. Throughout this journey anchors are cast which immanentize the passage, and these are the symbolic representations in all their forms. They aim to bring the transcendent within a manageable range, to bring it into human dimension by capturing and solidifying its potency in material analogy, in an edifice, whether built of words or built of tufa-blocks, whether as a mythical discourse involving personified gods, or as an architectural discourse involving walls, colonnades, peristyles, atria, door-ways, gates, occulae, etc. They are all compatible and mutually interactive, they are all contributory to the creative interpretation of the spatiality of 'being' through representation. But they do not fix anything for the sake of what is fixed, they fix it for the sake of what eludes fixation, the field in which they sit, and this is their authentic value to humanity faced with the insurmountability of the cosmos. We make a vessel in which to collect the redolent juices from a fruit forever out of reach; but the vessel is inadequate, the fluids seep away as fast as they are acquired, thus demanding constant vigilance.

The Pompeian house, then, is just such a perforated vessel. It is a nebula of thresholds, a coming together of empierced layerings and interstitial domains inhabited by gods and humans. It has analogical connections with the articulation at the civic scale. Here, a numinous hierarchy is overlaid upon these interstitial domains with great explicitness. The shared territory of gods and men is modulated – a place on earth is singled out for the gods, lent to them as a site for the anchoring of divine presence, the delimitation of the sacred precinct. In its simpler occurrences we can cite the mundus, the hole in the ground, or the early Etruscan temple with its cella, pronaos, podium and enclosing compound. In its more complex occurrences we can cite the imperial fora of the flourishing Empire. The symbolic reference is identical but in the latter its elaboration attains a greater degree of sophistica-tion and exuberance.

The Pompeian house has similar ambitions; the creative ingenuity that articulates its spatiality is spurred on by similar intent, but the means at its disposal are more modest. As a coalescence of thresholds the house is vibrant with a sense of transience, a sense of undogmatic space that receives and nurtures the reciprocity of human dialogue upon which the idea of patronn-age, that characterizes Roman culture, depends. The structural solidity of stone and the potential finality of enclosure are defied at every turn by the perception of a 'background' made present by a surrounding gathering of thresholds both architectural and painterly. For instance, pressing upon the interior of the atrium there exists the 'beyond' of the lararium, the world of the dead; the 'beyond' of the cubiculi, simultaneously the world of sleep and nocturnal regeneration and the world of the family 'penates', the storehouse of sustenance; the 'beyond' of the tablinum, the world of public standing and the power of the 'paterfamilias'; and on to the peristyle garden, the world of the natural order of things. Each is held by the dominant centrality of the compluvium and impluvium, like a 'groma' (the Roman surveyor's instrument for aligning the cardo and decumanus), simultaneously penetrating the earth and gesturing to the sky, a great vertical axis rooting the space, around which human beings may amble (Figure 6.10).

The significance of this single source of emanating light in the context of the ritualized existence of the Roman citizen must, I feel, outstretch any pragmatic criteria. The contribution of the quality of light to the mood of the atrium is held hostage to the diurnal contingencies of the passage of the sun across the vault of the heavens; the 'pantheon' effect ensures that throughout the day the Roman, at business in the atrium, walks with the sun. Within this context, where the materiality of architectural embodiment reaches its limits, the pictorial takes over, and where the pictorial reaches its limits the mythical narrative takes over. However, it is artificial to view it in this manner, since each is present, to a greater or lesser degree, as a coexistent contributor to a continuum of experience. Each borrows from the domain of the other, each articulates the symbolic content in its own particular way: for instance, a built row of columns differs from a built row of engaged columns, which differs from a painted row of columns or engaged columns, which differs yet again from a literary description of either. However, as we have encountered with the phenomenon of doorways, all of these differentiations are part of the same depth of experience as far as any participant is concerned; they are all regulatory components of the spatiality of being, opening us always, in their own way, onto the very same world, but providing us always with new and reoriented perspectives onto it.

This can be very well illustrated by the oecus in the House of the Labyrinth which opens off the colonnaded peristyle (Figure 6.11). Just in front of its east wall stands a colonnade. Beyond this is the wall upon which is depicted a series of receding layers: first a podium; then a colonnade supporting a split pediment and an altar set between the two halves; then a low wall which is also divided centrally with its opening closed by a suspended drapery screen; then a circular colonnaded structure which invokes the round vestal temples of Tivoli and Rome and the two analogous civic structures in Pompeii (in the Macellum and in the Triangular Forum); then a tall, pierced wall or row of pillars. What these exhibit is the appropriation of the domain of one mode of embodiment (architectural) by another (pictorial). The latter brings possibilities to visibility in its own way that the former is unable to do in the confines of the domestic environment. It

Figure 6.10 'Gesturing': thematic study

Figure 6.11 Corinthean oecus of the House of the Labyrinth (Deutsches Archäeologisches Institut)

extends the possibilities of representation and therefore the potential fruit-fulness of the embodied situation; it brings to bear upon the domestic setting a richness of significance that just would not arise if the walls were, say, whitewashed. All the ceremonial grandeur and spiritual belongingness of the civic order (temples, colonnades, sacrificial altars, ritual implements, sacred precincts, etc.) reverberate throughout the house. The pictorial analogue introduces and sustains the fecundity of the civic analogue; together they enforce the cosmological situatedness of the participant. The 'depth' of the present, in Merleau-Ponty's sense,[12] wells up, is drawn forth and coaxed into a more rooted condition of existence by the content of the setting, or rather, it is the setting that moves the participant's presencing towards that rootedness. The tension set up between a built colonnade and a pictorial colonnade is the key to the homogenization of the setting, by asserting a continuum of spatiality that transgresses the distinctions between architec-tural space and pictorial space (Figure 6.12).

The pictorial expression never relinquishes its connection with the dialec-tic of openness and closure, of bounded and unbounded space. The differ-ences between the explicit architectonic manner of the so-called first and second styles and the highly elaborate filigree-like articulation of architec-tural elements of the third and fourth cannot necessarily be understood as merely evolutionary refinements, but rather as alternative imaginative re-sponses to the delimitation of the setting. The scope for the creative in-terpretation of colonnades, screen-walls, apertures, doorways and so on is opened to new possibilities in painterly articulation. Nevertheless, their responsibility as contributors to the 'place-making' intention of the poetic act is never renounced, indeed it is enhanced. Built architectural embodi-ment, itself a paradigmatic manifestation of the Roman way of acting which is saturated in all its detail by the pressure of a cosmic order, is taken beyond the narrowness of its mere physicality to participate in a wider field of significance presented by the visuality of the painting. The setting moves us, perceptually, in such a way that we inhabit a world of meaning, a content-world in which the physical world of our body and the illusory world of the painting cohabit. But it is not a case of fooling the participant into believing s/he is in some detached imaginary landscape with such convincing skill that it cancels out his/her bodily presence in the physicality of the room with its enclosing walls; but rather, it is to do with specifically bringing the imagin-ary to bear on his/her presence in such a way that s/he is taken bodily into it. The imaginary is geared towards and demands the co-operation of the body in order to become an integrated and meaningful aspect of the general setting in which participants lose themselves, or rather, find themselves lost. In this manner the dining room, say, of a Pompeian house is never merely a small room with four decorated walls and a door – it becomes a setting of immense richness, fuelling and substantiating a participant's situatedness in the imper-ial scheme of things, and thus in the cosmic order.

Figure 6.12 Continuity of architectural and painterly space

Figure 6.13 Theban Room in the House of the Vettii

This is taken still further by the incorporation of images of mythical figures, both sculptural and pictorial. In the true spirit of the intracosmic collaboration of gods and humans that typifies the imperial context, we find the symbolic fecundity of human gestural expression, of personified gods in action in their mythical settings, overlaid upon the spatial setting of the interior of the house. The virtuous content of the depicted events saturates and modifies the domestic setting and is balanced or offset against the virtuous aspirations of the human cohabitants. The influence of drama and literature, the narrative in which the mythical figures enact their roles, comes alive in the perceptual domain; with human features they gesticulate to each other and to the participants, who themselves gesticulate to each other. Here, the Roman finds a further creative facet to the representation of the community of being, a further injection towards a pregnancy of meaning. Indeed, the civic propensity for theatrical performance as an integral part of an urban experience involved in the celebration of numerous religious festivals made theatre and dramatic enactment a powerful source of pleasure and knowledge inevitably affecting the content of the wall paintings. The development of the scenic backdrop to the civic theatres was transformed during the Empire towards a phenomenal degree of complexity, with multi-storey and multi-layered constructions becoming prevalent.

Two rooms in the House of the Vettii illustrate this phenomenon admirably – the Ixion Room and the Theban Room (Figure 6.13) – as Brilliant

(1984: 53–89) has endeavoured to describe. The figuration of both these rooms follows, he suggests, the tripartite arrangement developed in the 'scaenae frons' of contemporary theatre. This is introduced into the rooms on two levels: first the tripartite differentiation of the three main painted walls as a whole (forming a U-shaped enclosure), and second by the triptychal nature of each wall, established with a main central panel containing the elaboration of a mythical event, and two flanking panels resembling windows which open onto perspectively receding architectural elements. The division is accomplished by the use of a painted articulation of architectural elements such as columns, cornice, dado, podium, etc. Brilliant suggests that the purpose of the central panels is the illustration of a moralizing intent by the depiction of demoralized conduct: Pasiphae's infatuation with the bull, Ixion's punishment for attempting to seduce Hera, and Dionysus's rescue of Ariadne after her abandonment by Theseus. He pinpoints the connection of these events by analogy to the central themes of betrayal and lust, and in so doing emphasizes the most important aspect governing the use of the separate mythological episodes, that is, their similarity through difference. It is the metaphorical force of the disparate events when set in cohabitation in the spatiality of the Ixion Room that reveals their value and significance. The panels were

> set at right-angles to one another in a tripartite composition so that in small rooms their projecting images were thought to intersect. The discreet nature of the panels and the sharp demarcation of their projecting images by careful enframement on the walls would, by implication, enhance the effect, emphasizing the synthetic power of the viewer's imagination. Yet the very fact of projection and the deliberate association of the pendants in an affecting relationship together serve to break the frame of the individual panel and to replace it by the larger enframement offered by the room as a whole, as a hermeneutical field.
>
> (ibid.: 78)

To enter the room is like breathing in the vapour of meaning that fills it up; it is to take issue with the radiating content of the panels; it is to take on board and rise up through that content to a level of correspondence which sets the tone of the room.

Moving into the peristyle garden we find the situation is not altogether different, but here the representation of a natural domain predominates. The spatial territories that arise from the reciprocity of the sacred and the profane have their parallel in the Roman understanding and reverence for natural order and the articulation of its place in the general setting. Recalling, once more, the demarcation of the settlement we see, at an urban scale, the interiorization of the human dwelling with respect to a concomitant exteriorization of the natural. In this way a certain respect is maintained for the natural order of things and its self-motivated manifestation in the vegetation, foliage and animal life of a natural landscape. In every act of bounding there is a boundedness from something, a setting apart, a mediated detachment (Figure 6.14). In an analogous gesture at the scale of the domestic setting, this opening out onto the natural domain from the security of the domestic is incorporated by the articulation of the peristyle. Here, it is not sufficient to view the vegetated abundance that pushes in from all sides, clinging to the trellises and pergolas and infested with birds and creatures, as merely an artificial aspiration for a larger garden. The fruitfulness of the peristyle is not in its physical magnitude but in its referential potency – it provides a metaphorical opening onto the natural order. It is a representation which reintegrates the Stoic notion of the possibility of humanity's repossession of a place in the completeness of cosmic unity, a human being's subsumption into the natural order of things by his/her own virtuous actions. The gods themselves find a place in this natural setting in the form of statues, alongside the human inhabitants. The notion of this transcendent condition of unity with nature is a common enough theme in Roman literature, for instance, Virgil's *Georgics*, where it acquires special relevance in the agricultural setting of rustic piety – 'happy too is he who knows the gods of the countryside' (Virgil *Georgics* 1982 trans.: 93) – and again, in the *Aeneid*, where the ultimate destination of the dead is likened to an idyllic landscape:

> the pleasant green places in the Fortunate Woods, where are the Homes of the Blest. Here an ampler air clothes the plains with brilliant light, and always they see a sun and stars which are theirs alone'
>
> (Virgil *Aeneid* 1956 trans.: 166).

A desire for a perennial presence of flourishing plant life would account for the prevalence of evergreen varieties manifest in paintings, relief sculpture and actual plantings which dominate the garden setting, such as ivy, myrtle, oleanders, box, and laurel (Jashemski 1979). The special significance of the latter, as one example among many, arises from mythical connotations evolving around the metamorphosis of the nymph, Daphne:

> Even as a tree, Phoebus loved her. He placed his hand against the trunk, and felt her heart still beating under her new bark. Embracing the branches as if they were limbs he kissed the wood: but, even as a tree, she shrank from his kisses. Then the god said: 'Since you can not be my bride, surely you will at least be my tree. My hair, my lyre, my quivers will always display the laurel.
>
> (Ovid *Metamorphoses* 1955 trans.: 43–4)[13]

The interpretation of the Roman domestic setting is one of limitless possibility and remains, for us, as creative a task as it was for the perpetrators of the Roman house with all its articulate nuances. The potency of interpretation persists as a constant force; the answer to the question of dwelling can never be viewed as an exhaustible task with a definitive solution. Such

Figure 6.14 'Mediating': thematic study

occurrences as the frequent redecoration of the houses of Pompeii (the earthquake of AD 62 notwithstanding) would suggest an awareness of an ongoing engagement with the transcendent (rather than the mere adoption of fashionable trends which is often presented as an explanation) which the domestic setting, in all its modesty, had just as much of a capacity and a need to address as the most elaborate temple complex. This is where the importance of the paintings set in the context of the architecture of the house must be emphasized, in terms of an essential mediating function, and a responsibility to preserve the inhabitant's relationship to the idea of a unified cosmic wholeness permeating every situation. Through what is immediate and visible the material articulation of the domestic setting is the key to bringing to bear the full potency of the invisibility of the mythical domain, which in its turn is the creative product of the response of human beings to an insurmountable world.

Lurking beneath the surface of this study and stimulating a particular perception of architectural reality has been a phenomenological understanding of spatiality as the receptacle of experience in its full synaesthetic sense, and one which, since Cartesian rationalism, modernity has learnt to subdue. The fullness of experience, its ethical dimension of virtuous conduct, its poetic dimension of mimetic, productive activity, have been captured and secured in the catacombs of a categorial prison. In earlier times they roamed free across the earthly domain in the human body, with virtue fixed in the direction of cosmic unity and material products laid down in evidence of a journey, mimicking bodily actions as they move ever on. At first human beings imitated the movements of the stars, in dance:[14] they participated in a celestial motivation that had its origin beyond the province of comprehension, so they appropriated it through the agency of the body and made it their own; they made a representational alternative that carried its celestial reference physiognomically and by doing so held within itself an opening onto cosmic truth, to be experienced each time the representation was encountered.

The symbolic content of the Pompeian house provides an instance of just such an opening. It is by interpretation that the virtuality of the house can transcend its mundane actuality, shifting the significance of dwelling into a region of ontological depth that is rarely addressed in the modern architectural context. Roman cosmology addresses reality through a screen of deities which succeeds in relieving human beings from the transcendence of the unknown by cohabiting their world and taking responsibility (in their eyes) for the perilousness of nature. In an atheist society, however, the problem would seem always to require a reasoning and logic that denies us access to an openness onto the world which remains perpetually present and appreciated as such by the manner in which we deal with it. Shaking off the dogmatic armour of mortals who serve under the tyranny of intellectualism has been the task that the phenomenologists have been grappling with throughout the past century. In this context I do not pretend to have placed more than, perhaps, a toe across the threshold of a rejuvenated understanding of the meaning of architectural works, but like all thresholds it holds the potential for the opening up of a new domain of experience:

> Well, said I, perhaps there is a pattern of it laid up in heaven for him who wishes to contemplate it and so beholding to constitute himself its citizen.
>
> (Plato *Republic* 1961 trans.: 819)

NOTES

1 René Cazelles quoted by Bachelard (1969: 51). The inspiration for the commencement of this search arose from a parallel interest in the phenomenological discussion of Merleau-Ponty on spatiality and the human body, and contemporary developments in hermeneutic theory, in particular, Ricoeur and the idea of the metaphorical work. Both have significant contributions to make when considering the interpretation of built artefacts and in understanding the meaning of architectural phenomena as an archaeologist, historian or architect. I owe the disclosure of this world of possibility to the insight of Dalibor Vesely at Cambridge.

Recent attempts to comprehend the structure and organization of the Roman dwelling in terms of 'social function' (Wallace-Hadrill 1988: 43–97; Gazda 1991) signify a welcome move towards reanimating the semantic dimension of Roman domestic architecture which has previously been stultified by generally descriptive accounts of form, pragmatic function and constructional technique. Whilst these provide substantial and useful quantities of information, the dangerously creative task of interpretation has often been avoided. The observation, gathering and sorting of material facts under the guise of objectivity has produced, to a great degree, a blinkered vision which denies the potential of the interpretative leap to reveal the role of Roman architecture in representing a certain way of being, a certain world view. A debt is owed to Wallace-Hadrill's account since it discloses through a discussion of social interaction and responsibility a profound condition of 'participation' which shapes and colours the Roman way of acting. My intention here is to begin an exploration of the Roman domestic setting as a built representation of human participation in a transcendent reality, mediated as it is by the mythical dimension of gods and heroes which is itself inextricably linked, through all Roman cultural manifestations, to the social reality inhabiting the dwelling. Indeed, the staggering research of John R. Clarke (1991) makes perhaps the most intriguing attempt so far to perceive all aspects of the domestic setting, its architecture, painting, sculpture, and its use, as mutually effective in representing the inhabitant's sense of identity and belonging.

2 See Merleau-Ponty (1962, especially Part Two, Chapter 2 entitled 'Space'). The idea of 'being situated' is further discussed in terms of its relevance to the making of architectural works in Vesely (1987; 1988).

3 'Spaces open up by the fact that they are let into the dwelling of man. To say that mortals *are* is to say that *in dwelling* they persist through spaces by virtue of their stay among things and locations' (Heidegger 1971: 157).

4 'The Stoic philosophy of nature is an attempt to provide a rational explanation for all things in terms of the intelligent activity of a single entity which is co-extensive with the universe. The history of the universe is the history of one thing, which can be signified by many names. Uncreated and imperishable Nature, God,

pneuma or universal logos exercises its activity in a series of eternally recurrent world-cycles. Beginning and ending as pure fire each world-cycle fulfils the goals of its active principle' (Long 1974: 168).

5 For 'man' please read 'human being'.

6 For 'men' please read 'human beings'.

7 See also Heidegger (1971: 156). 'When we speak of man and space, it sounds as though man stood on one side, space on the other. Yet space is not something that faces man. It is neither an external object nor an inner experience. It is not that there are men, and over and above them *space*; for when I say "a man", and in saying this word think of a being who exists in a human manner – that is, who dwells – then by the name "man" I already name the stay within the fourfold among things.' That is, earth, sky, divinities, mortals. For 'man' please read 'human being'.

8 The House of the Vettii has a painting of Priapus on the wall of its vestibule. Ovid recounts the relationship of the 'god of the extended Hellespont' to Vesta (*Fasti*, 1887 trans.: 225–6) wherein he attempts to violate her virginal integrity as she sleeps.

9 See also Lacey (1986). I agree entirely with Lacey that the significance of Janus is often underrated.

10 The close affinity between the veneration of the sacred fire and the worship of the dead is echoed in the symbolic value associated with the public Lararia. The possible origin of these has been discussed by Rykwert (1976) and may pertain to the inauguration ceremony. Having inscribed the templum and taken the auspices, the mundus could be located on or near the 'umbilicus', the intersection of the cardo and the decumanus. The mundus was the initial hole dug into the virgin soil of the new site into which offerings were made, often including soil brought from the settlers' home territory, and, following which the hole would be covered with a stone, an altar set up and a fire lit. It would seem reasonable to interpret this event at many levels, each serving to reinforce the significance of the household rituals. The penetration of virgin soil, the opening up of a subterranean domain, the making of offerings, whether to the infernal gods, the goddess of earth and crops, or the shades of the dead, each contributes to the establishment of a focus about which human activity can fluctuate, and through which it can acquire access to the 'beyond'. The mundus as a prototype of the civic temple can not be overlooked, along with its connection to the household lararia and, furthermore, as an early manifestation of what was to become, in Augustan times, the public lararia of the 'Compitales'. These shrines were set up at the site of all road intersections, simultaneously signifying in a singular phenomenon the orientation of the templum and the imperial orientation of urban life.

11 The festival of the Caristia was basically a family get-together in order to amend quarrels and disputes and where everyone brought their own contribution to a feast held in conjunction with the worship of the Lares. It was celebrated on 22 February (Dixon 1992).

12 Merleau-Ponty uses the term 'depth' to encapsulate the essential spatio-temporal nature of experience whereby: 'The "order of co-existents" is inseparable from the "order of sequences". . . . Perception provides me with a "field of presence" in the broad sense, extending in two dimensions: the here-there dimension and the past-present-future dimension' (Merleau-Ponty 1962: 265)

13 Evidently it is far beyond the scope of this discussion to do justice to the Roman understanding of nature in all its fascinating manifestations.

14 The earliest uses of the word group of which 'mimesis' is a member have been investigated by Koller (1954) and Else (1958) and seem to go back to the fifth century BC where it was connected with mimicry of natural phenomena, often in the form of dance.

BIBLIOGRAPHY

Aries, P. and Duby, G. (1987) *A History of Private Life*, trans. A. Goldhammer, Cambridge, Mass.: Harvard University Press.

Bachelard, G. (1969) *The Poetics of Space*, trans. M. Jolas, Boston: Beacon Press.

Brillant, R. (1984) *Visual Narratives*, New York: Cornell University Press.

Clarke, J.R. (1991) *The Houses of Roman Italy, 100 BC–AD 250, Ritual, Space and Decoration*, Berkeley: University of California Press.

Dixon, S. (1992) *The Roman Family*, Baltimore: Johns Hopkins University Press.

Eliade, M. (1958) *Patterns in Comparative Religion*, London: Sheed & Ward.

Else, G.F. (1958) 'Imitation in the fifth century', *Classical Philology* 53(2).

Gazda, E.K. (1991) *Roman Art in the Private Sphere*, Ann Arbor: University of Michigan Press.

Heidegger, M. (1971) 'Building dwelling thinking', in *Poetry, Language, Thought*, trans. A. Hofstadter, New York: Harper & Row.

Jashemski, W.F. (1979) *The Gardens of Pompeii*, New York: Caratzas Brothers.

Koller, H. (1954) *Die Mimesis in der Antike*, Bern: Francke.

Lacey, W.K. (1986) 'Patria Potestas', in B. Rawson (ed.), *The Family in Ancient Rome: New Perspectives*, London: Croom Helm.

Long, A.A. (1974) *Hellenistic Philosophy*, London: Duckworth.

Mau, A. (1899) *Pompeii: Its Life and Art*, trans. F.W. Kelsey, New York: Macmillan.

Merleau-Ponty, M. (1962) *Phenomenology of Perception*, trans. C. Smith, London: Routledge & Kegan Paul.

Ovid *Fasti*, trans. H.T. Riley, 1887, London: George Bell.

——*Metamorphoses*, trans. M.M. Innes, 1955, Harmondsworth: Penguin.

Plato *Republic*, trans. P. Shorey in E. Hamilton and H. Cairns (eds), *The Collected Dialogues of Plato*, 1961, Princeton: Princeton University Press.

Rykwert, J. (1976) *The Idea of a Town*, Cambridge, Mass.: MIT.

Suetonius (1957) *Twelve Caesars*, trans. R. Graves, Harmondsworth: Penguin.

Vesely, D. (1987) 'Architecture and the poetics of representation', *Daidalos* 25: 24–36.

——(1988) 'On the relevance of phenomenology', *Pratt Journal of Architecture* 2: 59–62.

Virgil *The Aeneid*, trans. W.F. Jackson Knight, 1956, Harmondsworth: Penguin.

——*The Georgics*, trans. L.P. Wilkinson, 1982, Harmondsworth: Penguin.

Voegelin, E. (1974) *Order and History, Vol. IV: The Ecumenic Age*, Louisiana: Louisiana State University Press.

Wallace-Hadrill, A. (1988) 'The social structure of the Roman house', *Papers of the British School at Rome* 56: 43–97.

Zeller, E. (1980) *Outlines of the History of Greek Philosophy*, trans. L.R. Palmer, New York: Dover.

7

SWAHILI ARCHITECTURE, SPACE AND SOCIAL STRUCTURE

Mark Horton

Swahili stone houses have been the subject of particular attention in recent years. Found in traditional settlements on the East African coast, where mud and thatch houses are normal, these have been used to explain the method by which particular groups asserted their identity and role within the community. By using 'house power' (Donley 1982), with complex symbolic and social associations, patrician groups who claimed Arab as opposed to African ancestry came to dominate trading activities on the Swahili coast in the eighteenth and early nineteenth centuries. The origins of this patrician group, known as the Waungwana, have been the subject of controversy. Linda Donley-Reid (1990) has argued through her oral historical and ethno-archaeological research that a middle Eastern origin was an important factor in the importance of this group (Figure 7.1). J. de V. Allen (1979; 1993) took a completely opposing view, that these claims were largely bogus, and that stone house architecture was just one facet of a complex indigenous society.

In this chapter, I wish to explore the relationship between the social organization, spatial structure and architecture of these Swahili communities, using archaeology to study these issues over a long time-period. Such an analysis rests upon the assumption that some communities may use the planning of settlements as a 'map' with which to express elements of their social and kinship structures. It may be possible to explain these relationships in functionalist terms of access and control of particular resources by specific social groups, or as cognitive expressions, which may incidentally have economic benefits.

THE SWAHILI AND THEIR SOCIAL STRUCTURE

The Swahili are a trading people, who live between southern Somalia and northern Mozambique as well as on the offshore islands of Zanzibar, Pemba and Mafia, the Comoro archipelago, and northern Madagascar (Nurse and Spear 1985; Middleton 1992). Traditional Swahili settlements are rarely

147

Figure 7.1 Waungwana stone house in Lamu. Dating to the late eighteenth century, the interior was decorated by fine plasterwork, prepared for an important wedding.

found more than a few kilometres from the Indian Ocean, and relied upon marine resources and mixed agriculture. The majority of Swahili settlements are of mud and thatch, although often with stone mosque and tombs. A small number of settlements with stone houses (but also containing mud and thatch houses) are also known, which historically had much larger populations of up to 20,000 people. Islam is today a key feature of Swahili society, and in many ways is a defining feature of ethnic identity, *vis-à-vis* the non-Muslim groups who live in the coastal hinterland. Their language, ki-Swahili, has become a widespread *lingua franca* throughout the region and consequently has become less useful as a defining feature of Swahili identity (Sharif 1973).

CLANS

'Who are the Swahili' is a most frequent question, posed by anthropologists and historians, and one which is almost impossible to answer in communities with such mobile and cosmopolitan populations (Eastman 1971; Arens 1975). Indeed the very term Swahili is rarely used by the local people and over the last 100 years has implied several different status, language, racial and ethnic groups.

The one feature which is held in common in traditional settlements is clan structure. It is membership of a particular clan, and the relationship with other clans, which gives an individual his/her identity in these cosmopolitan communities. Each settlement or group consists of a fixed number of clans, and membership is through patrilateral descent, although matri- or bi-lateral descent also occurs in different communities. These clans are often arranged in order of seniority and membership establishes status, marriage prospects, identity and to a limited extent economic activity within the community.

Although clans are encountered in virtually every coastal settlement, there is neither an accepted nomenclature nor a precise formula with which they can be described. Furthermore as clans are a feature shared by most other East African societies, especially the coastal Bantu groups (Prins 1952), it is difficult to single out features peculiar to the Swahili. The widespread differences in clan group terminology are matched by differing criteria for membership. Members of a *jamaa* in the rural areas of the southern Kenyan coast would not only be loose kin groups but also might include friends and neighbours (Prins 1967: 81). In Zanzibar an *ukoo* would contain members established through both patrilateral and matrilateral descent, so an individual can belong to up to four different *uko* at any one time (Middleton 1961). In Lamu, membership is established through patrilateral descent, but as residence patterns are matrilocal there is very little territorial significance to clan allegiance (Prins 1971). In Mombasa membership is established through patrilateral descent but marriage is traditionally endogamous within each moiety or deme, so that there is a general relationship between clan and

Figure 7.2 The spinal division at Siyu is marked by a path running to the entrance of the Congregational Mosque, which divides the patrician and commoner moieties in the community

moiety. In practice, however, exogamous marriage takes place and there is considerable flexibility in clan membership as a result (Prins 1967: 80).

Clan membership indicates an individual's hierarchical position within the society. In Lamu the clans are divided into the three, the nine and the twelve (Prins 1971; Zein 1974). The Wa-amu (the inhabitants of Lamu) are divided into twelve clans which comprise the nine clans of patricians (Waungwana) and the three clans of commoners (Washenzi). It was the nine clans that made up the Waungwana proper – those people who lived in stone houses and in whose hands the governing of the town was traditionally placed. The nine themselves have an order of seniority which determines which clan undertakes certain offices. The justification of Waungwana authority is that they 'founded the town'. The most senior clan are the Bereki who actually describe themselves as *wenye mui* or the owners of the town and tend to live in the old north moiety of Lamu – Zena. Strangers, tribal groups and other high-ranking sharif or merchant newcomers could not describe themselves as *wa-amu* but only *watu wa* Lamu (people of Lamu).

In other communities in the Lamu archipelago, the clan structure is similar although simpler. In Siyu there are nine clans comprising patricians and commoners with the patrician groups further subdivided (Figure 7.2). In Pate there are seven clans with a clear order of seniority. Among the Bajuni of the Kenyan and Somali coast, there are eighteen clans (described as *kamasi*) – ten Bajuni proper (fishermen and agriculturalists) and eight of the Katwa who are pastoralists and have a prohibition on the eating of fish (Grottanelli 1955: 199; Prins 1967: 82; Bujra 1968).

One problem that has made the study of Swahili clans particularly difficult is that although there is always a firmly established number of clans in each settlement, different informants will give conflicting names or more or less names than the stated number. Thus every well-informed person will tell of the twelve of Barawa, the nine of Siyu, the seven of Pate, the twelve of Lamu and the three and the nine of Mombasa. But when pressed, each will give a radically different list of the groups that qualify, a real problem for the oral historian attempting to reconstruct the origin of specific clan groups. For example, amongst the eighteen Bajuni clans there is little relationship between the names suggested to Grottanelli (1955: 202) and Allen (1993). The same conclusion can be reached from Brown's (1985) research in Siyu or Zein's (1974: 19) work in Lamu when compared with the earlier work of Prins (1967: 82).

A remarkable feature of this system of clan organization is the long-term stability of the number of clans associated with particular towns. Barawa is probably the best-documented example, where the 'twelve' clans were already in existence by 1503. A Portuguese account describes the organization of Barawa (Freeman-Grenville 1966: 78–9): 'As this town was governed by a corporation, these twelve moors being the principal heads of the government'.

The implication is that some feature of the settlement limits the actual number of clans although the identity of the clans shifts, both through perception and time. New clans may displace older ones, as was probably the case with the arrival of the Katwa in Siyu, but it appears that the total number of eligible clans that comprise the settlement is fixed. One possible reason for this is that each community has its clan numbers fixed by the physical layout of the town.

ENCLOSURES AND SETTLEMENT PATTERNS

A clue that a social/spatial relationship may exist comes from the Lamu area, where a clan is often referred to as a *mlango*, ki-Swahili for gateway or door (Krapf 1882: 237; Prins 1971). This somewhat curious term is used in a number of ways: *mlango moja*, literally 'from the same doorway', is a common phrase to identify the same clan member, whilst *mlango wa ufalme* is used to refer to the royal family (Sacleux 1935: 500).

A possible explanation for this usage comes from the Comoro Islands (Figure 7.3). Here the centres of several villages contain the *fumboni*, a stone enclosure where communal activity takes place including marriage rituals, funerals, dancing, poetry competitions, discussions and the meeting of the

Figure 7.3 A doorway leading into a *fumboni* located on the Comoro Islands (photo: British Institute in Eastern Africa)

elders. The *fumboni* often contains a mosque and a well, is normally square and measures about 75 m across. The entrance to the *fumboni* is through a number of gates which are the property of a single clan or moiety group. In Comoran society, *mlango moja* is simply an expression implying that a particular groups shares an entry into a communal *fumboni* – identity is thus expressed through the particular gateway one passes to enter the central *fumboni*.

Archaeological evidence for these 'central enclosures' within Swahili settlements comes from several sites, although ethnographic context has inevitably been lost. The seventeenth-century site at Takwa on Manda Island near Lamu has a large rectangular enclosure around the mosque and well, with a north and south entrance in classic Comoro style (Wilson 1982: fig. 2). At Koyama, on the southern Somali coast, Elliot (1925–6: 250) recorded a

Figure 7.4 The centre of Mogadishu in the late ninetheenth century was a large open communal area, entered through stone gateways (after Révoil, 1885)

central core walled enclosure which was 'simply being kept for worship and for purposes of defence' and the villagers lived out in the hills and valleys. The centre of Mogadishu in the late nineteenth century had a similar open space exactly between the two moieties, Shangani and Hamer Weyne (Révoil 1885; Alpers 1983: 443) (Figure 7.4). Hamer Weyne in Somali means 'stone enclosure'. This name is similar to the traditional name of one of the moieties at Mombasa, Haram el Kedima, meaning in Arabic 'ancient enclosure' (Guillain 1856: 111, 258–9).

This idea of a central communal enclosure is not confined to Muslim groups but also occurs in a modified form among the Mijikenda, who live along the coastal hinterland. This group is particularly relevant because their language is a member of the same sub-group of north-east coastal Bantu as ki-Swahili (Nurse 1983). They also share several traditions of origin in common with the Swahili (specifically the Bajuni Swahili), including a claimed common homeland called Shungwaya. Sacred enclosures were also found among the Pokomo, also Bantu speakers, but these are much less well known.

The typical Mijikenda enclosure is known as the *kaya* (pl. *makaya*) and these have attracted considerable ethnographic and historical attention (Spear 1978). Archaeological investigation and detailed mapping have also taken place at several sites (Mutoro 1987). The typical *kaya* is surrounded by

153

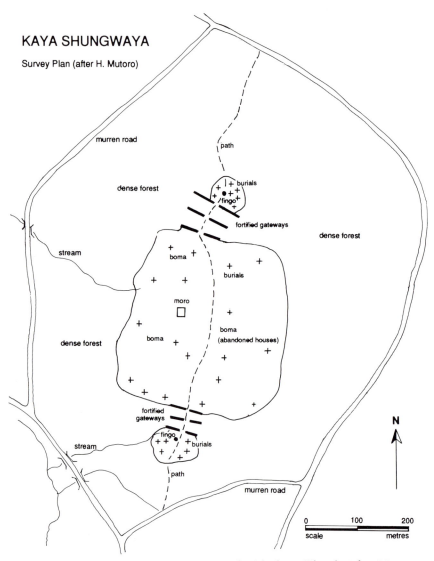

KAYA SHUNGWAYA

Survey Plan (after H. Mutoro)

Figure 7.5 Plan of *kaya* Shungwaya associated with the Mijikenda (after Mutoro, 1987)

dense coastal forest (Figure 7.5). In the centre is a rectangular clearing. Entrance into the clearing is from north or south through gateways; entrance through these gates is associated with particular clans or moieties. Up to four gates block the pathway; these are constructed of wood with a short length of stone wall leading into the forest. Near the outer gates the *fingo* pot is buried – traditionally a pot containing magic carried from Shungwaya. Within the clearing or *boma* and close to the centre, there is a single hut or *moro*. Here the main *fingo* pot is buried. The hut itself served as both the secular and ritual centre for the *kaya*, and contained items like the *muanzia* drum. Here the Council of Elders would meet (ibid: 46–50). Burial patterns are also of interest. If the death occurred within the *kaya*, then burial took place within the enclosure; if not, then the burial was located as close as possible to the outer gate. *Makaya* are no longer lived in, although they are respected as sacred sites, and the forest around them is still preserved.

THE ARCHAEOLOGY OF SWAHILI ENCLOSURES: THE SHANGA EVIDENCE

Close similarities between Mijikenda practice and the patterns of Swahili clan and spatial organization – both groups for example use *fingo* pots – might suggest a common origin. The excavations at Shanga, a site on the south side of Pate Island near Lamu and dating from the mid-eighth century AD, provided an opportunity to study the development of central enclosures through several centuries, along with the process of Islamization and changing architectural technology and style (Horton 1987; 1991; forthcoming).

Shanga is a typical Swahili town, with evidence for extensive overseas trading links, Islam (represented by three mosques and numerous tombs) and stone architecture. It was abandoned in the early fifteenth century, and a low rate of stone robbing resulted in the survival of a town plan into the twentieth century (Figure 7.6). The fourteenth- and fifteenth-century houses have several features in common with the eighteenth-century Waungwana architecture of Lamu studied by Donley-Reid, including decorated *ndani* niches, outer courtyards and an 'intimacy gradient'.

The 1980 survey of the houses, streets, mosques and tombs provided the basis of plan analysis and subsequent excavation strategy. While there was no surviving *fumboni*-style enclosure above ground, the central part of the town remained open and distinctive, with few houses and large numbers of burials as well as the Friday Mosque and community well. Analysis, based upon street position and house alignments, suggests that fourteenth-century Shanga developed from a fairly coherent underlying plan (Figure 7.7). The central area was rectangular, 80 m by 100 m, with the well at the exact geometric centre. Seven streets led into this area; these were spaced at regular intervals. There were traces of an outer enclosure, closely following the lines of the inner area; this too had the well at the centre, and was entered via four streets, each centrally placed on each side. Both enclosures were aligned almost precisely on cardinal north–south axes.

While this reconstruction is based upon plan analysis and is thus a hypothesis, excavation does provide a method of testing it. Indeed Shanga is

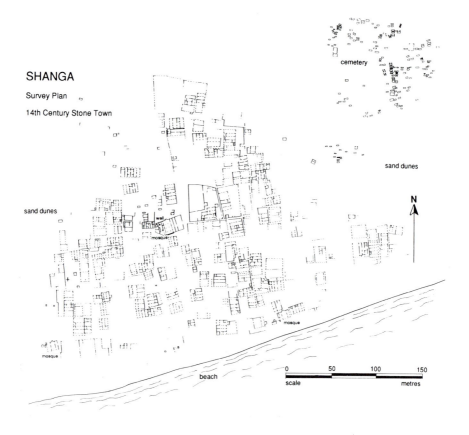

Figure 7.6 Plan of stone walls, Shanga, showing houses, mosques and tombs, largely dating to the fourteenth century.

a deeply stratified site, with up to 4 m of deposit, spanning six hundred years. Excavation was needed to demonstrate not only the original layout of the settlement that created this underlying plan, but also the subsequent six hundred years of continuity to the fifteenth-century abandonment. This was done by means of a series of contiguous excavations that extended across the east–west axis from both sides of the central area. The results are presented below.

156

SHANGA

Hypothetical Plan

Early Settlement Structure

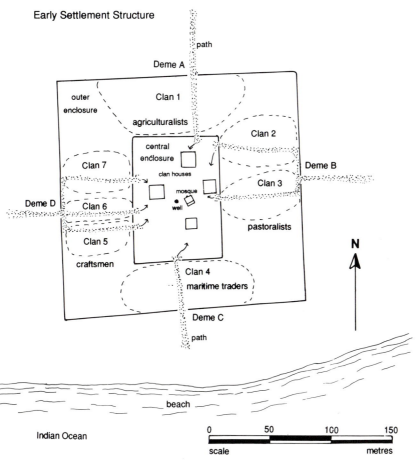

Figure 7.7 Hypothetical plan of the early settlement structure of Shanga

Original settlement

The earliest occupation, dating to the mid-eighth century AD, was located around a depression in the sand-dunes set back 150 m from the sea. In the centre, a well was dug into the natural coral rock, through the sand-dunes; this was an open hollow. This well, although rebuilt many times, remained in the same position through the entire occupation of the site.

Close to the well there was at least one large tree (and possibly three), scattered iron slag deposits, and the occasional post-hole. From a very early

Figure 7.8 Excavation of part of the central enclosure, Shanga, with external round houses marked by post holes in the foreground

date, there was settlement 'order'. On the east side of the central area a north–south gully split the trench into an open space to the west and an occupied area with a post-hole structure and rubbish pits to the east, with a path leading towards the well; a hoard of cowries marked the point where this path crossed the gully. On the east side, a mirror image of this occurs with a hollow way leading to the well, and an impressive enclosure wall marked by two lines of post-holes (Figure 7.8).

The consistent cardinal north–south alignment of the enclosure found on both sides indicated that a rectangular area was laid out from the period of primary occupation and reserved for communal activities. The position of the gullies, paths and well is very close to that predicted from the plan analysis. The central well, trees, cowrie deposits and spreads of iron slag all suggest that this area had a strong cultic significance. Domestic occupation lay outside the enclosure, as is evident from the domestic spreads.

Period B

Directly above the primary level of trodden sand and burnt-out tree stumps, a succession of early timber buildings was discovered, on an alignment of 310° (and thus not the cardinal alignment of the original enclosure). Located by the side of the well, these were directly underneath the prayer

Figure 7.9 Early timber mosques, Shanga, following a different alignment to the later stone mosques

hall of the later Friday Mosque. It is possible that these timber buildings were early mosques, serving a very small minority population of Muslims (Figure 7.9). Islamic burials on the same alignment of 310° were also found nearby.

The central enclosure persisted at the same location and alignment with a path and elaborate gate to the west and a much larger gully and path to the east. Outside the enclosure there was a mixture of round and rectangular huts of post-hole construction. Various craft activities were identified – iron working (including at least two furnaces), bead making and the preparation of shells.

What was the central enclosure for? The best evidence for this is structure 284, a square hipped-roofed building with three rooms, set within its own enclosure and gate, cardinally aligned. It was quite unlike the domestic buildings and a communal function is probable as with the central enclosure. It may have been one of a series of such buildings in the centre of the site, perhaps 'club houses' for each of the constituent clans, or it may have been unique, similar perhaps to the *moro* in the centre of the Mijikenda Kaya.

Period C

The first large-scale building – although still wholly reliant on mud, thatch and timber – appears in the late ninth century. This is marked by much larger post-holes in the construction of one of the timber 'mosques'. Structure 284 was itself replaced (and directly overlain) by a massive timber hall, structure 272, surviving as a grid of post-holes, each post-pit measuring over 2 m deep and 0.8 m wide. Reconstruction suggests a square building, with a hipped roof – basically very similar but on a much larger scale to structure 284. The enclosure still remains clearly defined, with pathways, gates and gullies.

Period D

Stone building was introduced in the early to mid-tenth century, using a technique that cuts porites coral from the sea bed. A stone mosque (with a mihrab) replaces the underlying timber structures, but basically follows exactly the same plan and alignment. The timber hall, structure 272, is succeeded by a square stone building, directly above, retaining the same basic plan and dimensions of the earlier timber hall. Other stone buildings were also found north, south and east of the well; that on the east had an identical plan to structure 272.

Walls in stone also appear, replacing the earlier timber gullies, on the very same alignment and position, making the archaeology of these boundary areas complex. The appearance of stone buildings is marked by two changes in the stratigraphy. First, the appearance of stone chippings, from the cutting of the porites coral, which forms an obvious horizon across the site. Speckled layers are also found around the central buildings and in the street/path levels; the central enclosure seems to have been covered in this deposit, which was brought from a beach some 5 km away from the site, perhaps to distinguish it from the domestic areas beyond.

One feature of the area around these stone buildings were the numerous timber kiosks (Figure 7.10). They had a very short life, were repeatedly redug, and may have been either craft workshops or market stalls. Similar kiosks can be seen in a nineteenth-century print of the central area of Mogadishu (Figure 7.4).

Period E

The Friday Mosque, built c. AD 1000, represents a major point in the history of the site; here for the first time was a building large enough to accommo-date the majority of the male adult population at prayer. Estimates of about ninety worshippers would serve a population of around four hundred.

Figure 7.10 Stone monumental buildings, Shanga, with slots marking the position of kiosks in the adjacent open area

Associated with this mosque and around it were the first stone tombs, of faced coral and plaster.

Shortly after the construction of this mosque, in the mid-eleventh century, much of the centre of the site was levelled flat and the porites buildings were systematically taken down – a thorough operation, in which hardly a stone was left standing. Thick levels of rubble covered the centre of the site. A lime kiln was excavated, which burnt up the timber (some of it expensive hardwoods) and stone from the buildings.

The permanent boundaries of the central enclosure were abandoned at this point, while significant numbers of burials were placed within the enclosure. Paths shifted their position slightly and a new path followed the original enclosure line. Between this path and the new boundary, infill buildings were constructed. These lay among the ruins of the former stone buildings and wall stubs were used as wind breaks for bread ovens. They were constructed entirely of mud, timber and daub walls.

These daub buildings may not have been domestic, even though there are a number of bread ovens associated with them. The large numbers of spindle whorls suggest the growing importance of textile working, while the discovery of spindle whorl blanks suggests some form of manufacturing; indeed these daub structures may have been weaving sheds. Another craft seems to have been leather working, with evidence for tanning pits, while

161

Figure 7.11 Coral and mud houses, Shanga, dating to the late thirteenth century, representing an intermediate stage in the evolution of the stone Waungwana house

there are also significant quantities of iron slag. A possible model for these infill structures is that they began as craft workshops, to which more permanent residential units were later attached.

Period F

In the mid-thirteenth century trading patterns shift from the Gulf to southern Arabia. Chinese pottery also rapidly increases in popularity. At the same time, textile working declines (as measured by the overall number of spindle whorls) and ironworking disappears. This may represent a shift from a craft-based exchange system to a more fully mercantile economy.

A two-stage evolution can be noted in the house architecture. First, in the mid-thirteenth century, the daub-walled structures make increasing use of coral rag, bonded by mud and removing the timber supports (Figure 7.11). The surface is plastered and whitewashed. The next stage is the replacement of mud with lime mortar; this occurs c. AD 1300. These new stone walls are often built directly over the foundations of the earlier walls. It is to this period of building that the present ruined town largely belongs with buildings which can be directly compared to the Waungwana houses of Lamu, but whose plan can be traced back directly to pre-stone daub houses.

The buildings within the centre of the site seem to have been converted

162

from workshops into houses. At least one has a tanning pit attached to it. Burial continues in the central area, with numerous tombs, often of monumental construction. This retains the notion of the central enclosure, which by the abandonment of the site in the fifteenth century has become little more than a cemetery.

CLANS, MOIETIES AND STONE ARCHITECTURE

Early Shanga seems to have been laid out very much in the fashion of a Mijikenda *kaya*. Each individual gateway into the central enclosure was associated with a particular clan – in the Shanga case, there seem to have been seven clans. Some support for this comes from the external cemetery at Shanga, where there were seven distinct areas of burial. Seven is a fairly common (and no doubt significant) number. At nearby Pate, for example, there were seven clans, and traditionally seven gateways through the town wall.

Analysis of the faunal remains from the excavations are of particular interest as they point to significant cultural differences across the site. An excavation in the north-west section (in an area which did not develop stone houses in the fourteenth century) was notable for its larger proportion of goat to cattle bones, numerous fish bones, wild animals, dogs and turtles. In the central part of the site there was far less fish, but cat bones and dugong were present. These differences seem to highlight an agriculturalist/pastoralist division in economic activity. Pastoralists had a strong taboo on the consumption of fish, but dugong (or 'sea cow') seem to have been acceptable. Agricultural activity took place on the mainland, and this may explain the presence of game and dogs (for hunting) in the assemblage.

The original model suggested four basic entrances to the settlement, and these may reflect four basic demes, which must have remained largely endogamous. These four demes may have reflected four basic groups living together in the community. The faunal evidence provides some clue as to their origins; architectural evidence from the standing buildings provides other clues, which suggest the following reconstruction:

Deme A: north, clan 1, agriculturalists with ironworking elements important. Very few stone buildings in this area during the fourteenth century; iron slag and furnaces present.

Deme B: east, clans 2 and 3, pastoralist. Major area of large stone enclosures (probably for the keeping of cattle, with accumulations of dung) and multiroom houses.

Deme C: south, clan 4, maritime traders. Uniform stone houses; main concentration of guest rooms for visiting merchants attached to courtyards. Significantly this group lies on the seaward side of the settlement.

Deme D: west, clans 5, 6 and 7, craftsmen. Stone houses of non-standard plan, suggesting modification of workshops. Excavations produced high concentrations of bead-making equipment and spindle whorls as well as tanning pits.

It is very tempting to link these four groups with the four stone buildings in the central area, located for easy and equal access for each clan. As such, these buildings could have served as the ritual and communal centre for each deme. The basic structure of the community would have been a multi-cultural alliance where each deme contributed to the success of the settlement through exchange conducted within the central enclosure.

EXCHANGE, CULT AND SOCIAL ORDER

One particular feature, which outside observers noted in their contact with the Swahili world, was the system of sponsorship – a common method of trade on the Somali coast as late as the nineteenth century (Cassanelli 1982: 156). One of the first descriptions of this practice was by Yakut (c. 1210), in the context of trade in Mogadishu:

> When a merchant goes to them he must stay with one of them, who will sponsor him in all his dealings.
>
> (Trimingham 1964: 5n)

Ibn Battuta met with such conditions when he visited Mogadishu in 1331 where, because he was a religious scholar, he was sponsored by the Qadi (Freeman-Grenville 1966: 27–8). Fragments of descriptions about much earlier trading practice on the east African coast suggest that these mechanisms established trust between widely differing ethnic groups. Although trade could take place in a 'neutral' location, specific institutions were often needed to ensure the security of the transaction and the avoidance of disputes. According to tenth-century Buzurg ibn Shahriyar:

> When merchants go to Berbera, they take escorts with them for fear that a native will seize them and geld them. The natives collect the testicles of foreigners.
>
> (Freeman-Grenville 1981: 66)

A ninth-century Chinese account written by Duan Chengshi describes trading on the coast of Bobali, with elaborate rituals involved in sponsorship:

> If Possu [Persian] merchants wish to go into the country, they collect around them several thousand men and present them with strips of cloth. All, whether young or old, draw blood and swear an oath, and only then do they trade their goods.
>
> (Duyvendak 1949: 13–14)

Blood-brotherhood rituals between traders and apparently large numbers of the local population ensured security in a segmented lineage system where the murder of a trader could be avenged by the sponsors' own lineage group (Cassanelli 1982). On the Sofala coast in the eleventh century, according to al-Biruni:

> It is the custom of seagoing merchants in their dealing with Zabej and the Zanj that they do not trust them in their contracts, so their chiefs and elders come and give themselves as hostages so that they are even held by fetters. Then the goods that the people desire are handed over to them for them to take to their land and divide among them. . . . They remove the fetters from them and let them go with honours and gifts.
>
> (Levtzion and Hopkins 1981: 58)

With sponsorship and associated rituals, it is also clear that these trading sites had an important cult component. Magical tricks are a recurring theme: they were seen as a major hazard of trading, and probably a method of controlling foreign merchants. For example at Zhongli, a late twelfth-century Chinese source describes:

> Many people are addicted to magical tricks; they can change their bodies into the shapes of birds and beasts and aquatic animals, and they frighten or bewilder the ignorant people. If in their commercial dealing with a foreign ship, there may occasionally be a quarrel, they pronounce a ban over it so that the ship can neither move forward nor backward, not until the participants in the quarrel have been wise enough to settle the dispute is it released. The government of the country have strictly forbidden this.
>
> (Duyvendak 1949: 21)

Buzurg recalled a similar story when a Zanj witch doctor placed a spell over a fleet of fifteen trading ships (Freeman-Grenville 1981: 36). The Zanj ports seem to have contained a strong religious component. Idrisi refers to the sorcerers by their Swahili name *maganga* while Bazawa (?Barawa), an early and important port, was:

> the last in the land of the infidels, who have no religious creed, but take standing stones, anoint them with fish oil and bow down before them. Their worship and their depraved beliefs consist of this and similar absurdities but they are steadfast in them.
>
> (Lewis 1974 ii: 117–18)

At Shanga, the archaeological evidence throws considerable light upon these references. The enclosure may have been seen as an area of ritual protection for the market, an area of neutrality that contained both communal buildings as well as a mosque. Indeed the timber kiosks at Shanga could mark the adoption of open trade within the enclosure.

However, for a foreigner to gain access to the enclosure, and thus this market, he would need to pass through one of the gates and therefore to become a clan member. In practical terms this meant that a foreigner had to be sponsored by a specific clan, who would adopt him and protect him. In return, that clan could gain a monopoly of the foreign trader's goods which, as prestige goods (such as cloth, glass, glazed pottery), were extremely valuable to them. Some clans (such as the northern-living agriculturalists) may have been denied the right to admit foreigners.

With the Islamization of the community, this system must have become increasingly untenable. First, with the mosque in the centre of the enclosure, it was very difficult to deny access to visitors – who according to Islamic tradition had free access to the mosque, even being allowed to sleep there overnight. Second, the 'magical tricks' and fear of castration, which were used to underpin the system, must have become very much less credible within a wholly Islamic society. It is therefore not surprising that the central enclosure was replaced with the adoption of majority Islam in the twelfth century. That this change may have been a violent one is suggested by the very comprehensive demolition of the stone buildings and the evidence that the mosque itself was burnt down at this time, and it is possible that this was associated with the arrival of a more militant form of Islam.

The line of the enclosure was preserved, and a plausible explanation is that pre-Islamic ceremonies continued to be followed, so the space remained significant. One such ceremony is the *zinguo*, still practised in Lamu, in which a bull is taken around the boundaries of the town (Zein 1974; Allen 1993: 230–1).

The system of sponsorship seems to have remained in place by the simple expedient of moving sponsorship into the house; Yakut suggests that by the early thirteenth century, merchants stayed in their sponsors' houses, and this was already considered the norm by the time of Ibn Battuta's visit in 1331. The architectural evidence for this, found in eighteenth-century Lamu houses as well as Shanga houses, is a separate guest room, attached to the courtyard of the house, which was known as the *sabule*. A result of this was that the house became the focus of trading activities, and that ownership of the house was the mechanism of monopolistic control, not that of the gateway into the central enclosure. If one did not own a stone house, then trade was impossible. Stone houses were constructed and occupied as a symbol of aristocracy and permanence. Permanence implied creditworthiness and in a society based on trade this was essential to the successful merchant.

At Shanga, it appears that such a system emerged in the twelfth and thirteenth centuries. It is clear, from the fourteenth-century town remains, that the southern part, with its guest rooms, emerged as the main stone house part of the town. The north-west quarter contains virtually no stone houses; indeed a complex of mud houses was excavated in this area. The difference in plan between the mud and stone houses was very slight, with courtyards and toilet areas. Building a stone house in fourteenth-century Shanga involved the use of lime mortar to bond the walls in a permanent way. One might be bold enough to state that this architectural change represents the emergence of the Waungwana as a distinct grouping.

In eighteenth-century Lamu, as well as Pate and Siyu, the right to build a stone house became the most important material culture feature separating the Waungwana clans from commoners. A whole series of ritual activities linked the Waungwana to their stone house. During the marriage ceremony, for example, elaborate plaster decorations were prepared. Other rituals, such as the *kutolewande*, directly link the new-born baby to the stone house (Donley 1982). The stone house constituted the private zone into which a commoner could only be admitted in certain circumstances as a servant, slave or concubine. Defiling activity took place in the inner private part of the stone house.

But of all the coastal settlements, it is at Pate that the patrician/commoner division is strongest. The stone houses in the north of the walled town have been abandoned and robbed for their stone. The population now lives in two villages, set either side of the Friday Mosque, with an open area beside the mosque (Chittick 1967: fig. 11). In the western village, Kitokwa, the houses are small with one or two rooms, rarely a courtyard, built together in a complex maze of streets and side alleys. Mud and coral rag walls are covered with thick coatings of lime plaster. To the east, at Mitaayu, the houses of the Waungwana are of a very different kind. The room plans are those of the typical stone house, with a courtyard and up to five rows of rooms to the rear. The streets in this settlement are more orderly, and all the walls are well built with stone, although often held together with mud.

CONCLUSION

Much controversy has surrounded the origins of the Swahili, largely concerning the Waungwana and their distinctive stone architecture. Those historians working within colonial milieux sought to stress the Arab roots of the Swahili, as essentially the descendants of Arab traders who married Bantu women, producing an Afro-Asiatic culture (Chittick 1977). For such an origin within a clan-based system, those Arabs who did marry into Swahili society must have done so within the existing structures. It is also very clear that the stone houses are no more than the product of an evolution of architectural form, which suddenly attracted significance through the abandonment of the central enclosure.

The archaeological evidence provides a model of a society whose basic structures have remained largely unaltered for a thousand years, but have remained flexible enough to incorporate major changes such as Islam, colonization, and latterly westernization. The study of space and social order provides a useful explanatory framework.

167

BIBLIOGRAPHY

Allen, J. de V. (1979) 'The Swahili house: cultural and ritual concepts underlying its plan and structure', in J. de V. Allen and T.H. Wilson (eds), *Swahili Houses and Tombs of the Coast of Kenya*, London: Art and Archaeology Research Papers.

——(1993) *Swahili Origins; Swahili Culture and the Shungwaya Phenomenon*, London: James Currey.

Alpers, E.A. (1983) 'Muqdisho in the nineteenth century: a regional perspective', *Journal of African History* 24: 441–59.

Arens, W. (1975) 'The wa-Swahili: the social history of an ethnic group', *Africa* 45(4): 426–37.

Brown, H. (1985) 'History of Siyu: The Development and Decline of a Swahili Town on the Northern Kenyan Coast', unpublished Ph.D. thesis, Indiana University.

Bujra, J. (1968) 'Conflict and Conflict Resolution in a Bajuni Village', unpublished Ph.D. thesis, University of London.

Cassanelli, L.V. (1982) *The Shaping of Somali Society*, Philadelphia: Pennsylvania University Press.

Chittick, H.N. (1967) 'Discoveries in the Lamu Archipelago', *Azania* 2: 37–68.

——(1977) 'The East Coast, Madagascar and the Indian Ocean', in R. Oliver (ed.), *Cambridge History of Africa Vol. 3*, Cambridge: Cambridge University Press.

Donley, L.W. (1982) 'House power: Swahili space and symbolic markers', in I. Hodder (ed.), *Symbolic and Structural Archaeology*, Cambridge: Cambridge University Press.

Donley-Reid, L.W. (1990) 'A structuring structure: the Swahili house', in S. Kent (ed.), *Domestic Architecture and the Use of Space*, Cambridge: Cambridge University Press.

Duyvendak, J.J.L. (1949) *China's Discovery of Africa*, Occasional Paper, London: School of Oriental and African Studies.

Eastman, C. (1971) 'Who are the wa-Swahili?', *Africa* 41: 228–36.

Elliot, J.A.G. (1925–6) 'A visit to the Bajun Islands', *Journal of the Asiatic Society* 25: 10–22, 147–63, 338–58.

Freeman-Grenville, G.S.P. (1966) *Select Documents from the First to the Earlier Nineteenth Century*, 2nd edn, London: Clarendon Press.

——(1981) *The Book of the Wonders of India by Captain Buzurg ibn Shahriyar of Ramhormuz*, London and The Hague: East West Publications.

Grottanelli, V.L. (1955) *Pescatori dell'Oceano Indiano*, Rome: Cremonese.

Guillain, M. (1856) *Documents sur l'histoire, la géographie, et la commerce de l'Afrique orientale*, 3 vols, Paris: Bertrand.

Horton, M.C. (1987) 'Early Muslim trading settlements on the east African coast: new evidence from Shanga', *Antiquaries Journal* 67(2): 290–323.

——(1991) 'Primitive architecture and Islam in east Africa', *Muqarnas* 8: 103–6.

——(forthcoming) *Shanga; The Archaeology of a Muslim Trading Community on the Coast of East Africa*, Nairobi: British Institute in Eastern Africa.

Kraft, L. (1882) *A Dictionary of the Suahili Language*, London: Trubner & Co., reprinted 1969, New York.

Levtzion, N. and Hopkins J.F.P. (1981) *Corpus of Early Arabic Sources for West African History*, Cambridge: Cambridge University Press.

Lewis, B. (1974) *Islam: from the Prophet Mohammed to the Capture of Constantinople*, 2 vols, London: Macmillan.

Middleton, J. (1961) *Land Tenure in Zanzibar*, London: HMSO, Colonial Research Studies no. 23.

——(1992) *The World of the Swahili*, New Haven and London: Yale University Press.

Mutoro, H.W. (1987) 'An Archaeological Study of the Mijikenda Kaya Settlements in the Historical Kenya Coast', unpublished Ph.D. thesis, University of California at Berkeley.

Nurse, D. (1983) 'A linguistic reconsideration of Swahili Origins', *Azania* 18: 127–50.

Nurse, D. and Spear, T. (1985) *The Swahili. Reconstructing the History and Language of an African Society, 800–1500*, Philadelphia: Pennsylvania University Press.

Prins, A.J.H. (1952) *The Coastal Tribes of the North-Eastern Bantu*, Ethnographic Survey of Africa, vol. 3, London: International African Institute.

——(1967) *The Swahili Speaking Peoples of the East African Coast*, rev. edn, Ethnographic Survey of Africa, vol. 12, London: International African Institute.

——(1971) *Didemic Lamu. Social Stratification and Spatial Structure in a Muslim Maritime Town*, Groningen: Instituut voor Culturele Antropologie der Rijksuniversiteit.

Révoil, C. (1885) 'Voyage chez les Benadirs, les Comalis et les Bayouns en 1882 et 1883', *La Tour du Monde* 49: 1–80; 50: 129–208.

Sacleux, C. (1939) *Dictionnaire Swahili-Français*, Paris: Institut d'Ethnologie.

Sharif, I.N. (1973) 'Wa-Swahili and their language: some misconceptions', *Kiswahili* 43(2): 67–75.

Spear, T. (1978) *The Kaya Complex*, Nairobi: Kenya Literature Bureau.

Trimingham, J.S. (1964) *Islam in East Africa*, London: Clarendon Press.

Wilson, T.H. (1982) 'Spatial analysis and settlement patterns on the east African coast', *Paideuma* 28: 201–20.

Zein, A.H.M. (1974) *The Sacred Meadows: A Structural Analysis of Religious Symbolism in an East African Town*, Evanston.

8

ORDERING HOUSES, CREATING NARRATIVES

Matthew H. Johnson

This chapter is about architecture and order. It is about different ways of creating order through ancient buildings and landscape, whether by building houses in traditional or different ways, or by writing about ancient buildings and landscape in traditional or different ways. It is thus about our understanding of the built environment around us and the way we actively structure that understanding, through moving within built space, altering that space or attempting to grasp that space through a written discourse. Such a written discourse must ultimately be one of narrative.

A central dimension of such an attempt is the relation between past and present, a relation often conceived of or modelled by the use of a spatial metaphor. Landscape is all about a sense of place; architecture is simultaneously a moulding of landscape and the expression of a cultural attitude towards it. Our attempt to make sense of the old, the traditional, the past, thus merges with our attempt to create and maintain a sense of place, of location. The past is a foreign country, is very far away; we travel that distance both intellectually and emotively, through movement from present to past landscapes and back again; we are after all, in Shanks and Tilley's (1987: 17) memorable phrase, on a return ticket.

In attempting to create an intellectual order out of architecture, the archaeologist or historian tries to weave old buildings into a story. This story exists in and gives sense to the present. The story doesn't belong to the past, though it does refer to it. The story you are reading now is heavily influenced by the notion of cultural translation (Geertz 1975), of taking a system of meaning that is Other and exploring it while (perhaps unsuccessfully) avoiding a reduction to sameness.

In what follows, then, I shall present different aspects of my research into one Suffolk community, its buildings and landscape. Only one or two of these aspects might be considered as 'legitimate' forms of argument within the discipline of archaeology, though the others fall within recent developments in interpretive anthropology and the study of discursive thought as a whole.

170

OLD HOUSES

Brent Eleigh is a quiet parish in rural Suffolk. At its centre is a small village, whose houses are ranged along a high street running down to a small stream. At one end of the street a junction leads to the largest house and church. Around this village lie what to an East Anglian are rolling hills, to anyone not brought up in this gentle scenery some slight undulations. On the crest of these hills, on the edges of the parish, lie farmsteads, timber-framed barns and houses, apparently isolated but often intervisible within a complex pattern of ancient fields.

The high street is now a quiet cul-de-sac; the main road between the medieval towns of Lavenham and Hadleigh has been diverted to the south, presumably to avoid the tight corner at the junction which gives the most impressive traditional house in the village, Corner Farm, its name.

Brent Eleigh, in many ways a 'normal' Suffolk parish, is the scene of an historical accident, a statistical freak. In the reign of Charles II, in the 1670s, the Hearth Tax commissioners recorded the number of hearths and name of householder for every house in the kingdom. Coming to Brent Eleigh, the local dignitaries had recorded a small community: seventeen households. Three centuries later the local listings officer had done a similarly mundane circuit of observation and listing, this time recording what the Department of the Environment defined as 'buildings of architectural and historic interest'. He had noted thirteen buildings dating to the seventeenth century or earlier. By chance then, a sufficiently high survival rate made it possible to attempt a reconstruction of which name lived in which house.

Such an intersection of different planes of evidence is rare and deceptive. It seemed to offer a direct route into the past, of reconstructing a living picture of a seventeenth-century community with all its working parts, both physical – the houses, the church and the fields, and the web of lanes connecting them – and the documentary – the names of the people. Of course, any paid-up reader of Foucault knows that such a route must be theoretically naive; it was appealing nevertheless. (Unfortunately it was also a dead end empirically; no convincing match between the two lists could be made to emerge.)

Most early modern descriptions of a community start with its most prominent members and work downwards, so it is plausible to follow this tradition here with the houses. The main house in Brent Eleigh is Brent Eleigh Hall, now a nineteenth-century reconstruction of an earlier structure. The earlier structure, the place, had gone, though its trace in the landscape remains. Next to Brent Eleigh Hall is the church, a modest building by Suffolk standards, much restored and affected by later alterations.

Down the road from the church is Corner Farm, a large building, too much affected by extensive Victorian restoration to be really fully understood. Corner Farm is unusual in that instead of plastering between the timbers it had a herringbone pattern of bricks, termed in the professional jargon 'brick nogging'. Its central core was a large, handsome hall; on either side were various wings, additions and extensions.

The first sixteenth-century owner had built an impressive house, with lavish use of scarce and expensive timber as well as brick nogging. Successive generations had extended, modified, fiddled with, and rearranged the interior layout right up to an extensive Victorian restoration and further extension which had masked much of the earlier development. This is a typical history of a Brent Eleigh timber-framed house.

Timber-framed architecture is like a puzzle, with the different parts fitting together, elements being reused in different ways, often a single peg-hole, mortice or joint being the only clue to a complete rebuilding. The student of vernacular architecture works through the building fitting the pieces together, trying to understand each piece by creating a *narrative* that explains all the various anomalies that can be seen and acts as a commentary on any plans and sections. The final stage in many workers' analysis in the field, including the author's, is to go round the house checking for any contrary evidence for such a story. It is a narrative with its own jargon and discursive rules, and one has to conform, to solve the puzzle in accordance with those rules for one's findings to command academic respect. Here, unedited, is such a narrative for another house in Brent Eleigh, whose first phases were close in date to those of Corner Farm.

Hill Farm, Brent Eleigh: a C16 continuous-jetty house with service cross-wing, with the parlour end remodelled later. There is a jetty and exposed close studding to N. Some of this has been renewed. There are butt-joints in E and W wings against the main range, but the sill and bressumer have many cuts and have probably been renewed. The two-bay wing to W had arch-braces to both spine beam and tie over. The sill-beam appears cut to E, and the tie over was arch-braced without a partition: therefore a probable third bay at the E end of the wing has been destroyed. Probable screens-passage are to N of this. Though the present partition at this point is an insertion, there is a tie over in this position. The central tie is arch-braced with a partition inserted around this. There is a peg-hole for a crown-post. The stack is partly blocked and rebuilt. There is a shutter groove in the wall to S of stack and mortices for studs to N (i.e. no lobby entry in this position). Various shutter grooves and diamond mullions in the cross-rails and wall-plates of the main range. The wing to E was probably added around 1600. It has breaks in cross-rails and sill-beams against the main range. It may also have extended to S. The W wall-plate has a partly obscured splayed scarf of medieval type, but there is nothing else in this wing to indicate such a date; probably reuse. The wing has a jetty and close studding, tension-braces above and below the cross-rails, and a clasped-purlin roof. There are three large C16/17 barns to W of property. A large front range added in pseudo-traditional style in the C20: rears of wings probably destroyed at this point.

Such a 'description' is derived from the model narratives at the back of Royal Commission volumes (for example Pearson 1985); the adoption of such a style and the 'correct' use of technical terms (bressumer, spine beam, screens-passage) act in various ways. The description is dense, impenetrable, repeating the initial experience of confronting a timber frame in all its complexity; its impression of dry technical expertise affords the writer a certificate of scholarly competence. The description acts to disperse agency, to fetishize, to render organic. It does so in the sense that the actions of individual builders are lost in the passive tense and the building seems to sprout wings, additions, extensions of its own accord. Just as the agency of the past subject is lost, so is that of the contemporary observer; there is no account of the excitement of discovery, of the excitement of the medieval interior found behind the Victorian shell of the house, of the hospitality of the occupant, of the subjectivity of the fieldworker.

Such a descriptive narrative might be constructed in a different way:

Once upon a time a prosperous yeoman of the parish of Brent Eleigh decided to rebuild his house. The farm had stood on its site, an isolated location on the edge of the parish with a fine view to the north, for centuries; but recently it had known prosperity, with fine harvests being sold off at good prices and a bit of money on the side from cloth production. He was keen to display his new wealth and specified a new house rather like those just built over the hill and in the village. He did compromise though on traditional shuttered windows and an older style of room arrangement, insisting only on a fine brick fireplace in his new chamber over the hall. Towards the end of his life he had the old barns rebuilt, one by one. Though demand for cloth slackened off, mixed farming grew ever more profitable. The next owner built a new wing, but decided to leave the house facing down towards Lavenham and away from Brent Eleigh and his neighbours . . .

And so on. There is, of course, no positive evidence for the identity of the first builder, the persons who built the second phase and thereafter; assumptions made in the story such as the gender and lifespan of the owners are probabilities rather than certainties.

The central point to be made here is that *the first narrative quoted fails to make sense unless placed against the implicit story told in the second*. For the reader to understand anything approaching the implicit meaning of the first story, the Royal Commission-style 'description', one has to be aware that such an account of chronology and development is a typical one for the period in which the house was built. It is 'typical', it is 'coherent', in that it all ties in with other stories told of the region in this period, stories of increasing wealth, population growth, and the rise of capitalism.

The implication of this argument is that without the second story as a likely *model*, the first cannot be decoded by the reader. The order governing and underlying the first story, and which the first story reproduces, is a discursive order referring to the unobservable. Its implicit assumptions thus refer in turn back to a social and academic order of students of vernacular architecture, those who know and those who have much to learn.

The first story also embodies a uniquely architectural order; it concentrates on the houses in themselves at the expense of the landscape as a whole. One house, an isolated unit, ties in with another; the pattern of fields between them is lost. But a different order might be discerned, one much older still, prefiguring and moulding that seen in the architecture. Most of the isolated farms in wood-pasture Suffolk lie on much older sites, many surrounded by moats of the twelfth and thirteenth centuries, within still earlier property boundaries, all set within a pattern of field boundaries that may be a thousand years earlier still (cf. Williamson 1984). So the houses sit within and refer back to a millennia-old structuring of the landscape. The village of Brent Eleigh itself fits into such an older structuring; the church and hall lie a short distance from the rest of the village, perhaps indicating some settlement shift over the centuries away from the higher ground to the north towards the stream.

NEW READINGS

So the houses are not isolated items to be acounted for by way of inventory; they merge with the old landscape around them. However, a further danger must be avoided. It is very tempting to move from such a recognition of the way architecture and the physical landscape structure our thoughts to an assumption of timelessness, a renunciation of agency, an assertion of continuity or a naive view of tradition. It is easy to move from a view of rural Suffolk as an ancient landscape in which the actions of men and women take place within a very ancient dance, to a simplistic reading of an unchanging pattern of life reminiscent of Constable or Hardy. Such a move, however, is as false as it is easy. The landscape may remain an enduring structure but each generation fashions its own view of it. The Puritans took the old medieval church and plastered its walls, formerly covered in wall paintings; the old divisions between chancel and nave within the church were removed to create a wider space for the spoken word and a less mysterious atmosphere (Fitch 1986). Thus was the old retained and referred to, but in a way reflecting and asserting the new. Across early modern Suffolk the old Roman fields were being improved, being used for new crops, feeding the growing market of London and providing the income to pay for new consumer goods, new barns, and new houses (Dymond and Betterton 1982: 32–6).

Such a wider story, then, is ultimately one of material affluence, of the origins of capitalism, of the roots of modernity, of ourselves. Therefore it is as impossible to move through a timber-framed house in Brent Eleigh and not think these thoughts, not refer to this wider teleology, as it is to escape one's own cultural categories.

Such a conclusion is inescapable once it is recognized that the story being told is one of modernity and that one's own 'humanity' and 'self' are constituted by modernity. Working on houses, therefore, is an essentially hermeneutic exercise, a process of drawing together meanings and creating new levels of meaning from existing practices. The study of traditional architecture as a scholarly discipline is just such an exercise, held together by disciplinary solidarity often reminiscent of an Anglo-Saxon shield-wall. Nine centuries on from Hastings, however, such a wall seems invulnerable to puncture by the barbs of French philosophers.

Such a shield-wall is rather dissolved from within. There has always been a strong emotive element in British landscape studies, sometimes naively seen as nostalgic, whose genealogy may be traced back to Iowerth Peate's (1944) search for Celticism in Welsh long houses, W.G. Hoskins' (1957) search for tradition in the English countryside, and the assumed self-evident nature of most assumptions in vernacular studies. The Royal Commission-style accounts cited above are examples of this also. Thus today we see the hostile and admirable reaction of most vernacular architectural scholars to attempts to introduce an avowedly neutral descriptive methodology into recording (Meeson 1989; Smith 1989).

As vernacular architectural scholars we create an objective order through subjective narrative, narrative that works at at least three levels. First there is the level of grand narrative, of the Hoskins tradition, in which the English countryside becomes a metaphor for so many cultural values and meanings threatened by the modern world. The order being asserted here is a humanistic, spiritual one – the elevation of the humane, however defined, over the implicit and absent modern. In this sense it may be traced back to Richard Tawney and the view of human values as rooted in material culture of William Morris and John Ruskin.

Second there is a middling level, a strongly teleological account of a succession of architectural and landscape forms; thus 'most seventeenth-century houses in this area were of the three-cell lobby-entry type', or 'crown posts become less ornate over time'. This is the level of *habitus* for the working scholar, of so many assumptions indispensable to his or her work, and the level at which research on architecture can be seen as a craft, trailing in the wake of the craft tradition that produced the houses themselves. Here the order being created is a typological one, a succession of classes and types, though it is an order still partly implicit.

Finally, of course, there is the micro-level, that of account of individual houses – a level dictated by craft convention in its approach (the standard Royal Commission-style description and plan). In this, the order created, one of a narration of successive phases, is quite explicit; an order which, before the technique of deconstruction became a familiar one, would be considered to be the objective empirical bedrock on which other orders were based. But as deconstruction might indicate, such an apparently hard empirical bedrock is merely yet another text, with all that that implies in terms of the impossibility of assigning any final meaning. It is a level of discourse most effectively dissected through parody:

> The farm was crouched on a bleak hillside, whence its fields, fanged with flints, dropped steeply to the village of Howling a mile away. Its stables and out-houses were built in the shape of a rough octangle surrounding the farmhouse itself, which was built in the shape of a rough triangle. The left point of the triangle abutted on the farthest point of the octangle, which was formed by the cowsheds, which lay parallel with the big barn. The outhouses were built of rough-cast stone, with thatched roofs, while the farm itself was partly built of local flint, set in cement, and partly of some stone brought at great trouble and enormous expense from Perthshire.
>
> The farmhouse was a long, low building, two-storied in parts. Other parts of it were three-storied. Edward the Sixth had originally owned it in the form of a shed in which he housed his swineherds, but he had grown tired of it, and had it rebuilt in Sussex clay. Then he pulled it down. Elizabeth had rebuilt it, with a good many chimneys in one way and another. The Charleses had let it alone; but William and Mary had it pulled down again, and George the First had rebuilt it. George the Second, however, burned it down. George the Third added another wing. George the Fourth pulled it down again. . . . Like ghosts embedded in brick and stone, the architectural variations of each period through which it had passed were mute history.
>
> (Gibbons 1938: 34–5)

In this passage Stella Gibbons not only indulges in parody but also brings out how buildings have character, how their personality conditions an emotive response even in the apparently driest narratives – a point familiar to readers of the descriptions of Nikolaus Pevsner. Yet she is wrong on one point. History, of course, is not a thing which can be called mute; old stones on the other hand are. Yet our unavoidable constitution of those stones as history places them at the centre of a web of meanings whose nature we have to explore – meanings whose constitution is rooted in the order of our daily lives as scholars and as human beings.

NOTE

Discussions with Becky Smalley influenced the content and style of this paper. I am grateful for her support and advice.

BIBLIOGRAPHY

Dymond, D.P. and Betterton, A. (1982) *Lavenham: 700 Years of Textile Making*, Woodbridge: Boydell.

Fitch, J. (1986) *Brent Eleigh Church: A History and Guide*, Brent Eleigh: no publisher stated.

Geertz, C. (1975) *The Interpretation of Cultures*, New York: Basic Books.

Gibbons, Stella (1938) *Cold Comfort Farm*, Harmondsworth: Penguin.

Hoskins, W.G. (1957) *The Making of the English Landscape*, London: Hodder & Stoughton.

Meeson, B. (1989) 'In defence of selective recording', *Vernacular Architecture* 20: 18–19.

Pearson, S. (1985) *Houses of the Lancashire Pennines*, London: HMSO.

Peate, I.C (1944) *The Welsh House: A Study in Folk Culture*, Liverpool: Brython.

Shanks, M. and Tilley, C. (1987) *Re-constructing Archaeology: Theory and Practice*, Cambridge: Cambridge University Press.

Smith, J.T. (1989) 'The archaeological investigation of standing buildings: a comment', *Vernacular Architecture* 20: 20–1.

Williamson, T. (1984) 'The roman countryside: settlement and agriculture in north-west Essex', *Britannia* 15: 225–30.

9

SPATIAL ORDER AND PSYCHIATRIC DISORDER

Annie E.A. Bartlett

The obituary of the asylum may have been written too soon – and published before its death. More than anything else the asylum towers over the history of Victorian and early twentieth-century psychiatry. Asylums housed, and as the nineteenth century wore on, increasingly warehoused, the mad of western Europe and North America (Jones 1972). More than at any other period in history they exemplified the creed that the mad, however defined, must be separate from the rest of society. The asylums' Italianate facades and red brick pavilions withstood attack by social reformers until the 1950s. Since then, there has been a progressive reduction in the population of psychiatric in-patients (Thornicroft and Bebbington 1989). A small number of these institutions have closed. Many more continue to exist in attenuated forms, with far fewer individuals actually resident. The emphasis in the rhetoric and the practice of psychiatry, be it concerned with the young and schizophrenic or the elderly demented, is on care in the community (HMSO 1989; Dept of Health 1991). While recent years have seen a genuine increase in the range of settings in which psychiatric practice occurs, there has of late been considerable anxiety about the efficacy of community care. Critics have wondered whether resources are adequate, whether the community, in so far as it can be said to exist, cares at all about anyone with mental health problems. What was heralded as an advance in psychiatric care in the 1950s is seen as a potential social disaster. That this possibility exists must be evident to anyone familiar with Britain's metropolitan areas where substantial numbers of the homeless population live on the streets. It is increasingly well documented that a high proportion of such individuals are mad (James 1991). This population is particularly vulnerable to criminalization; they are arrested for trivial offences, remanded to prison because they have no permanent address, and are thus warehoused in a more contemporary fashion (James and Hamilton 1991; Joseph 1992). The imprisonment of the mad is a reminder of the pre-asylum era, and to a historian it might seem as if we have come full circle. To those who believe that not only asylums, but also madness, were a nineteenth-century invention this may be more of a surprise. Unsurprisingly, there have been calls from interested parties for a return to the days of the asylum (National Schizophrenia Fellowship 1992). The attempt to provide care in the community is now suspected of being a cynical attempt at cost cutting (Scull 1984); families receive little financial support for looking after relatives who previously might have been accommodated in an asylum. This would not be the first time that the provision of services to the mad was affected by financial considerations; a glance at the archival material relating to the private madhouses of the eighteenth century, the county asylums of the nineteenth century indicate that thrift was always the order of the day (Crammer 1990; Ripa 1990). Not for nothing is psychiatry known as one of the cinderella services of the current health service.

This chapter, however, is not primarily concerned with social history. Rather, its focus is a theme running through both the conceptualization of psychiatric disorders and the professional and societal responses to those socially constructed mad. It will be argued that the spatial segregation of the mad, done differently at different historical points, is not independent of the prevailing concepts of insanity. As the nineteenth century progressed the views that carried weight were increasingly the views of a professional group, the alienists, soon to become the psychiatrists. The Association of Medical Officers for Hospitals for the Insane, the precursor of the current Royal College of Psychiatrists, was established in 1841. More specifically, the language of psychiatry demonstrates a concern with the boundaried person, the discrete individual, recognizably intact and separate from others – and with a complex internal world. Madness begins when the demarcation of internal psychic space from external social space dissolves. Psychiatry's response to this dissolution has been, in several different ways, to reinforce the regimentation and order of the madperson's social space. It is therefore worth considering first the professional concepts of mental disorder as they emerged, and then, in more detail the responses of both the nineteenth-century alienists and the twentieth-century psychiatrists to the 'practical problem' of the mad. Psychiatry should be taken seriously, but not too seriously; seriously because the psychiatric profession has power over individuals in a way that must be unique outside of the criminal justice system, but not too seriously because, as Porter has said, 'psychiatry is itself part of the problem not the solution – it is just another rival, plausible mythology' (Porter 1987a: 3–4).

That there are multiple and competing discourses on madness is not in dispute, but the task of this chapter is to look at how the *formal* discourse on madness consciously and unconsciously invokes spatial imagery and how this is reflected in aspects of psychiatric practice.

CONCEPTS OF MADNESS

The lunatic has had a longer life than many would imagine. Allderidge's (1979) scrupulous examination of English records notes that as early as the twelfth century the term 'mad' was in use. Many of those who might now be considered mad could well have been socially acceptable, their experiences of God being a reward for religious fervour. Common law dating from the fifteenth century mentions 'lunatyks' and provides a justification for their detention which lasted until 1714, at which point the Vagrancy Act took over. What is more difficult to establish is exactly what was meant by such terms. As Porter (1987b: ix) remarked, the enthusiasm of historians of madness for the nineteenth century is only matched by their neglect of earlier epochs. In the same review of concepts of madness immediately pre-dating the Victorian era he notes that 'Madness advertised itself in a proliferation of symptoms, in gait, in physiognomy, in weird demeanour and habits. It was synonymous with behaving crazy, looking crazy, talking crazy' (ibid.: 35).

Madness, to be identified as such, needed a behavioural manifestation. Some differentiation into types of madness occurred prior to the nineteenth century. Melancholy, described at length in its various forms by Burton in *The Anatomy of Melancholy* ([1621] 1806), appears to have become frankly fashionable in the eighteenth and early nineteenth centuries (Skultans 1979), provoking parallels with the contemporary use of the word 'neurotic' and the appeal of psychoanalysis for the middle classes. The spleen became a focus of interest; the four stages of spleen culminated according to Robinson (1729) in madness, passing en route through melancholy. Cullen, writing in the late 1790s, mentions both hypochondriasis and hysteria (Mace 1992). However, these excursions into classification pale by comparison with the exhaustive efforts of later psychiatric botanists.

In the early part of the nineteenth century articles were still being written on 'insanity'. Such articles relate to the origins, manifestations and care of the insane. There is evidence, however, of more complex typologies emerging. Morison (1824) uses illustrations of facial features to demonstrate several of the monomanias, imbecility and idiotism (Skultans 1975: 71–8). Ripa (1990: 26), writing on the involuntary admission of women to French asylums in the nineteenth century, notes that the three most frequent diagnoses for 'curable mental illnesses' were mania, monomania and lypemania. Crammer (1990), a psychiatrist, gives a detailed account of diagnoses attached to those admitted to the Buckinghamshire County Pauper Lunatic Asylum in 1868; seven types of mania are listed and the commmonest cause for admission is mania of recent onset. Lower down the list come melancholia, three types of dementia, imbecility and idiocy (cf. Connolly [1847] 1968). Although there were depressingly few treatments at their disposal, the nineteenth century saw the increasingly large number of alienists expand their diagnostic categories to include certain sexual practices and the conse-quences of excessive use of alcohol (Maudsley 1873: 86–7). They speculated on the origins of this range of complaints; Skultans (1975: 1–25) suggests that as the century wore on there was a shift from 'moral' ideas to the belief that hereditary factors determined insanity. What these ideas had in com-mon was the location of insanity within the individual. The exponents of moral treatment saw the moral determinants of insanity as 'unreason' – the mad individual lacked self-control. Later on the attention paid to hereditary factors showed the mad as hapless victims of forces beyond their control. Women were seen by virtue of constitutional factors to be particularly vulnerable (Showalter 1987). The onset of such determinist arguments coin-cided with a decline in therapeutic optimism. It became clear that the population of the asylums was there to stay and the proportion of 'curable lunatics' very small (Walton 1981). The alienists were at their wits' ends.

EARLY RESPONSES TO MADNESS

The prevalence of ideas about possession states and the acceptance of the divinely inspired confounds attempts to document responses to madness prior to the eighteenth century (Allderidge 1979). The rather sporadic nature of records, which continues until halfway through the nineteenth century, makes this yet more difficult. However, it seems that the mad were cared for amongst the sick in the few general hospitals that existed (ibid.). The exception was the Bethlem Hospital; from the start of the fifteenth century this was exclusively for the mad. Not until the eighteenth century did other sizeable institutions specifically for the mad emerge. Quite what happened in between, and why, has been the subject of some debate. There is a school of thought that suggests, crudely, that all was well with the mad until they were locked up. Foucault (1967) describes a Europe-wide 'great confine-ment' between 1600 and 1800 which was the start of the institutionalization of the mad. By this account they and others were scooped up and put away – and only latterly sorted out into various categories such as the disabled and the criminal. The advent of the large asylums in the nineteenth century is thus part of a continuing but more subtle segregation of the mad from mainstream society. Leaving aside whether or not this version of events does, at least, apply to France, there is substantial historical evidence to suggest that during the eighteenth and the nineteenth centuries in England some of the mad were contained in private madhouses (Parry-Jones 1972). These appear to have some similarities with the landlady schemes of the present day: small numbers of individuals located in domestic circumstances.

Whilst stories of 'corrupt and brutal practices' emerged sporadically during the eighteenth century (ibid.: 9), concern for the plight of the mad only culminated in 1807 in the Select Committee of Inquiry into the state of criminal and pauper lunatics. The mad were discovered to be distributed amongst workhouses, houses of correction and the private madhouses. A small number appear to have been included in the public subscription hospitals built from the second half of the eighteenth century. A wave of further investigation, scandal and lunacy reform over the next forty years resulted in the development of county asylums for the mad (Scull 1979: chapters 2–3). The social forces responsible for this are complex. Two points are clear, however. First, in some of the facilities for the mad, conditions were abominable. Browne, commenting on evidence collected about the Fonthill Asylum in 1815, quotes the following description of an inmate's plight: 'He was confined in one of the oblong troughs, chained down; he had evidently not been in the open air for a considerable time, for when I made them bring him out, the man could not endure the light . . . he had been allowed to get out of the trough, he said, perhaps once in a week, and sometimes not for a fortnight' (Browne 1990: 129).

Inhuman conditions existed in all *types* of institution. Second, the campaigners for 'moral treatment', with its emphasis on cure and non-restraint, gained ground (Digby 1985). A few county asylums were built prior to 1845 but it was after tougher, and more prescriptive legislation that both their number and size grew rapidly (Scull 1989: 239–49). Private madhouses continued for the rich (Parry-Jones 1972: 23). The principle that the best place for lunatics was in specific institutions away from mainstream society had been established by halfway through the century, indicating a major ideological shift from a hundred years previously.

What is of particular interest is the uniformity – or the poverty – of the treatment approaches for the majority of those who found themselves thus confined. 'Moral treatment' was pioneered by Tuke in the York Retreat, a small private madhouse with a marked Quaker influence. In marked contrast to the imprisonment of many of the mad, it propounded that each individual should be treated with dignity and, certainly relative to previous levels of confinement, allowed to roam free. Furthermore, the intention was that the mad should be encouraged to reassert self-control.

This view was hotly debated. Medical men of the time advanced the view that restraint 'contributes to the cure of insanity' (Haslam 1817). Despite some uncertainty both about what constituted moral treatment and the fact that it was prescribed wholesale for all forms of lunacy (Browne 1990: 140), the practices of Connolly, who was for a time medical superintendent at Hanwell (a public asylum), held sway. Connolly gained considerable prestige, and unlike Tuke, was a doctor. Within a short time of becoming medical superintendent at Hanwell Asylum, he demonstrated that mechanical restraints such as chains and manacles could be abandoned. The effect of these restraints had been that large numbers of lunatics were kept locked in cramped conditions and confined spaces. He was subsequently lambasted in his obituary, written by his rather more successful son-in-law, Henry

Maudsley, for the sin of overenthusiastic institutionalization (Showalter 1987: 116). However, in his heyday Connolly could arguably be said to represent the most agreeable face of Victorian psychiatry. This was no mean feat in that Hanwell at that time contained over eight hundred patients (Connolly [1847] 1968).

Indeed, the size of the asylum and the organizational consequences were in some ways the key to their ultimate failure. Without doubt the average size of asylums grew consistently throughout the Victorian period. Jones (1972) gives average population sizes of 542 in 1870, 961 in 1900 and 1,221 in 1930. Yet these were originally intended to be homely institutions. Walton (1981: 188) notes that Lancaster Asylum had 650 patients in 1852, 745 in 1863 and 1,026 in 1870. This asylum had been praised by the inspectors of the Lunacy Commission, but as the numbers grew the standard of care declined. Colney Hatch, one of the largest London asylums, brought back mechanical restraints in the 1860s.

Economic reality competed with the ideals of the reformers and the architecture of the asylums changed. The early emphasis on small buildings gave way to large buildings whose design facilitated classification and grouping of patient types (Taylor 1991). Like, it was intended, would be placed with like. Women and men were firmly segregated. Patients were thought to be more or less behaviourally disturbed and segregated to different wards accordingly. Gardiner Hill ([1839] 1975) considered three categories of patient – the convalescent and orderly, the moderate and the disorderly. Dormitories were used for patients prone to self-destruction and single-bedded rooms for the 'harmless, noisy, violent and insensible'. Social class could also dictate where and in what facilities inmates would reside (Tomes 1975). In England a small number of nineteenth-century private madhouses were built, at considerably greater per capita cost, which provided more spacious accommodation (Taylor 1991: 158).

More commonly, dormitory-style accommodation was suggested when the cost of expanding the number of asylum beds was causing the planners concern. One of the reasons why expansion of bed numbers was deemed necessary was because in 1859 whilst 15,000 individuals were in asylums, a further c. 7,500 individuals located in workhouses were thought suitable for admission to asylums (ibid.: 141; Connolly [1847] 1968: 2). One response to this early 'needs assessment' was to build the cheap brick asylums at Caterham and Leavesden. These contained forty bedded dormitories. In some instances, at least the behavioural classification system of the early Victorians broke down under the later weight of subsequent admission numbers (Crammer 1990: 131). Mixed bags of patients were detained on single wards. One reason for this may have been the failure to maintain staff–patient ratios capable of dealing with the influx.

However, a persistent feature of the large asylums was their generous grounds. In the Epsom Cluster, where five hospitals were built, these were sited on 1,040 acres (Taylor 1991: 152). Extensive gardens were planted, and villas placed around the main building. Long Grove had a large administration block with wards on two floors leading off a semicircular covered way. The grounds were sufficient for the much later addition of an Industrial Therapy unit not to interfere with their basic layout. Even in recent years, right up to its closure, junior doctors called out at night would drive from their overnight accommodation in the administration block to the wards based in the surrounding villas.

Throughout the country, the absence of more specific treatment interventions meant that the pattern of daily life constituted the treatment. Work, though not the patient's normal employ, exercise and association with others of a similar degree of disability were desirable. Writing about Hanwell, Connolly comments:

> Among the means of relieving patients from the monotony of an asylum, and of preserving the bodily health and, at the same time, of improving the condition of the mind, and promoting recovery, employment of some kind or other ranks the highest.
>
> (Connolly [1847] 1968: 77)

He gave detailed instructions as to suitable dress for the mad (ibid.: 63). Staff and patients, who at least in some institutions all lived on the same ward in the absence of separate staff accommodation, were equally subject to the same routines. Regularity was in itself thought to be therapeutic, countering the chaos of insanity. As the century wore on, however, the difficulty of maintaining adequate levels of care and occupation in overcrowded conditions became apparent (Scull 1989: 235–8). The greatest irony of the therapeutic ethos of regaining self-control was that it was undermined by the reality of the institutions to which patients were assigned; they had little say in how they ran their lives. The greatest irony of the desire to provide *domestic* asylums was that individuals were admitted not only from institutions to asylums but also from home. As the asylums got larger they must have appeared less and less like what patients were used to in their own houses, or indeed like the exemplary York Retreat.

Insanity had been countered during the nineteenth century by regimentation and segregation. There had been a wholesale move of lunatics out of the cities into countryside 'bins'. The asylum itself divided them up again, according to their behaviour and their gender. Once there, their days were divided up by place and time. As a consequence of universal involuntary admission, individual patients were entirely dependent on the authorities for discharge. Many found themselves permanently siphoned off from society.

TWENTIETH-CENTURY PSYCHIATRY

This century has seen substantial changes in psychiatric thinking, as well as an increase in the range of treatments available and the choice of therapeutic settings (Gelder et al. 1983).

The history of twentieth-century psychiatry is made more complicated by attempts to render it a biological science, a school of psychoanalysis and a branch of the social sciences. Spatial imagery is readily apparent in the formal writing of the phenomenologists and the psychoanalysts. Placing emphasis in this way on 'the psychiatrists' in contemporary accounts of madness is a risky business; equally foolhardy for a contemporary psychiatrist would be to paraphrase patients' experiences. It is clear that despite the (at times) coercive power of the machinery of mental health, patients' voices are increasingly audible (Chamberlain 1988; Millett 1990; Mental Health Act Commission 1991). Clearly there are connections between lay accounts of madness and the formal writing of psychiatry. The taxonomies of psychiatry, be they the defence mechanisms of Freud (Breuer and Freud 1953–73; Freud 1953–73; Freud 1986) or the phenomenology of Jaspers (1962) emerge from the accounts of patients. Both these men radically altered the direction of twentieth-century psychiatry. It is in these explanatory frameworks and their successors that an implicit and at times explicit discourse on the 'boundaried self' is evident. This differs from the two prevailing concepts of the person readily discernible in the psychiatry of the nineteenth century – the autonomous individuals who can be encouraged to conquer madness by taking control of themselves, or the victims of their inherited defect for whom little help is available. What remains the same is the continuing focus on the individual.

The province of psychiatry is often to adjudicate on the subjective experiences of the individual – what are the norms of abnormality? The most recent psychiatric taxonomy includes more than 290 diagnostic categories (American Psychiatric Association 1987) and probably more will be included in the next version. The burgeoning of categories has not gone unnoticed within psychiatry although the absurdity of this exercise is not acknowledged. From the outside it would appear that psychiatry is appropriating more and more psychological territory – continuing the nineteenth-century trend. Psychiatry's ability to expand depends ultimately on the acceptance of its distinction between normal and abnormal psychological experiences. Jasperian phenomenology laid the foundations for these distinctions and continues to provide the basis by which contemporary psychiatry makes diagnoses. Standing on a crowded underground train you will often find your nose pressed up against the back of a stranger's head. You will move back, defining an almost imperceptible space between you and the person in question. If you find yourself on the same train facing someone at very close proximity you will avoid eye contact. The bizarre ritual of standing in tube trains performed twice a day by the inhabitants of many major cities is in defiance of almost all the rules of social contact with strangers. Equally, they could be said to have developed their own code about the use of interpersonal space. Tube train practice is normally abnormal.

How might space be perceived that its perception and use be thought abnormally abnormal? How then might such abnormality find itself incorporated into contemporary classificatory systems of madness? Modern psychological ideas suggest that acts of perception, involving the sensory modalities of touch, taste, smell, sight and hearing, involve the recognition of an event in external space followed by the neuro-transmission of this recognition to the brain and the translation of that recognition into cognitions which can be expressed verbally. Normal human development involves pattern recognition and consensus labelling of such perceptual experiences. Thus, we agree for the most part that the cat is on the mat. To what extent the neuro-physiological mechanisms by which humanity comes to this remarkable consensus are the same in each person is not so clear. Madness could be said to begin, however, not where the neuro-physiology is necessarily different, but where the consensus about perceptual experience breaks down and where unusual perception occurs.

Jasperian phenomenology detailed how this happens. Psychosis best illustrates this lack of consensus. Psychotic individuals experience the world in a unique way. What they share is a disturbance of the appreciation of what is normally present in external space, as well as the disintegration of the boundary between their mind and the world. Things are not where they are supposed to be. Curiously, any anxiety about the strangeness of these phenomena is often absent. Psychotic individuals are often sure that their own ordering of external space is valid and are sometimes surprised to find others disbelieving. Their experiences are varied, but hallucinations are frequent. Here, the person hears a voice, or voices, possibly conversing about them, possibly giving instructions. Commonly these are the voices of people they know, often the voices are unpleasant. They hear these voices as they hear ordinary voices, coming from outside their heads, in external space. Where the boundary between social and psychic space is dissolved, the inside of one's head is no longer private. The body offers no protection against invasion. In this world the walls are bugged and the telephone is tapped and the neighbours are spies for an evil power so that the thoughts inside one's head can be rendered public. The neighbours can read your mind in defiance of your wishes, your body can be moved at the whim of your enemies and someone seems to have planted a sophisticated listening device inside your ear canal. They are recording everything you think at night. At night other people come into your room and you experience them having sex with you against your will. No one else agrees that any of this is happening to you. A consistent feature in all these experiences is that bodily and mental intrusions of this type are never recognized as being created by the self. The account given of these experiences by Jasperian psychiatry is a simple taxonomy of beliefs and percepts, and it is to psychodynamic writing that we must turn for a framework that considers the meaning of these experiences.

One of the most significant contributions of the object relations school of psychoanalysis has been to emphasize the normality of such psychotic experiences in infancy (Segal 1989). Their destructive potential in adult life is recognized and importance is attached both to the psychodynamic mechanisms involved and to the content of such psychotic thoughts. Within this school of thought experiences which constitute unacceptable psychic material and which give rise to intolerable anxiety are projected outwards and thus disowned and attributed either to a real or fantasy other, thus the voices are apparently those of other people. Thus, that which is internal is made external to the self because it is intolerable. It can be interpreted in terms of the individual's life history.

Certain individuals sit on the borderline between normality and frank psychotic experiences of the kind outlined above. The following case example shows how this can be experienced.

Case history A

Ms A had been admitted to hospital after threatening her father with a knife. She had not injured him but had cut her own wrists very badly. She was happy to be in hospital because she felt as though she was disintegrating and that she might act on her continuing urges to kill her father. Ms A said she could sometimes hear her father's voice. Most of the time she heard this inside her head and was clear these were her own thoughts. When she was upset, the voices were external and their intensity was such that she lost sight of the idea that they were a product of her own mind. The voices said she was a whore. On these occasions she could feel her father near her, though her rational self knew this was not true. She found this perception most distressing. Cutting herself relieved the feelings of tension these experiences induced. The only other thing that helped at these times was being alone, and she would use the area of the ward designed for this purpose – a space with no furniture or windows where she could not hurt herself. In this area she felt both contained and free from interference. This last point was of particular significance. As a child Ms A had been sexually abused by her father, over a period of some years. Her quasi psychotic experiences replicated that experience and reinforced her already poor self-image.

The intermittent breakdown of certainty as to where the self ends and the rest of the world begins – experienced in this example as the phenomena of hallucinations and pseudo-hallucinations – can be construed within a psychoanalytic framework. In Ms A's case the establishment of boundaries as a child had been badly disrupted by abusive parenting – she had not been clear what rights she had over her body. The recognition and characteristics of 'other' had been distorted. In addition to the problems above, Ms A had developed erotic attachments to therapists and could only poorly tolerate separation from them, believing in some way that she 'owned' her therapists.

Thus there may be a spectrum of experience, from the psychotic to the neurotic. The psychotic notices invasion and extrudes intra-psychic experiences, effectively disowning them. The borderline person, with fragile but not destroyed boundaries, only sometimes distorts and dissolves the boundary between self and the world. The neurotic fears that social and psychic space will be taken over, although this does not happen. S/he never loses sight of the fact that such thoughts originate in his/herself.

Although there are several different neurotic syndromes in which symptoms of anxiety, depression, hysteria, depersonalization obsessions and compulsions occur to various degrees, issues of spatial order are most obvious in those with obsessions and compulsions.

In obsessive compulsive states, individuals experience intrusive thoughts, which provoke anxiety. The anxiety is linked to a feared consequence, such as the death of a child, the house burning down. Their response to initial anxiety is frequently to develop anxiety-reducing mechanisms – the compulsive rituals of psychiatric phenomenology. In addition they will often try and avoid situations which provoke such obsessional thoughts in the first place. The major difficulty for the obsessional is the short-lived nature of relief from anxiety – soon more thoughts occur and a pattern ensues of obsessional thoughts and compulsive actions repeated many times in the course of a single day. Such symptoms are in many cases exaggeration of traits which can be very useful – who would trust the doctor who did not check the contents of a syringe before injecting you. Most people are grateful for the 'ritual' of instrument checking pilots go through before the plane takes off.

However, obsessional/compulsive phenomena can cause enormous subjective distress. For the obsessive, catastrophe is always close at hand in two senses, both in that disaster is about to strike *and* because it can hinge on the appropriate ordering of his/her *domestic* environment. It is only by repeated attempts to control the physical environment that s/he averts 'the feared consequence'. Frequently fears are those of contamination such that either the individual's body or domestic setting will become polluted with various bodily fluids – urine, faeces or semen. Great efforts are made therefore both to prevent any such material entering the house or, if inevitably present, to prevent it contaminating the rest of the household. Rooms have to be cleaned and cleaned again, bathing happens several times a day, children remove their shoes and leave them outside. Ritualistic activity involves order, even in the action itself and necessitates further repetition, if such order is broken. Equally, this is often reflected in the perfectionistic approach to household spaces; walking into the obsessional's home you are confronted with rows, lines and piles of things, nothing can be moved without fear of recrimination. The effort of maintaining such behaviour is considerable and physical exhaustion and consequent domestic chaos can intervene. Only mildly more benign is the hoarding of everyday objects which in extreme cases can lead to similar chaos. In this case fears of discarding household items are so great that they pile up until no domestic space is left for the inhabitants. Some of these features are evident from the brief case history below.

Case history B

Mr B had a preoccupation with HIV. There was no reason to assume he was more at risk than many others and he had tested negative for the virus on several occasions. Despite understanding actual methods of virus transmission, he undertook frequent cleaning of the house, being concerned that the virus might have come in through open windows. He would spend several hours a day preparing the bathroom prior to washing and again cleaning it after use. He would wear overcoats in hot weather lest he become contaminated walking along the street. When helping to bathe his children one night he had rubbed their heads until they bled for fear too that they might become infected. When thinking about the possibility of infection Mr B would feel anxious, but his excessive cleaning activities would temporarily relieve his anxiety.

Such histories are some distance from 'The Rat Man', Freud's original case ([1909] 1979). In this long account of an obsessional young soldier, Freud describes the significance of the symptomatology in terms of repressed and displaced feelings, whilst his obsessional fears can be reinterpreted as actual wishes (ibid.: 60). The patient's anxiety about his father's death is actually a desire for this to happen. An important similarity between Mr B, a real and not uncommon type of case, and the rat man, is the fear of bodily invasion. Unlike the case of the psychotic, the sensation of bodily invasion never occurs.

These are a few examples of the way in which current classificatory systems describe, and in describing define normal and abnormal experience. There would equally be examples from other areas of psychiatry, for example the organic states and eating disorders. Both the psychodynamic and phenomenological approaches utilize a notion of self congruent with a physical body. This is a self with edges; where beliefs, perceptions and anxieties threaten or do blur the edges, psychiatry steps in, sometimes with the intention of simply obliterating the distressing experiences, at other times with the intention of resolving what are believed to be internal conflicts through understanding them.

CURRENT PSYCHIATRIC SERVICES

Just as the range of diagnostic categories and the number of classificatory frameworks is greater than a hundred years ago, so too are the number of treatment modalities and the treatment settings in which the psychiatric encounter can occur. Once again the emphasis is on cure rather than simply on care. Psychiatry now has at its disposal medication, cognitive behavioural interventions and a range of dynamic psychotherapies, all with specific indications. However, the relationship between patient and therapist continues to be a subject of debate and at times a source of concern (Committee of Enquiry into Complaints about Ashworth Hospital 1992). The language of psychiatry and the social relations established by the therapeutic encounter ensure that the patient continues to be 'other'. In the language of therapy, there is appropriate distance to be established and maintained between therapist and patient, although this is clearly breached at times (Fahy and Fisher 1992). This process is evident not only in the formal discourse of academic psychiatry but also in psychiatric practice. It is readily apparent in negotiations about the ownership of space within psychiatric settings.

By the end of the nineteenth century, the law of 1845 and the increase in the number of identified 'lunatics' meant that the landscape of Britain was dotted with large, densely populated asylums. Inmate numbers continued to rise until the 1950s; since then they have fallen steadily. The care of the mad is now done at home, in hostels, in general practice surgeries, in community centres, in district general hospitals and in a not insignificant number of cases in asylums. Since the introduction of new mental health legislation in 1930, when it became possible to be a voluntary patient, most people are voluntary patients.

As Chamberlain (1988) has pointed out, this shift, at least towards the principle of community care, has interesting symbolic implications for users of services. Areas of activity previously free of the threat of psychiatric intervention or interference – depending on your point of view – have now been opened up to possible invasion. This is exemplified in Britain by the debate on community treatment orders, whereby it would be possible for psychiatric practitioners, both forcibly and legitimately, to enter people's houses to administer medication. The appropriation of psychological territory indicated in the preceding section is matched by a concrete expansion of territory.

In-patient care is provided in explicitly medical settings. The medical model of psychiatric disorder is echoed in the siting of in-patient beds alongside beds for general surgery and coronary care in local hospitals. The staffing structures are as for other medical specialities. The architectural features are often similar. Barefoot, a designer who recently surveyed psychiatric environments, commented: 'the worst place to build an acute

190

psychiatric facility is in a medical or surgical ward block of a general hospital' (Barefoot 1992: 99).

He goes on to point out the continuing value of providing a domestic type of environment. However, the continuation of dormitory accommodation, the absence of kitchen space on wards with the consequent delivery of often cold food from central kitchens, enormous sitting rooms lacking in table lamps and lit from neon tubes (which show all too clearly the rows of chairs below), can contribute to the failure to produce such an atmosphere. Features like these raise important issues about the ownership and control of ward space with implications for privacy and safety. Despite a spate of social science reports in the late 1950s and 1960s, relatively little work has been done in this area subsequently, notwithstanding more sophisticated theoretical suggestion about legitimation of power and authority in social arenas (Stanton and Schwartz 1954; Goffman 1961; Thompson 1984). Levels of interpersonal violence are often high on psychiatric wards (Noble and Rodger 1989). Having arrived seeking asylum, in the true sense of the word, patients can find themselves further intruded upon. A particular concern of late has been the threat of sexual violence, particularly to female patients (McMillan 1992). Ward structures can make it difficult for patients to find safe places. Where there is thought to be a significant risk of suicide, patients tend to find themselves under surveillance – being either 'closely observed' or 'specialled'. Whilst such measures are taken to protect the patient and to protect the hospital from medico-legal complications, they require the continuous scrutiny of patients, often extending to accompanying them to the lavatory. Staff can therefore 'own' all ward space. Patients tend to be excluded from ward space such as the 'nursing office' – on some disturbed wards this area will be locked and patients have to knock at the door to speak to staff members. The net effect of this type of ward management is to reinforce the hierarchy of the 'them' and 'us' distinction.

Wards catering for high levels of disturbed behaviour usually have seclusion rooms. This is a room which can only be unlocked from the outside, and which contains no furnishings except perhaps a rubber mattress. In the door there is a keyhole-sized observation point. The explicit purpose of these rooms is to allow violent patients to calm down. However, their use has been controversial (Grounds 1990) and there is little doubt that they can be considered punishment cells. They are one of the most powerful symbols of the power of psychiatry.

This can be contrasted with the nature of out-patient contacts. Attendance at such clinics and community centres is almost always voluntary. The patient can almost always walk out. The nature of the contact is more likely to be truly confidential. None the less, the most frequent social interaction is one that is familiar to anyone visiting a GP surgery, the doctor ensconced behind the desk, the patient being viewed. The social rules of engagement are clear. Should the patient break these rules – sit too close, ask the doctor personal questions – this is likely to be interpreted within the language of pathology. A psychoanalytic colleague of mine, accustomed to dealing with the small number of dangerous patients, remarked half seriously, half self-deprecatingly that after an interview with one particular individual she had found herself searching the waste bin to see if she had inadvertently dropped an envelope with her address on it. Her concern was of physical invasion; would this man turn up on the doorstep? She realized that her fears mimicked his; would she turn up on his doorstep and compulsorily admit him to hospital? A more positive scenario was that both sets of fears could be contained within the therapeutic setting and not spill over into life. The boundaries of therapy can be used to maintain appropriate boundaries around the person in life.

These issues are not new. It is clear that the nineteenth-century alienists and attendants were guided at best by a benign paternalism and at worst by gross indifference to suffering; the mad were often separated from their doctors by their social class and gender as well as their madness. Within the routine of institutions difference must similarly have been negotiated and reinforced.

CONCLUSION

It is clear that the cornerstones of contemporary psychiatric thought are built on the foundation of the boundaried individual, with congruence of the physical and psychic self. The professional response to madness has been, and still is, an attempt to impose order on the chaos indicated by disruption of this entity. Order is achieved through structuring therapeutic settings, in both their architectural layout and the permissible use of space. In this century changing fashions in psychiatric thinking have meant that this is at times a conscious therapeutic endeavour, where misuse of interpersonal space is deemed indicative of the psychological problem. At times it seems a less conscious and perhaps less benign undertaking, as in the imposition of arbitrary rules about who can use the kitchen without staff supervision. That these issues are an integral part of both psychiatric categories and inter-ventions is perhaps unsurprising, implicit and explicit division and symbolic investment of territories being such an inevitable part of human behaviour. But the incorporation of these issues into a professional discourse can also be seen as the recognition by a powerful professional group of the modalities by which its authority can be perpetuated – part of the way in which the everyday gets smaller as the professional gets larger.

BIBLIOGRAPHY

Allderidge, P. (1979) 'Hospitals, mad houses and asylums. Cycles in the care of the insane', *British Journal of Psychiatry* 134: 321–34.

American Psychiatric Association (1987) *Diagnostic Criteria DSM II R.*

Barefoot, P. (1992) 'Psychiatric wards in DGHs?', *Psychiatric Bulletin* 16: 99–100.

Breuer, J. and Freud, S. (1953–73) 'Studies on Hysteria, 1895', in *The Standard Edition of the Complete Psychological Works of Sigmund Freud*, 24 vols, vol. 2, London: Hogarth Press.

Browne, W.A.F. (1990) 'What asylums were, are and ought to be', in A. Scull (ed.), *The Asylum as Utopia: W.A.F. Browne and the Mid-Nineteenth Century Consolidation of Psychiatry*, London: Routledge.

Burton, R. (1621) *The Anatomy of Melancholy*, London: J.E. Hodson, 2nd edn 1806.

Chamberlain, J. (1988) *On Our Own*, London: Mind.

Connolly, J. [1847] (1968) *The Construction and Government of Lunatic Asylums and Hospitals for the Insane*, London: Dawson.

Crammer, J. (1990) *Asylum History. Buckinghamshire County Pauper Lunatic Asylum – St John's*, London: Gaskell.

Department of Health & Social Security (1989), *Caring for People. Community Care in the Next Decade and Beyond*, London: HMSO.

——(1991) *Community Care: Services for People with a Mental Handicap and People with a Mental Illness*, government response to the 11th report, Social Services Committee Session 1989–90, London: HMSO.

——(1992) *Report of the Committee of Enquiry into Complaints about Ashworth Hospital*, 2 vols, London: HMSO.

Digby, A. (1985) 'Moral treatment at the Retreat 1796–1846', in W.F. Bynum, R. Porter and M. Shepherd (eds), *The Anatomy of Madness. Essays in the History of Psychiatry. Vol. 2 Institutions and Society*, London: Tavistock.

Fahy, T. and Fisher, N. (1992) 'Sexual contact between doctors and patients', *British Medical Journal*, 13 June: 1519–20.

Foucault, M. (1967) *Madness and Civilization. A History of Insanity in the Age of Reason*, trans. R. Howard, London: Tavistock.

Freud, A. (1986) *The Ego and the Mechanisms of Defence*, London: Hogarth Press and Institute of Psychoanalysis.

Freud, S. (1953–73) 'Inhibition symptoms and anxiety, 1926', in *The Standard Edition of the Complete Psychological Works of Sigmund Freud*, 24 vols, vol. 20, London: Hogarth Press.

——(1979) 'Notes upon a case of obsessional neurosis (The Rat Man) [1909]', in *Case Histories II*, Harmondsworth: Penguin.

Gardiner Hill, R. (1839) 'Total abolition of personal restraint in the treatment of the insane', London: Simpkin, Marshall Co., quoted in V. Skultans (ed.) (1975) *Madness and Morals: Ideas on Insanity in the Nineteenth Century*, London: Routledge & Kegan Paul.

Gelder, M., Gath, D. and Mayour, R. (1983) *The Oxford Textbook of Psychiatry*, Oxford: Oxford University Press.

Goffman, E. (1961) *Asylums*, Anchor Books, Harmondsworth: Pelican.

Grounds, A. (1990) 'Seclusion', in P. Bowden and R. Bluglass (eds), *Forensic Psychiatry*, Edinburgh: Churchill Livingstone.

Haslam, J. (1817) *Considerations on the Moral Management of the Insane*, London: R. Hunter, quoted in V. Skultans (ed.) (1975) *Madness and Morals: Ideas on Insanity in the Nineteenth Century*, London: Routledge & Kegan Paul.

James, A. (1991) 'Homeless women in London: the hostels perspective', *Health*

Trends 23: 80–3.

James, D. and Hamilton, L. (1991) 'The Clerkenwell Scheme: assessing efficacy and cost of a psychiatric liaison service to a Magistrates' Court', *British Medical Journal* 303: 282–5.

Jaspers, K. (1962) *General Psychopathology*, trans. M.W. Hamilton and J. Hoenig, Manchester: Manchester University Press.

Jones, K. (1972) *A History of the Mental Health Services*, London: Routledge & Kegan Paul.

Joseph, P. (1992) *Psychiatric Assessment at the Magistrates' Court*, London: Home Office.

Mace, C.J. (1992) 'Hysterical conversion 1: a history', *British Journal of Psychiatry* 161: 369–77.

McMillan, I. (1992) 'Out of the shadows', *Nursing Times* 88(32): 18.

Maudsley, H. (1873) *Body Mind*, London: Macmillan & Co., quoted in V. Skultans (ed.) (1975) *Madness and Morals: Ideas on Insanity in the Nineteenth Century*, London: Routledge & Kegan Paul.

Mental Health Act Commission (1991) *Fourth Biennial Report 1989–91*, London: HMSO.

Millett, K. (1990) *The Loony Bin Trip*, New York: Simon & Schuster.

Morison, A. (1824) 'The physiognomy of insanity', in *Outlines of Mental Diseases*, Edinburgh: McLachlan and Stewart, quoted in V. Skultans (ed.) (1975) *Madness and Morals: Ideas on Insanity in the Nineteenth Century*, London: Routledge & Kegan Paul.

National Schizophrenia Fellowship (1992) *Window Dressing – A Report from the National Schizophrenia Fellowship*, London.

Noble, P. and Rodger, S. (1989) 'Violence by psychiatric in-patients', *British Journal of Psychiatry* 155: 384–90.

Parry-Jones, W.L. (1972) *The Trade in Lunacy: A Study of Private Mad Houses in the Eighteenth and Nineteenth Centuries*, London: Routledge & Kegan Paul.

Porter, R. (1987a) *A Social History of Madness: Stories of the Insane*, London: Weidenfield & Nicolson.

——(1987b) *Mind Forg'd Manacles. A History of Madness in England from the Restoration to the Regency*, London: Athlone Press.

Ripa, Y. (1990) *Women and Madness. The Incarceration of Women in Nineteenth-Century France*, Cambridge: Polity Press.

Robinson, N.A. (1729) *New System of the Spleen Vapours and Hypochondriack Melancholy*, London: Bettesworth.

Scull, A. (1979) *Museums of Madness*, London: Allen Lane.

——(1984) *Decarceration: Community Treatment and the Deviant – a Radical View*, Cambridge: Polity Press.

——(1989) *Social Order and Mental Disorder. Anglo-American Psychiatry in Historical Perspective*, London: Routledge.

Segal, H. (1989) *Klein*, London: Karnac Books/Institute of Psychoanalysis.

Showalter, E. (1987) 'Nervous women, sex roles and sick roles', in *The Female Malady: Women, Madness and Culture 1830–1980*, London: Virago.

Skultans, V. (ed.) (1975) *Madness and Morals: Ideas on Insanity in the Nineteenth Century*, London: Routledge & Kegan Paul.

——(1979) *English Madness: Ideas on Insanity 1580–1890*, London: Routledge & Kegan Paul.

Stanton, A.H. and Schwartz, M.S. (1954) *The Mental Hospital: A Study of Institutional Participation in Psychiatric Illness* New York: Basic Books.

Taylor, J. (1991) *Asylum and Hospital Architecture in England 1840–1914*, Building for Health Care, London: Mansell.

Thornicroft, G. and Bebbington, P. (1989) 'Deinstitutionalization – from hospital closure to service development', *British Journal of Psychiatry* 155: 739–54.

Tomes, N.J. (1981) 'A generous confidence: Thomas Story Kilbride. Philosophy of asylum construction and management', in A. Scull (ed.), *Mad Houses, Mad Doctors and Madmen. The Social History of Psychiatry in the Victorian Era*, London: Athlone Press.

Thompson, J.B. (1984) 'Symbolic violence, language and power in the writings of Pierre Bourdieu', in *Studies in the Theory of Ideology*, Cambridge: Polity Press.

Walton, J. (1981) 'The treatment of pauper lunatics in Victorian England: the case of the Lancaster Asylum 1816–1870', in A. Scull (ed.), *Mad Houses, Mad Doctors and Madmen. The Social History of Psychiatry in the Victorian Era*, London: Athlone Press.

10

THE TEMPORAL STRUCTURING OF SETTLEMENT SPACE AMONG THE DOGON OF MALI: AN ETHNOARCHAEOLOGICAL STUDY

Paul J. Lane

> Time elapses in a sequential way in all societies, but in those in which tradition is pre-eminent, processes of social reproduction are interwoven with different forms of awareness of past, present and future than in the contemporary industrialized world.
>
> (Giddens 1979: 200)

In this chapter I draw on an analysis of the organization and use of settlement space among the Dogon of Mali to address a number of issues of wider relevance to archaeology. The first of these concerns the temporalities of material forms, and especially the possibility that these are multiple as well as historically and contextually specific. Following on from this, I provide an examination of the active role of material culture, in this case physical space and architecture, in the reproduction and transformation of society. Finally, the paper also considers the use of alternative concepts of time in the discipline and in a more general sense the significance of time for the interpretation of space and material culture patterning.

Although there has been a general lack of consideration of the more philosophical issues of time throughout the discipline (Bailey 1983), this is especially true of spatial archaeology. There are at least two reasons which may help to account for this. The first concerns the tendency to consider space and time as separate and neutral dimensions which provide an environment for human behaviour. The second is the related tendency to equate time simply with change. As a result, most discussions of the temporal aspects of spatial patterning have been restricted to discussions of chronology, and especially the methodological difficulties of determining different phases of site use and occupation.

Despite this lack of theorization about time–space relationships, temporal issues are nevertheless inherent to a number of concepts that are widely used in spatial archaeology. Examples include the notions of seasonality, site maintenance and artefact curation and recycling. The more general assumption that most archaeological patterning is the outcome of aggregate and cumulative behaviour carries with it a similar tacit acknowledgement of temporality. Moreover, the importance of these factors in the structuring of archaeological contexts has been reaffirmed by a number of site formation studies (e.g. Ascher 1968; David 1971; Binford 1978; 1982; McGuire and Schiffer 1983), to the extent that archaeological sites can be considered to have their own 'life histories' (Stevenson 1991: 286).[1]

Many of the insights provided by such studies, however, have tended to 'underscore the difficulty of determining whether observed variability is caused by past behaviours or by formation processes' (Seymour and Schiffer 1987: 554). As a result, the aggregate and cumulative properties of archaeological contexts have come to be seen as imposing certain constraints on archaeological inference. It has even been suggested that these features of archaeological materials entail the use of particular temporal concepts in the discipline rather than others – specifically, those which concern long-term temporal processes such as evolution and environmental change (Bailey 1983: 180–6; 1987: 8).

Other proposed solutions to the problems of inference are similarly instructive, since they provide a further indication of the manner in which the issues of time in spatial archaeology are perceived. Specifically, an emphasis is placed on distinguishing between different categories of events and their sequence of occurrence, through the development of appropriate techniques,[2] and the establishment of relevant material correlates of behaviour. Significantly, however, this emphasis on sequence and event is partly a product of the dominant conceptions of time in the discipline as a unilinear and infinitely segmentable dimension, and partly the result of the use of a spatial concept, stratigraphy, to determine variation in time (Shanks and Tilley 1987: 118–20).

Abstract and mensurable notions of time such as these lie at the root of most forms of western science. Nevertheless, as Leone (1978) pointed out some years ago with particular reference to archaeology, these ideas are the outcome of particular historical and intellectual developments, especially those related to the emergence of industrial capitalism. As such, there is no particular reason to assume that these ideas should resemble the manner in which time and its relationship to space were perceived by the members of past societies, or even that the modern, scientific representations of time and space are necessarily correct formulations of their essential properties.

Western models of time also contrast strongly with contemporary 'folk' and 'peasant' approaches to time. Among the more important differences are that in 'peasant' societies, time is generally marked rather than measured, reversible as opposed to directional, and substantive rather than abstract

(Shanks and Tilley 1987: 126–32). At a more analytical level, since space and time are inherent to all forms of behaviour, that is, behaviour is both spatial and temporal in its execution and does not simply occur in space–time, it can be argued that space and time need to be considered as constituents of, and not just environments for, behaviour (Bourdieu 1977; Giddens 1979; 1981). As constituents of action, this would imply that the times and spaces of society do not exist independently of social practices, and instead can be regarded as being in a state of 'becoming', of being constantly generated and reformulated through social action.

The notion that space and time are as much constitued by, as constituents of, practice has been taken further by Giddens in his examination of the existence of multiple times and their different structuring effects on activity. In particular, following Heidegger, Giddens has suggested that all forms of social action involve at least three intersecting 'planes of temporality'. These are, the rhythms of daily routine, the biography or lifecycle of the individual, and the inheritance or *longue durée* of social institutions (Giddens 1979: 198). This observation also has important implications regarding the temporal properties of material culture, which have rarely been considered in archaeology (although see Hall 1987). Specifically, it can be suggested that rather than having a single temporal significance, material culture and spatial forms are imbued with several different temporalities that arise from their articulation with the patterns of daily, biographical and institutional time within society. In addition, these forms also have their own relative and absolute histories, which coexist alongside these other temporalities, and it is these which are used conventionally in archaeology to establish chronology.

An understanding of these different temporalities, and their generative power, is thus of central importance to the interpretation of spatial patterns, and in this chapter I provide several examples of how this works in practice within a contemporary society. However, because of constraints on space, I shall limit my discussion to the importance of the temporal structuring of space to the reproduction of the dominant ideology, and particularly the emphasis that this places on the need for the maintenance of 'tradition'. By this I do not mean to imply that other readings of space and architecture do not exist, or that there is no room for strategic and negotiated responses to the lineage dynamic. The power of certain material forms as representations of an ideal past, however, is especially strong, and it is because of this that the temporal structuring of settlement is so effective in helping to maintain the existing relationships of power and authority. Again, this should not be taken as an indication that I consider Dogon society to be unchanged, or that Dogon themselves do not acknowledge these developments. The Dogon have a long history of contact with neighbouring groups, and as elsewhere in Mali the events of the last century have had some profound consequences for Dogon communities, of which they are well aware. Nevertheless, at the time of my fieldwork the invocation of notions of tradition was a major motif in

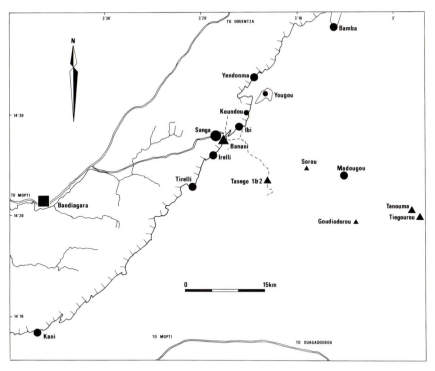

Figure 10.1 Location of study village (Banani Kokoro) and neighbouring settlements

expressions of the dominant ideology, and it is an analysis of this aspect of Dogon society which I present below.

THE DOGON

The Dogon live in the area of the Bandiagara escarpment and the neighbouring Gondo Plain of eastern Mali (Figure 10.1). They are predominantly subsistence agriculturalists, and are speakers of one of the Gur group of languages. Settlement is generally in the form of nucleated villages, and these are found scattered along the foot of the escarpment, as well as on the rolling plain to the east and on the sandstone plateau to the west. The research on which this paper is based was carried out between 1981 and 1983 in one of these villages, located at the foot of the escarpment and roughly midway along its length (Figure 10.2).

As a patrilineal society, the Dogon are divided according to the principles of lineage organization into a number of agnatic descent groups. In terms of their genealogical structure, these are of progressively narrower social extent and shallower time depth. With the exception of the four sub-tribes, which represent the largest social unit, each of these has a spatial equivalent

199

Figure 10.2 Banani Kokoro, 1981

(Tait 1950; Dieterlen 1956). Thus, each village (*ana*) is made up of a group of agnates descended from a common founding ancestor, and who share a common patronym. As a result of lineage segmentation, villages on occasion can be divided into a number of wards, or *togu*. In turn, each ward comprises a number of smaller social units. Known as *tire ginna*, or more usually as simply *ginna*, these segments can best be described as minor lineages.

Although the more inclusive groups fulfil a number of important functions and provide individuals with a different aspect of their social identity, on a day-to-day basis the minor lineage, or *ginna*, is by far the most significant. In terms of their social composition, these generally cover three, or more rarely four generations. Thus, ideally a *ginna* will consist of the conjugal family of the lineage head, who is always the eldest male member of the group, along with the families of any of his junior brothers, married sons and married nephews, and even married grandsons. The actual composition of these groups, however, is usually more varied, largely because at any particular moment lineages are at different stages in their developmental cycle.

As an independent unit of production, each *ginna* holds and controls rights of usufruct in agricultural land on the slopes and valley floor neighbouring the village. Most of this land is farmed collectively by lineage members, and both men and women participate in the annual tasks of sowing, weeding and harvesting. There is some division of labour between men and women over certain of these activities. For instance, during sowing, men do the hoeing while women plant the seed. Similarly, at harvest-time it is men who harvest the crop while women have the task of transporting it back to the village. The sexual division of labour also governs the allocation of other routine tasks. Specifically, women are responsible for crop processing, collecting firewood, food preparation and child minding, while men look after herds and do most of the work on building and maintaining houses and other structures.

These two themes of collective participation by lineage members in routine tasks of production and consumption, and the complementary division of labour between the sexes, are central elements of the lineage ideology. The most overt expressions of this occur during the various calendrical rituals of lineage renewal. These ceremonies generally take place within the courtyard or some other sector of the compound (*ginu na*) occupied by the lineage head. Where the ritual involves two or more lineage segments, as happens for example during certain stages of the annual sowing festival, or *bulu*, the ceremonies will be held at the *ginu na* of the most senior segment. Most members of the *ginna* will be in attendance during such rituals. The principal officiant, however, is generally the lineage head or some other senior male member, who will offer a selection of prayers and benedictions to the appropriate ancestors. These are accompanied by a sacrifice of either gruel, beer, chicken, goat or some combination of these, over either the outside of a shrine, the ritual artefacts within it, or a small altar in the courtyard.

Although the specific content of the various prayers and benedictions which are offered up to the ancestors varies from ritual to ritual, the range of liturgical devices that are employed is fairly constant between the various ceremonies and also between different lineages. Published versions of the same category of prayers collected between the 1930s and 1950s suggest that these techniques have been in use for at least two generations (for a discussion of these texts, see Lane 1986: 400–7).

One of the most recurrent elements of these prayers is the request for the ancestors to ensure that the younger male members of the lineage are provided with food, wives and children, in that order. Frequently, these prayers are invoked specifically for those junior males who are temporarily absent from the village, especially those who are engaged in wage-labour in one of the towns in the region, and those who have established farms away from the cliff-line in the Plain of Gondo. This concern is contextualized as an 'objective interest' in the welfare of these individuals, and the lineage elders who utter these prayers portray themselves as seeking ancestral support for the common good of the lineage. Under the existing relations of production and consumption, however, it is the elders who have most to lose economically by the absence and growing independence of the younger men, since they rely on these men and their wives for agricultural labour, and hence their subsistence.

Meillassoux (1978) has noted for segmentary lineage societies in general that there is normally an imbalance of power and authority between elders and juniors in favour of the former. This is despite the fact that elders are both numerically and physically the weaker category. In order to retain their position of authority, it is necessary for elders to maintain a monopoly over certain kinds of knowledge which are deemed to be central to the reproduction of the group and hence its very survival. In this regard, the Dogon are no exception. What is perhaps more interesting is the specific way in which Dogon lineage elders approach the problem of the reproduction of their authority and in particular the role of material symbols, including architecture and space, in the process.

SOCIAL AND TEMPORAL ORGANIZATION OF SPACE

One of the most apparently contradictory elements of lineage organization, and thus potentially threatening to the dominant order, is the distribution of its members through space. For, whereas great emphasis is placed on the collective participation of lineage members in daily production and consumption, they do not all reside in the same compound. Instead, each *ginna* owns and controls a number of individual compounds which are allocated to the different members of the lineage. In some cases these abut one another, however, for the most part they are scattered throughout the village amongst the compounds of other lineages. In Figure 10.3, for example, Compound Nos. 7, 8, 22, 28, 30, 36 and 40 all belong to the same lineage.

Physically, there is little to distinguish between these different compounds. (Figures 10.3 and 10.4). Typically, each will contain between one and four houses grouped around an open multi-purpose activity area, and bounded on all sides by a combination of drystone walling and large sandstone boulders. A number of other structures can also be found within the enclosed area of a compound. These include tall, rectangular millet granaries, as well as smaller versons which are used for storing secondary crops and personal possessions, stone seating platforms, hen-coops, weaving looms, livestock pens and entrance porches. Not all of these are represented in each compound, and some have a more restricted distribution than others. In particular, millet granaries, livestock pens, seating platforms and entrance porches tend to be found in the compounds of lineage heads, for reasons which will be elaborated upon below.

Despite the lack of architectural differentiation, the various compounds occupied by different members of a lineage are distinguished from one another, according to the age, gender and marital status of their principal occupants. The Dogon recognize four basic categories. These are:

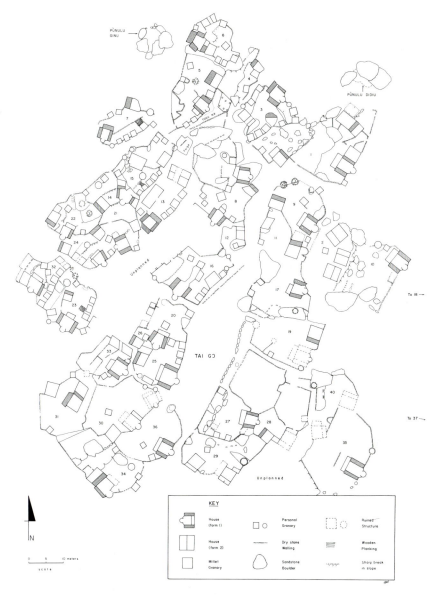

Figure 10.3 Plan of the village of Banani Kokoro

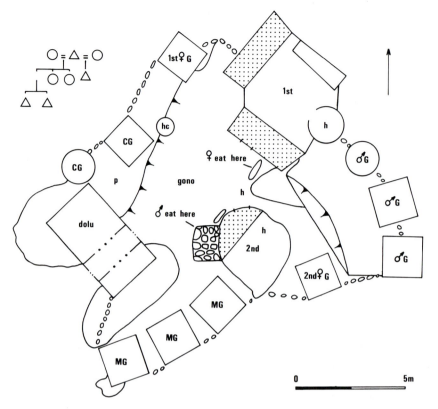

Figure 10.4 A *ginu na* compound. MG: millet granary; CG: secondary crop granary; G: personnal granary (husband's or wife's); 1st: first wife's house; 2nd: second wife's house; h: cooking hearth; p: potting equipment; gono: courtyard; dolu: entrance porch; dotted area: first floor room

1 the compounds occupied by lineage heads, their spouses and certain dependent children,[3] which are known as *ginu na*, or more simply as *ginna* (e.g. Compound No. 7);
2 the compounds used by other married or divorced men and women, along with their dependent children, which are called *ginu sala* (e.g. Compound Nos. 8, 22, 30 and 36);
3 the compounds inhabited by widowed women, who may also share this space with unmarried adolescent, female agnates, which are termed *yana peney dunoy* (e.g. Compound No. 28);
4 the compounds allocated to unmarried adolescent males, for which the term *sagadara dunoy* is employed (e.g. Compound No. 19).

The social and moral significance of these different spaces is partly revealed through the choice of terms for the different categories of residence. Thus, as has already been noted, the compound of the lineage head, who is the eldest male member of the group, strictly speaking is known as *ginu na*, or great house. However, in everyday usage this term is contracted to simply *ginna*, which is the same term for a minor lineage. Through the use of this single term, therefore, an important homology is established between the social group and the residential space of the person who heads it.

The inclusion of the word *ginu*, meaning house, in the terms for only two of the four categories of compound is also significant. Specifically, a basic distinction is being made between these compounds, that is, the *ginu na* and *ginu sala* categories, whose occupants under normal circumstances belong to conjugal families and so contribute to the reproduction of the lineage, and those compounds used by individuals who have either passed the age of reproduction (elderly widows)[4] or have yet to reach that stage in their lives (unmarried adolescent males).[5] In each case, the term *dunoy*, which roughly translates as sleeping room, is used rather than the word for house, even though there may be no physical difference between the different categories of compound and the houses they contain. Compare, for example, compounds 10, 17 and 29 in Figure 10.3, which were all occupied by widows between 1981 and 1983, with compounds 2, 9, 34 and 36, which all belonged to the *ginu sala* category, and compound 19 which was used by two unmarried males with compound 11 which was occupied by a widow, and compound 31 which was occupied by a young, married couple. For the Dogon, therefore, a house is not simply a physical structure but must also be occupied by a socially approved reproductive unit.

Since each of these residential categories is linked to the biographical position of the principal occupants, they are also subject to change as the age and marital status of these individuals alters. Consequently, at periodic intervals throughout the history of a lineage, there is a need for the recategorization of dwelling space. In fact, as well as the reclassification of space, the specific response to the developmental cycle of the lineage also requires individuals to move from one compound to another. The precise sequence of moves an individual will follow during the course of his or her life varies considerably (Lane 1986). Not all men become the lineage head, not all women outlive their husband. There are, nevertheless, basic regularities to the moves that both men and women are likely to make during the course of their lives. Initially, the sequence followed by both sexes is identical. Later in life, however, a number of important differences begin to emerge (Figure 10.5).

The ideal pattern for males is as follows. They are born at the *ginu na*, and as children will either sleep here or at their parents' compound. Following circumcision, boys move into their own sleeping quarters, termed *sagadara dunoy*, which they may share with one or more age mates. The next move comes after marriage, when men establish their own households for the first time. The compounds they occupy at this stage in their lives all belong to the *ginu sala* category. However, if later in life they become the eldest male of

Males

Birth   Adolesence   Marriage   Old Age

Ginu na ⟶ *Sagadara dunoy* ⟶ *Ginu sala* → *Ginu na*

Females

Birth   Adolesence   Marriage   Old Age   Widowhood

Ginu na→ *Yana peney* → *Ginu sala*→ *Ginu na*→ *Yana peney*
                 dunoy   *dunoy*

Figure 10.5 Schematic representation of ideal sequence of residential moves for male and female lifepaths

their patrilineage, they will be required to move into their *ginu na* so as to assume the position of lineage head, or *ginu bana*.

The pattern of residence for females up until puberty is identical with that for males. During adolescence, however, rather than having their own space, girls are required to sleep at the house of one of the widowed women in the village, and preferentially that of a close relative. On marriage, they will move from here to join their husband in his *ginu sala* compound. Since the rule of post-marital residence is virilocal, and there is a strong preference for village exogamy, most women after marriage have to leave their natal settlement and will spend much of their adult lives amongst affines. If sometime after marriage their husband becomes the lineage head, then they too will move with him into the *ginu na* of his patrilineage. If, however, they outlive their husband, then they may have to move again, or at the very least their compound will be recategorized as a *yana peney dunoy*.[6]

Time, as manifested by the developmental cycle of the lineage, therefore, is an important principle governing the organization of space, and its categorization links individuals at different stages in their lives to specific localities. However, because the means of production are relatively straightforward, dividing residential space in this way provides much greater opportunity for individuals to establish independent households than would be the case if all lineage members lived in the same compound, which is the more common situation elsewhere in west Africa. From an archaeological point of view, it would certainly be easy to assume that the fairly even distribution of the material evidence of the means of consumption, such as hearths, crop-processing areas and granaries, was an indication that each compound was occupied by an independent productive unit. The fact that despite being dispersed throughout the village, members of different compound groups continue to co-operate in routine tasks of production and consumption therefore requires explanation. An important clue to understanding why this is the case is provided by the way in which time is encapsulated in the material fabric of settlement space.

TIME IN THE MATERIAL WORLD

When individuals move from one compound to another, the compound they vacate becomes available for other members of the lineage to occupy. Only in the case of the *ginu na* compound is the social position of the next occupant predictable – he will be the new lineage head. In contrast, there is no rule governing who will move into, for example, a recently vacated *ginu sala* compound. According to the residential requirements of the lineage, the compound may be occupied by another married couple, in which case it will remain in the *ginu sala* category. Alternatively, it may be used by a widowed woman or unmarried man, in which case it will cease to be considered as a *ginu sala*, and instead will fall into either the *yana peney dunoy* or *sagadara dunoy* category.

This basic contrast between the *ginu na* and the remaining residential categories is further compounded by another relationship. Specifically, of all the extant occupied compounds belonging to a lineage, the *ginu na* is considered to be the oldest. Thus, since the lineage head is always the eldest male of the group, an important isomorphic relationship – of the kind 'the eldest lineage member in the oldest living space' – is established. No such stricture on the age of the occupant governs the residential use of any of the other compounds belonging to a lineage. Thus, for instance, Compound 29 in Figure 10.3 was occupied in late 1981 by an elderly, widowed woman. Some months after this woman died in 1982, members of the lineage to whom it belonged began working on repairing the roof and walls, prior to it being occupied by a married couple and their children, who were still living there in mid-1983.

A basic set of contrasts between *ginu na* and all other categories of compound can now be established. On the one hand, the former are durable, permanent and predictable spaces, while in comparison the latter are transient, impermanent and unpredictable in terms of the status of their occupants (Figure 10.6). There is also a distinction between the guiding criteria of occupancy. In the case of a *ginu na* it is age, whereas in the case of the others it is marital status. This distinction also makes sense in terms of the other

Ginu na	Other categories
Durable	Transient
Permanent	Impermanent
Predictable	Unpredictable

Figure 10.6 Conceptual features of *ginu na* compounds compared with those of all other categories

three, in that a person's marital status is always subject to change, whereas the position of lineage head is determined by a man's relative age *vis-à-vis* that of other male members of the lineage, and which, unlike his absolute age, is unchanging.

It is precisely because of these properties of durability and predictability that the *ginu na* is contextualized as a symbol of the lineage. It is as if its material presence is a reaffirmation of the continued existence of the lineage, thereby confirming the practical logic of the lineage ideology. It is no surprise, therefore, that in everyday speech the term for this space is contracted to simply *ginna*, that is, to the same term used to define the social group. One of the recursive consequences of this contextualization of the *ginu na* as a symbol of lineage continuity is that it is made to appear as the legitimate and logical space for the storage of the product of the collective labour of the group, the preparation and consumption of food, the veneration of lineage ancestors and the birth of children, since the continued survival of the lineage depends on all of these. In turn, the routine use of the *ginu na* for these practices reaffirms, in a similarly recursive fashion, this same symbolic scheme. Such contextualization also explains why such features as large storage granaries for the staple crops, stone seating platforms for use during communal meals and gatherings, and the ancestral shrines all tend to be concentrated in *ginu na* compounds.

A further consequence is that as a symbol of the continuity of the lineage, the physical fabric of the *ginu na* is preferentially maintained. Other lineage structures will also be repaired while occupied. However, if through the contraction of the lineage some should fall vacant, the buildings they contain will be left unattended and may even be allowed to collapse (Figure 10.7). Only when that space is required again by the lineage will the structures be renovated, but in some cases this never happens.

Finally, there is an added potency to the *ginu na* as a material metaphor for the lineage, which arises from the fact that its own existence is something of a paradox. As an agnatic descent group, there should be a single *ginu na* for the entire village. In reality, however, there are several because over the centuries lineage segmentation has led to the creation of numerous units of

Figure 10.7 An abandoned compound, 1983

narrower span. Thus each *ginu na* is the outcome of the complex contingencies of genealogy, and in one sense is tangible evidence of the failure rather than the success of the lineage ideology. For, despite all the emphasis placed on the need for mutual co-operation and collaboration in the tasks of lineage production and reproduction, groups in the past have split away from one another to form new units. This process is a continuing one, and between 1981 and 1983 the demographic and social dynamics of several lineages ensured a potential for fissioning in the near future.

Unlike the other compounds belonging to it, therefore, in the constitution of the *ginu na* the lineage appears to have mastered time. Its existence is simultaneously an outcome of time's arrow – an event in the history of the steady fragmentation of the original kinship group – and also a confirmation of the continuities of time's cycle – a physical manifestation of lineage renewal.[7] In effect, it is only at the *ginu na* that the different rhythms of daily routine and generational time, and the tensions between time's arrow and time's cycle, all coalesce in a single form, and it is this encapsulation of time which assures its potency as a metaphor for the lineage.

TOWARDS AN ARCHAEOLOGY OF DOGON SETTLEMENT

As well as being of importance to the generation and reproduction of symbolic values, the temporal organization of space has a related bearing on the 'archaeology' of Dogon settlement. There are at least two ways in which this occurs. The first concerns the structuring effect of these temporalities on the formation of the 'archaeological record' of Dogon villages. The second pertains to the manner in which the Dogon perceive and construct their past.

There are a number of ways in which the encapsulation of time in the material fabric of settlement has a determining effect on site formation processes. The preferential preservation of *ginu na* compounds is perhaps the clearest example of these. As previously noted, each lineage considers this to be the oldest extant compound belonging to it. The age of these compounds relative to others which are also in current use can be confirmed through the use of genealogical information. Specifically, in many cases the names of the original builders of the various extant, and also ruined, compounds belonging to a lineage are known. In all recorded cases, the genealogical position of the founders of those compounds now designated as *ginu na* is senior to the genealogical position of the founders of the other compounds that are currently in use. More significantly, it is clear from this information that several of the ruined compounds in and around the village are also of more recent construction than any of the *ginu na* compounds. The power of the *ginu na* as symbol of the lineage, which arises in part from the relative age of the space itself, can thus be said to have a determining effect on architectural curation and maintenance practices, and hence on the rates of abandonment of different categories of compounds.

The use of space and architectural forms as ways of *presencing* the past also has a direct effect on the manner in which Dogon perceive and construct aspects of the past. Specifically, the Dogon recognize the entire assemblage of architectural forms, their spatial distribution, associations and relative condition as material traces of the past, that is, as 'archaeological evidence'. In their historical constructions, however, different spaces have different valences. Thus, although the historicity of each compound is acknowledged, the differences between these compounds may mean that this refers not simply to different moments along an unbroken continuum, but to two or more entirely separate temporal orders.

In illustration of this, differences between the interpretative readings of the archaeological and architectural traces of earlier settlement activity from different parts of the village can be compared. One of these areas is situated along the south-western border of the present village (i.e. adjacent to Compound Nos. 29, 31 and 39 in Figure 10.3), where the outlines of a number of abandoned compounds are marked by piles of rubble and eroded wall footings. Information on the genealogical position of the founders of these compounds indicates that all were of fairly recent origin relative to other buildings in the village. Moreover, in their discussion of these compounds, the heads of the lineages which own these spaces all attributed their abandonment to the catastrophic effects of the drought and ensuing famine which afflicted the area between 1913 and 1916.[8] In other words, these remains are interpreted as the outcome of particular events in the unfolding history of the settlement, and as such they document the changing fortunes of the various lineages.

However, it is highly improbable that the inhabitants of the compounds on the south-western edge of the settlement were the only ones to be affected by the famine, as a literal reading of the Dogon interpretation implies. Given the existing relations of production and consumption, other households would have had an equal chance of becoming unviable in the aftermath of a famine, just as those on the south-western side would have had an equal chance of survival. Subsequent recycling of some of these compounds elsewhere in the village, however, has obscured the precise pattern of the impact of the 1913–16 drought. In other words, although the Dogon consider the ruined compounds on the south-western edge of the village as material evidence of particular events, the historical reference of these 'archaeological traces' is of a symbolic rather than a strictly empirical nature. The vacant and abandoned state of other compounds in the village is interpreted in a similar fashion as symbolic of various other processes of settlement growth and contraction.

A final distinction, however, needs to be drawn between this kind of historical referencing and that of *ginu na* compounds. For, although the latter is of an even more symbolic nature, it is concerned with a quite different temporal order. Specifically, whereas the physical location and condition of other categories of compounds are used as a kind of mnemonic in Dogon constructions of the linear history of settlement, the temporal referents of *ginu na* compounds are to those of 'tradition', to legendary time or 'the time of the ancestors'. As indicated in this paper, the linking of particular areas of contemporary space to the ancestors is something which emerges from routine practices. Significantly, however, these links are explicitly reaffirmed through the naming of individual ancestors during various rituals of lineage and village renewal, and in a more general fashion in the various oral traditions of Dogon origins and migrations. In both cases, the principal objective of making these links between people, times and places is to establish the legitimacy of settlement over potential claims by other lineages, and in the case of the oral traditions, also other peoples. The selective conservation of certain structures thus provides a tangible confirmation of the antiquity of settlement and the durability of the institutions which lay claim to the land. The 'time of the ancestors', of 'tradition', therefore, although it draws on notions of cyclical repetition, cannot be reduced in a simple fashion to 'cyclical time' with all the connotations of cultural conservatism and changelessness that accompany this latter concept. Instead, the invocation of 'tradition' in practice and discourse, however strategic this may be,[9] is the invocation of an enduring time, of the eternal presence of the past through which Dogon attempt to mediate their future.

CONCLUSIONS

The temporal structuring of material culture and space is more than just an issue of chronology, although this is clearly important. Other facets of time also contribute to the generation and reproduction of spatial patterning, of which two of the most significant are the cultural division and management of the different temporal rhythms of activity. Since many of these are of a cyclical nature, their material traces might be expected to be both spatially discrete and of a fairly uniform composition. However, as indicated, although the patterns of daily activity can be highly repetitive in their nature and spatial organization, this does not always lead to the generation of regular patterning of the material traces of these activities because of their articulation with other 'planes of temporality'. This can be seen clearly in the contrast between the *ginu na* category of compounds and those belonging to other categories. In the former case, the institutional and biographical temporalities of these spaces help ensure that routine practices relating to the preparation and consumption of food are regularly and repetitively performed there. As a result, the debris produced by such activities accumulates in these localities, and becomes associated with the various facilities and material equipment used for these tasks which also tend to be clustered in *ginu na* compounds. A number of other uses are made of these spaces, some of which also generate spatially discrete, activity-specific material culture patterning. Examples include the shrine material associated with ancestral cults, and the animal pens, inclusive of manure deposits, used for keeping small livestock overnight. Although similar routine activities may also be performed in other categories of compounds and according to similar daily, weekly and annual cycles, because the institutional temporalities of these spaces are more varied and subject to change, there is a much greater likelihood that the traces of these activities will become mixed.

This type of 'smearing and blending' of different types and episodes of activity (*pace* Stevenson 1991: 294), of course, has been noted before on numerous occasions. The data presented in this chapter, however, suggest that the differences between these and more homogeneous types of deposits have alternative significances to those conventionally assigned to them by site formation studies. In the first place, differential patterns of discard, site maintenance, building reuse and abandonment cannot be explained purely in terms of cross-cultural laws of behaviour or some generalized notion of utilitarian value. Instead, they need to be understood as the outcome of specific societal approaches to the binding of space and time, which regulate individual access to, and use of, different places.

The creation of legitimate localities of practice in this manner is also an important source of power, both in the sense of individual practical capacities to control and transform, and in terms of more strictly jural abilities. As Bourdieu (1977), Giddens (1979; 1981) and others (e.g. Moore 1986) suggest, both aspects of power are inherent to most forms of practice, and many of the tensions that exist between these are exhibited in the specific ordering of space. These differing elements of power, however, are not fixed but need constantly to be reproduced and renegotiated, and it is partly this which makes time so central to an understanding of society. These points are amply illustrated by the example of Dogon settlement organization which, as argued above, is subjected to regular restructuring. In that these changes in residence are linked to social and biological processes of ageing, each move can be said to represent further accumulation of practical power and/or jural authority. In a general sense, this is so for both sexes. The wider significances of these moves for men and women, however, differ in some important respects.

Dogon men tend to reside for most of their lives in their natal village. As such, each residential move they make can be regarded as marking their increasing jural as well as practical control over the resources of their patrilineage. For some, but not all men, the culmination of this process is marked by their assumption of the position of lineage head and the occupancy of their *ginu na*, which stands as both a material symbol of the social group and the ideology which binds its members. In contrast, women spend most of their adult lives away from their natal villages in spaces over which they have only limited jural rights. However, because of their central role in daily tasks of household production and consumption, women excercise considerable practical power over these spaces. This also increases as they get older and acquire greater allocative authority over the labour of more junior female members of the lineage. Nevertheless, at crucial points in their lives, of which widowhood is one, women are spatially marginalized, and it is significant that on their death women are rarely buried in the same cemetery as their husband. Instead, their corpse is returned to their natal village to be interred there. The fundamental difference between male and female trajectories, therefore, is that men move *into* space whereas women move *through* space, and frequently do so less according to their own strategies and more in response to those of their natal and affinal patrilineages.

These differences also have a profound effect on the patterning of architecture and movable material culture. For men, their movement into space is a confirmation of history, and as indicated above the material fabric of settlement provides an important source of genealogical identity to which, ultimately, they may also contribute. The architectural traces of female identity, on the other hand, are far more ephemeral. In response to this, women endeavour to construct their own identities through investment in the material inventories of their own households, over which they have considerable practical power. The ultimate disposal of these, however, is far less localized than is the case for men, whose investment is directed more towards space and architecture. This is not just because pots, baskets, cloth

213

and other artefacts are more portable than buildings, but also because the spatio-temporal trajectories of women are more dispersed, as are those of the inheritors (female agnates) of these particular symbols of identity (Lane 1986).

Thus, the binding of space and time has rather different implications for the patterning of portable material culture than it does for the organization of residential space. In both cases, however, the acts of maintenance, recycling, discard and abandonment which govern the formation of the archaeological traces of Dogon settlement involve the articulation of symbolic and historical values, as well as more narrowly utilitarian ones. The importance of the historicity of objects and spaces also points to the significance of societal representations of time in the generation of material culture patterning. As argued above, these too have multiple consequences. Most crucially, however, the presencing of the past through space and architecture leads to the creation and maintenance of the type of long-term continuities, of cumulative material traditions, that are especially visible in archaeological contexts.

This is a rather self-evident, if often overlooked point, since any concept of 'tradition', whether invented or not, must entail a notion of 'history', of origins and genealogy. Moreover, the Dogon are not unique in their use of space to construct and represent their own history. As Beidelman has argued with reference to the Kaguru of Tanzania, a major achievement of the symbolic orchestration of time and space in many small-scale societies is that change becomes 'encapsulated within a broader frame of constancy' (Beidelman 1991: 44), thereby providing an important sense of 'ontological security' (Giddens 1981). With its access to long periods of human history through such material traditions, archaeology would seem to be an ideal means of gaining further insights into human understanding and transformations of time. Without the type of conceptual changes proposed in this paper, however, such a goal will always remain beyond our reach.

NOTES

This research was funded by the Department of Education and Science, with additional fieldwork and writing-up grants from the Crowther-Beynon Fund, Cambridge; the Tweedie Exploration Fund, Edinburgh; St John's College, Cambridge; the Allen Scholarship Fund, Cambridge; and the Worts Travel Fund, Cambridge. Permission to carry out fieldwork was obtained from the Government of the Republic of Mali and the Office of the Directeur Général des Enseignements Supérieurs et de la Recherche Scientifique, under Permit Numbers 0626/DNERS and 1596/DNERS.

An earlier version of this paper was presented at the 12th TAG Conference, held at the University of Wales, St David's College, Lampeter in 1990. I would like to thank the organizers of the session for inviting me, and the University of Dar es Salaam Archaeology Unit for financial support. Special thanks are due to Ian Hodder for supervising the original research and for his continued encouragement. I would also like to thank Henrietta Moore, Nick James and the editors for their constructive comments on aspects of this paper, and Debbie Cannon and Liv Gibbs for preparing the illustrations. Finally, thanks also to Keith Ray for starting me off among the Dogon and his subsequent critical support.

1 See also Oswald 1987.
2 Examples include the use of refitting and micro-stratigraphy.
3 In the first few years of life, children will sleep at their mother's place of residence. Thereafter, they will sleep at their father's *ginu na*, until they reach the age of circumcision in the case of males and puberty in the case of females, when they will move again.
4 Most women who are widowed while still of child-bearing age will remarry.
5 In point of fact, even after a man and woman are married they will not reside together until the birth of at least one child, and possibly not until their third child is born. This delay is said to be necessary so that the man's lineage can be assured that the union will bear issue.
6 Only where a woman is living in a *ginu na* will she always be required to move if her husband dies. In other situations, she may continue to live in the same compound she occupied with her husband. Alternatively, because of other lineage demands on that space she may have to move, and it is quite common under these circumstances for women to return to their natal village.
7 The Dogon do not make explicit reference to the metaphors of arrow and cycle when discussing the passage and ordering of time. However, much of society is structured to cope with the conflicting pulls of time's arrow and time's cycle, and like Gould I regard the contrast as 'a particularly good "dichotomy" because each of its poles captures a deep principle that human understanding of complex historical phenomena requires absolutely' (Gould 1988: 191–4).
8 See also Gallay (1981: 143) for references to this famine in the Dogon area.
9 For a discussion of this, see Lane (1986: 401–7).

BIBLIOGRAPHY

Ascher, R. (1968) 'Time's arrow and the archaeology of a contemporary community', in K.C. Chang (ed.), *Settlement Archaeology*, Palo Alto: National Press Books.

Bailey, G.N. (1983) 'Concepts of time in Quaternary prehistory', *Annual Review of Anthropology* 12: 165–92.

——(1987) 'Breaking the time barrier', *Archaeological Review from Cambridge* 6: 5–20.

Beidelman, T.O. (1991) 'Containing time: rites of passage and moral space or Bachelard among the Kaguru, 1957–1966', *Anthropos* 86: 443–61.

Binford, L.R. (1978) 'Dimensional analysis of site structure: learning from an Eskimo hunting stand', *American Antiquity* 43: 330–61.

——(1982) 'The archaeology of place', *Journal of Anthropological Archaeology* 1: 5–31.

Bourdieu, P. (1977) *Outline of a Theory of Practice*, Cambridge: Cambridge University Press.

David, N. (1971) 'The Fulani compound and the archaeologist', *World Archaeology* 3(2): 111–31.

Dieterlen, G. (1956) 'Parenté et mariage chez les Dogon (Soudan Français)', *Africa* 26: 107–48.

Gallay, A. (1981) *Le Sarnyere Dogon, Archéologie d'un Isolat (Mali)*, Paris: Éditions Recherche sur les Civilisations, Mémoire 4.

Giddens, A. (1979) *Central Problems in Social Theory*, London: Macmillan Press.

——(1981) *A Contemporary Critique of Historical Materialism*, London: Macmillan Press.

Gould, S.J. (1988) *Time's Arrow and Time's Cycle: Myth and Metaphor in the Discovery of Geological Time*, Harmondsworth: Penguin.

Hall, M. (1987) 'Archaeology and modes of production in pre-colonial southern Africa', *Journal of Southern African Studies* 14(1): 1–17.

Lane, P.J. (1986) 'Settlement as History: A Study of Space and Time among the Dogon of Mali', unpublished Ph.D. thesis, University of Cambridge.

Leone, M.P. (1978) 'Time in American archaeology', in C.L. Redman, M.J. Berman, E.V. Custin, W.T. Langhorne, N.M. Versaggi and J.C. Wanser (eds), *Social Archaeology*, London: Academic Press.

McGuire, R.H. and Schiffer, M.B. (1983) 'A theory of architectural design', *Journal of Anthopological Archaeology* 2: 227–303.

Meillassoux, C. (1978) 'The "Economy" in agricultural self-sustaining societies: a preliminary analysis', in D. Seddon (ed.), *Relations of Production*, London: Frank Cass.

Moore, H.L. (1986) *Space, Text and Gender: An Anthropological Study of the Marakwet of Kenya*, Cambridge: Cambridge University Press.

Oswald, D.B. (1987) 'The organization of space in residential buildings: a cross-cultural perspective', in S. Kent (ed.), *Method and Theory for Activity Area Research: An Ethnoarchaeological Approach*, New York: Columbia University Press.

Seymour, D. and Schiffer, M.B. (1987) 'A preliminary analysis of Pithouse assemblages from Snaketown, Arizona', in S. Kent (ed.), *Method and Theory for Activity Area Research: An Ethnoarchaeological Approach*, New York: Columbia University Press.

Shanks, M. and Tilley, C. (1987) *Social Theory and Archaeology*, Cambridge: Polity Press.

Stevenson, M.G. (1991) 'Beyond the formation of hearth-associated artefact assemblages', in E.M. Kroll and T.D. Price (eds), *The Interpretation of Archaeological Spatial Patterning*, London: Plenum Press.

Tait, D. (1950) 'An analytical commentary on the social structure of the Dogon', *Africa* 20: 175–99.

11

ORDER WITHOUT ARCHITECTURE: FUNCTIONAL, SOCIAL AND SYMBOLIC DIMENSIONS IN HUNTER-GATHERER SETTLEMENT ORGANIZATION

Todd M. Whitelaw

To judge by the number of edited volumes appearing in recent years, space has become a hot topic in both archaeology and ethnoarchaeology, as archaeologists have begun to think creatively and critically about the fundamental dimension within which archaeological data is recorded on site. While much of the theoretical attention is exciting, too often more attention is given to polemics than to critical examination of the behavioural issues, or to productive exploration of ways to pursue such approaches with archaeological data. Along the latter lines, this chapter will examine and try to dispel two notions which seem to have crept into recent writings, and which are inhibiting progress in understanding human spatial behaviour.

The first concerns contrasts in the way ethnoarchaeologists and archaeologists have approached spatial behaviour among different types of societies, and is exemplified by the focus on the functional organization of space among hunter-gatherer societies (e.g. Yellen 1977; Anderson 1982; Binford 1987; Kroll and Price 1991; Gamble and Boismier 1991), and the symbolic organization of space among sedentary agricultural societies (e.g. Cunningham 1964; Tambiah 1969; Douglas 1972; Tuan 1977; Bourdieu 1979; Donley 1982; Moore 1986; Kent 1990a; Samson 1990). This contrast reflects a bias in the orientation of anthropological work on each type of society, rather than any real difference in behaviour between such societies, a bias which we have inherited and reify in our ethnoarchaeology and archaeology, a bias which treats hunter-gatherers as less complex behaviourally, socially and symbolically, and which accepts a less elaborate explanation for their behaviour as satisfactory. This perpetuates Victorian notions of social evolutionism and teleological assumptions of progress in the contrast

217

between so-called simple and complex societies – with its implicit ethnocentric, imperialist, and indeed racist biases.

Second, in the context of the past decade of polemical debates between processualists and post-processualists, these two perspectives are usually set against each other as competing and antagonistic explanations for the same phenomena. In contrast, both may be argued to be relevant and necessary components of any full explanation or understanding of human spatial behaviour – they deal with different but equally relevant dimensions of the same phenomena. Such a view is one of the most emancipating perspectives developed in the early writings of the New Archaeology (Binford 1962), but seemingly lost sight of by both sides in much recent debate. In addition, both perspectives have espoused overly simplistic notions of what the archaeological record is, and how we can learn from it, as well as limiting the scope of model-building toward archaeological inference.

The remainder of this chapter will explore these problems from an anthropological and ethnoarchaeological perspective, using some of the few ethnographic studies of hunter-gatherer societies where information on the functional, social and symbolic context of spatial behaviour has been documented. It should become clear that these oppositions are of our own creation, and are not inherent in human spatial behaviour; furthermore, our perpetuation of such contrasts in archaeological debate guarantees that we will never approach more than a partial understanding of the phenomena we are trying to explain.

FUNCTIONAL PERSPECTIVES ON SPACE

A functional perspective on the organization of space has been developed in some detail, both theoretically and methodologically, by processual archaeologists over the past fifteen years, championed by Lewis Binford in his work on hunter-gatherer site structure. Such work aims at reconstructing the behaviour responsible for the debris patterning observable on-site. This built initially from the dimensions and simple mechanics of the human body, to explore the constraints this imposed and tendencies this encouraged in small-scale behavioural patterns (Binford 1977; 1978; 1983; 1987).

The classic example is Binford's hearth-centred activity model, with its debris drop and toss zones (Binford 1978; 1983; Anderson 1982; O'Connell 1987; Audouze 1987; Stevenson 1991). This has been widely applied by Binford and others to both ethnoarchaeological and archaeological data, with varying degrees of success (Binford 1983; 1987; Audouze 1987; Julien et al. 1987; Simms 1988; Gallay 1988; Petrequin and Petrequin 1988; Fisher and Strickland 1991; Cribb 1991a; Carr 1991). The same approach is used widely in our own society in design and architecture, to work out design needs, facilitate user comfort, or even to manipulate or control patterns in the use of space (e.g. Sommer 1969; 1974; Kira 1976). When applied to the interpretation of a site, it can give us a very basic, mechanical structure against which to compare actual debris patterns. In this way, it becomes a middle-range tool for measurement; it provides an expectation for debris patterning, under a rather simple model of spatial organization. As with any model, the degree to which the debris patterns do not conform to expectations encourages us to look for other causal processes.

Obviously, this is only a partial model of behaviour. Comparing overall patterns of behaviour at different points in time on the same site (e.g. Binford 1978: figs 8–10) suggests that the model is not particularly helpful in explaining the details; it may suggest the pattern of bone dumping by a few individuals sitting around hearths eating and talking, but it does not account for why certain activities are performed in different locations, and how they will contribute to the overall debris patterning. It is obviously not a complete explanation for the spatial organization of behaviour, but does provide a framework for further investigation.

Applying this model to another ethnoarchaeological context, one of John Yellen's maps of a !Kung camp site, a site structural approach can give us insights into the spatial organization of individual family activity areas around each domestic hearth, but it does not provide an understanding of overall camp layout – why households are situated the way they are with respect to each other (spacing, orientation), or with respect to natural features or other activity areas, etc. (Figure 11.1). We are left with a bunch of pieces, but cannot explain why they are assembled the way they are. Such an explanation must involve issues of perception and meaning – the social and symbolic elements in spatial behaviour.

THE SOCIAL ORGANIZATION OF SPACE

Recent work has begun to turn to some of these social and symbolic elements in hunter-gatherer spatial behaviour to try to develop some idea of what we should be looking for, if we accept that a functional and behavioural perspective alone is not sufficient (Whitelaw 1983; 1989; 1991; O'Connell 1987; Kent and Vierich 1989; Binford 1991a; 1991b; Gargett and Hayden 1991; Kent 1991).

This can be illustrated through the example of the !Kung San, who have dominated the anthropological and archaeological literature on hunter-gatherers since the Man the Hunter conference in the mid-1960s (Lee and DeVore 1968). This is because in addition to the ecologically oriented ethnographies of the 1960s and 1970s, such as the work of Lee (1979), Silberbauer (1981) and Tanaka (1980) among the !Kung and neighbouring San groups, there are also good traditional, normative ethnographies, such as those by Marshall (1960; 1961; 1976), and a detailed set of ethnoarchaeological data collected by John Yellen (1977; see also Brooks et al. 1984; Gould and Yellen 1987), still unique in the ethnoarchaeological literature. The latter

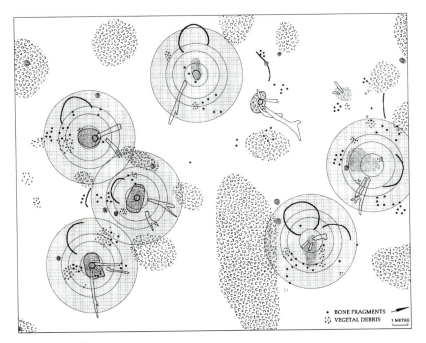

Figure 11.1 Temporary campsite, Dobe !Kung San,//Gakwe ≠Dwa, April 1968. Hearth-side activity areas shaded (modified from Yellen 1977)

are now beginning to be supplemented by ethnoarchaeological work among neighbouring San groups (Hitchcock 1987; Kent and Vierich 1989; Bartram et al. 1991).

Starting with depositional behaviour, it is simply worth noting, though hardly surprising, that there are differences in behaviour between different !Kung households, for instance in the scale, if not in the general organization of behaviour in space. In Figure 11.2, the aggregate debris patterns produced by the large nuclear families of two brothers at a number of sites are mapped at the top, while the camps of their parents are mapped at the lower left, and that of their bachelor brother at the lower right.[1] In all cases, the overall spatial behaviour is broadly comparable, with primary refuse zones focused on the hearth in front of the shelter, and secondary refuse areas displaced to the side or behind the shelter; the major difference is in the size of the scatter, reflecting the greater production and spread of debris by the families with more members, particularly children.

Despite these idiosyncratic differences between families, a normative view of the organization of !Kung domestic space can be developed by rotating and superimposing all domestic hut-sites from Yellen's sample, seventy-three domestic units from sixteen camps. This both amplifies the exiguous patterns which are difficult to identify on any one camp plan (Gregg et al.

220

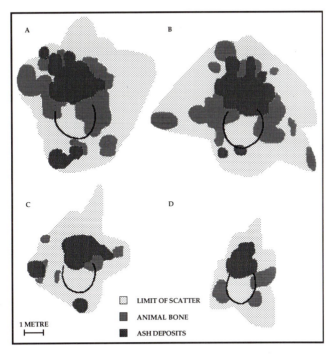

Figure 11.2 Aggregate debris produced by four !Kung San households. A: family with 2 adults, 4 children (14 camps); B: family with 2 adults, 3 children (14 camps); C: family with 3 adults (9 camps); D: single adult (12 camps)

1991), and averages out the uniqueness of each individual or family pattern of behaviour, and context-specific differences at individual camps – in other words, one has a chance of distinguishing normative or general from individual and idiosyncratic patterns of behaviour. This is particularly crucial, since the behavioural, social and symbolic models which are available to understand such spatial patterns are also normative, not individual and idiosyncratic.[2] In general, attempts to match data patterns with model resolution are rare in ethnoarchaeological and archaeological explorations of spatial behaviour, a point also highlighted in the second example (below).

Ash distribution (Figure 11.3a) defines the focal hearth in front of the family shelter, and more peripheral secondary ash dumps, usually used in longer occupations, when sites may be cleaned and maintained (Yellen 1977; Murray 1980). The distribution of animal bone (Figure 11.3b) conforms fairly well with Binford's drop-zone model, with primary areas of deposition associated with seating positions around the rear side of the hearth, near the shelter. Food-processing debris (Figure 11.3c), mostly nut shells and melon shavings, also conforms to the drop-zone model, although there are significant contrasts with the previous pattern; vegetal refuse is

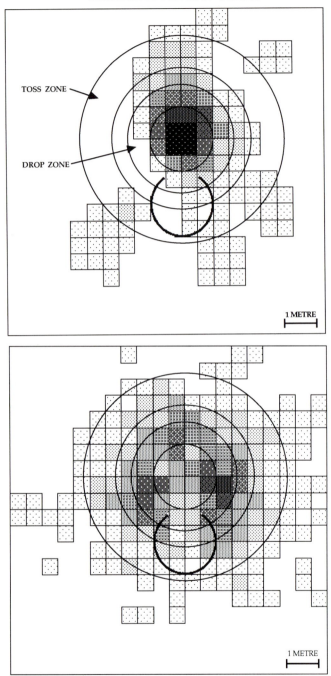

Figure 11.3 Gridded aggregate debris mapped from 73 !Kung San hearth activity areas. *a* (top): distribution of ash; *b* (bottom): distribution of animal bones;

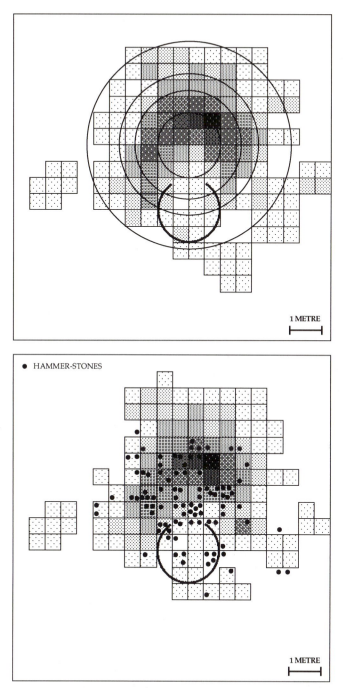

1 METRE

● HAMMER-STONES

1 METRE

c (top): distribution of vegetal food processing debris; *d* (bottom): distribution of mongongo nut processing debris

223

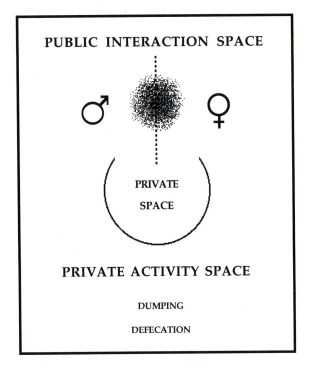

Figure 11.4 Normative model of !Kung San hearth-side spatial organization

particularly concentrated on the side of the hearth opposite the shelter, in the area that Binford (1983: 153) would suggest as a 'forward toss zone'. This contrast differentiates between animal bone discarded during direct consumption, and vegetal food debris disposal in the context of focused food-processing and preparation prior to consumption.

While imposing Binford's drop-zone/toss-zone model on the !Kung hearth debris pattern helps to highlight the contrast between food-processing and food consumption areas, this is about as far as a site struc-ture, behavioural model can go. Is there anything else of interest to be gleaned from the documented patterns? From the perspective of social and symbolic patterns in camp layout, one can note, particularly, the left/right imbalance of mongongo nut processing debris, focused on the upper right of Figure 11.3d.

Turning, not to Yellen's ethnoarchaeology, or Lee's ecologically oriented writings, but to the more traditionally oriented ethnography of Lorna Marshall (1976), allows us to account for this difference in terms of !Kung social and symbolic behaviour. As a self-contained unit, each domestic area is organized in terms of semi-public space around the hearth in front of the shelter, and private space within the shelter (Figure 11.4; Marshall 1976: 88;

Silberbauer 1981: 235). Given that the shelters are flimsy, or may not even be erected in the dry season, the privacy recognized is symbolic rather than effective. Cross-cutting this axis is a division between female and male space. This is manifest particularly in the rule that men and women must not sit where a mature member of the opposite sex has previously sat; to make this taboo maintainable, women and men are supposed to sit on specific, recognized sides of the hearth (Marshall 1976: 88). These two dimensions are important enough so that even at short-term camps, where actual huts may not be erected, sticks may be placed in the ground to define the doorway of a notional hut, defining private space behind the sticks, and providing a spatial fix for male and female orientation around the hearth (ibid.: 88; see Yellen 1977: map 15, features 1–4).

This has been identified as the normative pattern of !Kung hearth-side behaviour, though no time-and-motion studies of the degree to which it is actually practised have been documented.[3] The distribution of food-processing debris appears to be explained by the intersection of symbolic and functional models (Figure 11.4). Women, who collect and process most vegetal foods, sit to the right of the hearth. Being primarily right-handed, one can expect that the area most frequently used for disposal is to their right, and away from the seating areas on the inside circumference of the hearth area.

Archaeologically, while the right/left division of space might be identifiable by a trend in the material record, identifying it as gender-based would be rather more arbitrary, unless the analyst was willing to make the assumption that women were those primarily involved in processing vegetal food. In this case, identifying patterning ethnoarchaeologically does not mean that it can just be mapped on to any archaeological record, without making a series of assumptions which may not, themselves, be justifiable. This problem plagues much post-processual ethnoarchaeology, where both variability in behaviour, and the archaeological recognizablity of symbolically generated patterning is rarely considered critically.

Pragmatically, and perhaps equally distressing for archaeologists, while the food-processing debris will decay and be lost archaeologically, mongongo nut cracking rocks, subject to curation and alternative uses, do not appear to preserve the same behavioural patterns as the organic refuse disposal patterns (Figure 11.3d). In this example, there is no statistically valid distinction between left and right in the distribution of nut-cracking rocks.

A more completely documented example of the ambiguities involved in converting normative or anthropologically idealized models to archaeological frameworks for interpretation is given by one of the few quantified ethnographic studies of variability in spatial behaviour, Henrietta Moore's (1986) work on gender and spatial behaviour among the Marakwet. There, she identifies a symbolic association between gender and refuse disposal patterns, which has been regularly cited by post-processual archaeologists as a specific model for interpreting archaeological data. Unlike most ethnographically generated normative models, however, she is also able to document that these map 'on the ground' rather less clearly, with numerous cases which break the rules, justifying only a 'tendency' toward patterning (ibid.: fig. 36, where only c. 65 per cent of the relevant cases studied were found to conform to the 'rule').

Add to this the ambiguities which are introduced to any record which is a palimpsest, by changes in the use and gender associations of different parts of a compound or domestic area during its life history, and corresponding changes in its residents through the domestic cycle (ibid.: 91–106; Oswald 1987), and it becomes, like the mongongo nut cracking stones, much less likely that traces will survive in the archaeological record which will be clear enough to be recognized as the result of patterned behaviour, let alone associate that behaviour with gender concepts. This is not to say that archaeologists should not look for such patterns. Rather, they should be more critically aware that ethnographic or ethnoarchaeological observations cannot be treated as if they are archaeological records, as a basis for naively optimistic claims for archaeological inference.[4] Archaeologists have to explore both the processes responsible for the formation of the record, and methodologies for analysing and interpreting it, both critically and realistically.

Attempting to move beyond a simple functional framework for understanding spatial behaviour raises the problem of accounting for overall camp layout, anticipating that social and symbolic factors may also be relevant. I have argued elsewhere that communities among hunter-gatherer groups are spatially organized according to patterns of social interaction, often resulting in a direct mapping of kinship relations in space: the spatial localization of kin groups within a community (Whitelaw 1983; 1989; 1991).[5] This pattern linking social and spatial behaviour is also manifest in other ways, such as in the spacing between different domestic units, and in their orientation. It also varies consistently with the nature of social and economic interaction between members of such a community, and the social scale of the community, as space is used to buffer social relations by controlling patterns of social interaction.

As an example, in !Kung rainy-season, extended family camps, shelters are located close together, and distributed without any clear overall spatial structure. In the longer-term, dry-season camps of an entire band, inter-hut spacing is greater, and a more formal camp layout is adopted, with huts generally oriented towards the centre, emphasizing the band as a cohesive social unit (Figure 11.5; Draper 1975; Yellen 1977; Wiessner 1982; Brooks et al. 1984). At a grosser scale of measurement, more commensurate with the resolution of archaeological data, these differences in spatial patterning result in very different residential density levels for camps that represent

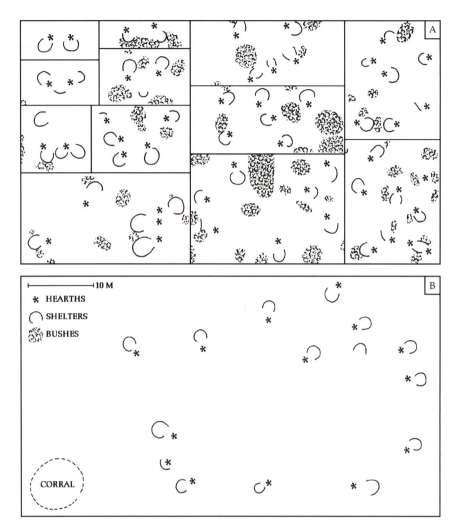

Figure 11.5 Contrasts in !Kung San spatial organization. A: twelve rainy season extended family campsites (modified from Yellen 1977); B: full band campsite, Dobe, 1968 (modified from Brooks et al. 1984)

different scales of social group with different patterns of social relations between members (Figure 11.6).

At a broad cross-cultural scale, variations in camp layout and density relationships can be related directly to variations in the social relations of production within such groups (Whitelaw 1989; 1991). Such spatial relationships vary systematically with environmental contexts, since the social relations of production relate to the patterns of co-operation and

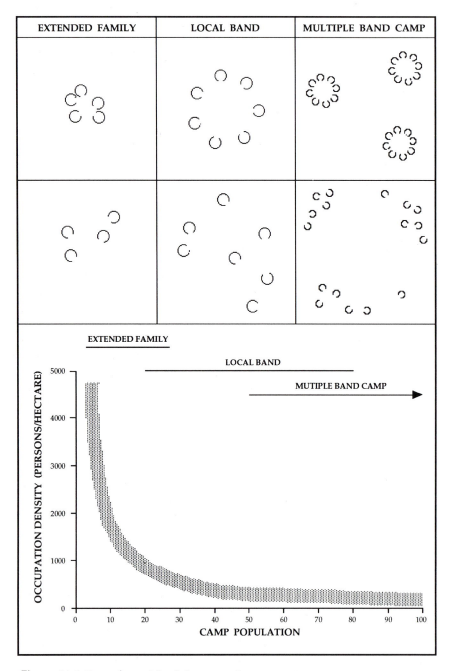

Figure 11.6 General model of hunter-gatherer social organization, community layout and occupation density

competition in the exploitation of the resources available in an environment. These issues need not be pursued further here, since they have been developed elsewhere in some depth (ibid.). Here, it is worth emphasizing that social, and therefore by necessity symbolic concepts and patterns of behaviour can be demonstrated to determine the spatial organization of hunter-gatherer communities, in regular and predictable ways.

THE SYMBOLIC ORGANIZATION OF SPACE

Having touched on functional/behavioural and social factors in the spatial organization of hunter-gatherer communities, the remainder of this chapter will explore in more detail the most neglected component of hunter-gatherer spatial behaviour, explicitly symbolic and ritual organization in space. This will be pursued through a consideration and comparison of the !Kung case with two of the limited number of ethnographic contexts where relevant data have been recorded for foraging societies.

Among sedentary agriculturalists, where the symbolic organization of space has been particularly investigated by anthropologists, two different sets of concerns have often been stressed. The first deals with the relative layout of particular parts of a domestic unit or even of a community, as components of the whole. The second concerns the absolute layout or orientation of individual domestic units or entire communities, with respect to characteristics of the surrounding environment – whether local landmarks (mountains, rivers, shore) or general geographic characteristics (the East, the rising sun, towards particular geographic points such as Mecca). In both senses, the house or community may give a concrete anchor, in the material world, to a series of concepts about the world, and specific inhabitants' position within that conceptual order.

From a symbolic perspective, spatial layout may embody particular associations or meanings attached to space, as a model of ideal domestic relationships between genders or between generations (e.g. Tambiah 1969), as a model of social relations or statuses within society, either by categories or by degrees of difference (e.g. Humphrey 1974; Donley 1982), as objectifying or legitimizing structural relationships of dominance or power (e.g. Bourdieu 1979), or as a microcosm of the universe and its order (e.g. Cunningham 1964; Ohnuki-Tierney 1972). With at least this range of documented options, the archaeologist interested in decoding spatial symbolism obviously cannot simply identify *order* as manifesting a particular meaning. As with the case of gender layout among the !Kung, the interpretation of meaning must be tied to other forms of patterning preserved in the record, to which we feel confident that we can attach meaning, to build up a pattern of contextual relationships (Hodder 1989; Whitelaw 1989: chapter 1).

An an illustration, a few characteristics of !Kung spatial organization may be re-expressed in this light. There is no evidence that compass directions have particular importance in !Kung spatial layout – what geographic factors are relevant appear to be more localized, such as wind direction and the location of shade trees and bushes (Marshall 1976: 85–6; Yellen 1977; Silberbauer 1981: 222, 230). On the other hand, social relations are crucial, both in the relative situation of individual shelters, and in their orientation (Whitelaw 1989: chapter 3). Within domestic space, spatial layout is organized around the nature of social interactions – public and private; no status is conveyed by location in this fully egalitarian society (though see Fourie 1928: 86–7). At the level of the community, the circular camp plan is particularly meaningful: !Kung bands are fluid social groups which exploit broadly defined territories. An individual gains access to the resources of the territory by being a member of that group (Marshall 1960; 1976: 187–91; Wiessner 1977), and exploits them in co-operation with other members of the group, emphasized by camp layout (Draper 1975; Wiessner 1982; Brooks et al. 1984).

One can, in a general sense, contrast this pattern with two characteristics of symbolic space among many sedentary agricultural populations. First, individuals, through categorization or status, may be more directly associated with fixed features or facilities of the domestic or community space (e.g. Tambiah 1969; Humphrey 1974; Bourdieu 1979; Donley 1982; Kent 1984; Moore 1986), with implications of differing social status. Second, such communities often have more formal geographical orientation, frequently with reference to the East and the sun-rise, more crucially important in the cosmology of agriculturally based societies (Tuan 1977). On the other hand, individual domestic units may be less formally organized with respect to each other, to the degree that access to the means of production is less tied to status or membership in particular social groups, which therefore may not be so explicitly represented in spatial arrangement.[6] Two other hunter-gatherer examples may make these points more clearly.

The Mistassini Cree are mobile hunter-trappers of the eastern Canadian sub-arctic. During the summer, they aggregate at a large trading community, while in the winter they disperse into small hunting groups of a few families, to specific habitual territories within the overall band range (Rogers 1963; 1972; Pothier 1965; Tanner 1979).

The symbolic organization of domestic and camp space has been the subject of an insightful study by Adrian Tanner (1979), and is presented in terms of normative models (Figure 11.7). Within the small tents or lodges, space is highly constrained and every individual has a place, determined by his/her gender and age within the domestic group (ibid.: 75–82). Status relationships are also expressed in the overall camp layout, or in the location of different families in the hunting group within a communal dwelling (ibid.: 82–7). In contrast with the !Kung, there is a far greater division of labour between males and females, and greater distinctions by age in the experience

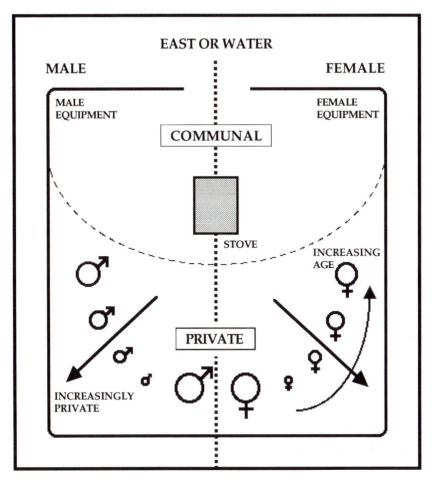

Figure 11.7 Normative model of Mistassini Cree interior spatial organization

and ability of individuals, recognized in social and spatial relationships. Between social units, there are greater status distinctions, based on the experience and success of the hunters, than among the !Kung, since hunting and trapping tend to be more specialized and complex operations in higher-latitude environments (Whitelaw 1989: chapters 4–5). Similarly, delayed-return foraging systems allow the exacerbation of inequalities in material terms, contributing to status distinctions (Meillassoux 1973; Woodburn 1980).

In addition to such social symbolism in spatial layout within the shelter and within the camp, there are also elements of cosmology in spatial behaviour. Shelters are usually situated on the western side of bodies of water, with tent and lodge doorways oriented to the East, and the body of water. Tanner (1979: 101–5) has emphasized functional characteristics in such layout, such as shelter from the prevailing and harshest north-west wind, and orientation toward water and the routes of access to the camp. On the other hand, he notes that such patterns have also become imbued with extra-functional meaning, relating to the symbolic attributes of the spirits of the winds, and of other features of the cognized physical and spiritual environment.

Complicating the identification and interpretation of such patterns are other levels of symbolically structured material culture patterning, such as Cree symbolic attitudes to animals, upon which the ideology and practice of hunting is based. Grossly simplified, animals give themselves up to hunters, as long as the hunters pay the proper respect to their prey. The latter involves the observance of particular rites, the proper display and treatment of animal carcasses, and the proper deposition of skeletal remains (ibid.: 153–81). The latter may involve complex patterns of disposal of bone elements, including their decoration and display, and deposition on platforms, tied in trees, or in bodies of water, out of reach of camp dogs and others scavengers. In addition, sites are rarely reoccupied, both for functional reasons (e.g. depletion of firewood and other resources in the immediate environs) and symbolic reasons – in the latter case, because they take on a ritual character as embodying a particular context of interaction with the world of the spirits (ibid.: 73–5).

Turning to ethnoarchaeological data from a Cree winter camp-site (Figure 11.8; Gordon 1980; see also Bonnischen 1973), only some of these dimensions of patterning are recognizable – as with the !Kung case, in the sense that there is identifiable, non-random (but seemingly non-functional) structure in the material record, though its identification may not be enough to indicate the actual symbolic significance of the individual patterns. The pairing of productive facilities such as meat caches, work tents and canoe racks fits with the evidence for a two-family dwelling, but suggests the economic independence of the two productive units. Some degree of interdependence might be inferred from the joint dwelling with common hearth – the context of consumption, and some shared facilities, such as a smoking tent. The symbolic attitudes toward animals are represented by the generally clean camp-site – very few stray bone elements are distributed around the camp. Instead, most faunal remains have either been placed on middens away from the lodge, or tied in trees, or burned in a series of fires lit especially for the clean-up at the end of the occupation (Gordon 1980). There is no clear evidence that different species or different anatomical elements were disposed of differentially, in midden, tree or fire, contra to normative expectations (Tanner 1979: 170–2). One might, on the identified patterns, suggest that particular care was afforded to the disposal of faunal remains, without being able to identify the specific symbolic content of such behaviour patterns. There is no reported evidence which documents the

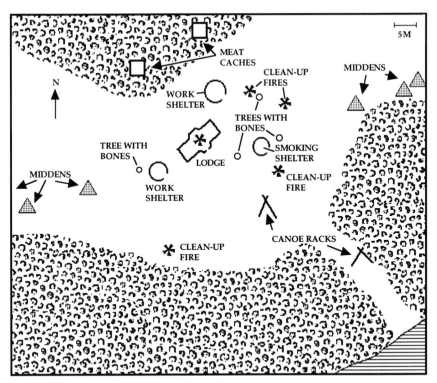

Figure 11.8 Winter campsite, Fort George Cree, Lake Washadimi, October 1977 to January 1978. Principal depositional contexts identified (modified from Gordon 1980)

rigid gender-specific activity areas, particularly within the lodge, which appear to be so significant in the organization of daily life.

Interestingly, in this case, the specific occupants of the site did not behave precisely in the normative fashion described by Tanner. In particular, the disposal of animal bones in middens had not been previously described, and less care appeared to be attached to separating the treatment of major and small game, or animals from the air versus animals of the land. The investigator attributes this to the fact that this camp was from a neighbouring group – the St James Bay Cree, rather than the Mistassini (Gordon 1980). However, as a one-off case, one cannot know whether the deviation from the idealized model is understandable in terms of a difference in norms between the groups not previously documented, whether the occupants of this camp were less rigorous in following the ideal models than the hunting groups studied by Tanner, or whether any camp actually mapped in ethnoarchaeological detail might differ from the expressed norms to a similar degree. Without an assessment of variability in actual behaviour, normative models are only of limited analytical value.

In contrast with the !Kung, the dimensions of inter-individual status distinctions by age, sex and accomplishment find spatial expression among the Mistassini (even if not clearly documented ethnoarchaeologically). Consciously cognized is the view that the camp may change location, but because of the consistency in layout, it does not change; it is at the centre of the individual's conception of the cosmos (Tanner 1979: 73–87). In addition, geographical orientation, in both a localized and absolute sense, is important with respect to water bodies and the East, and is given both functional and symbolic emic explanations (ibid.; 101–5).

This example highlights the potential importance of social and cosmological factors in the creation of material records, but also reinforces the caution expressed above concerning the difficulty of identifying and interpreting the significance of such patterns archaeologically and ethnoarchaeologically, deprived of emic accounts.

The third example is drawn from the Haida, a sedentary hunting and fishing society of the north-west coast of North America, one of the most socially hierarchical groups documented ethnographically among foraging societies. They lived in large village communities, occupied through most of the year, with populations occasionally exceeding a thousand people. Villages were composed of a number of lineage houses, each of which was a separate co-operative subsistence unit. Houses were socially ranked both within and between communities, and social affiliations, such as clans, integrated different houses into larger collectives (Swanton 1909).

The large timber houses sheltered up to a dozen or more families, who co-operated in collective hunting and fishing, and in amassing stores of food for consumption and competitive ceremonial feasting. The house also served as a material symbol of the lineage, and as its ceremonial focus (ibid.; MacDonald 1983). Each domestic unit within the house had its own private space against the outer wall of the structure, facing in on the communal social and ceremonial space (Figure 11.9). Physical locations within the house were ranked, with the house chief in the centre rear, the same location usually serving as a focus for ceremonial activities (McDonald 1983).

Cosmologically, each house was the centre of the universe for its inhabitants. The house faced the beach, which was both the source of access, and of most food, but particularly of socially prestigious foods such as large sea mammals. The sea was also viewed as the route to the underworld and the spirits which dwelled therein. Behind the house, towards the inland mountains, was the route to the overworld, and the private domain of each lineage, where mortuary houses were ideally located. In addition, communication with ancestors and spirits could be undertaken through the burning of offerings in the central fire of the house, defined as the pivot of the world (ibid.).

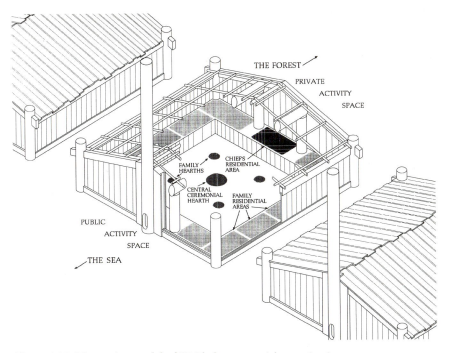

Figure 11.9 Normative model of Haida house spatial organization

Villages also had more secular symbolic dimensions. Ideally, the highest-ranking house in a village would be the largest, with the deepest hearth-pit, and be situated at the centre of the community; where there was more than one row of houses, those in the front row, with direct access to the beach, were of higher rank. Similarly, the lineages of the two main moieties, Ravens and Eagles, were ideally localized for solidarity within the community (ibid.). In practice, due to the changing demographic and economic fortunes of individual lineages, by the period of contact such ideal layouts were never found, though the model was approximated to, to a greater or lesser degree, depending on the history of the individual community (Figure 11.10). In addition, the pragmatics of a large community on a limited beach site often led to the construction of more than one row of houses, interfering with the ideal of direct access to the beach in front, and private space behind each house.

In comparison with the two previous examples, Haida spatial organization is yet more formalized, both socially and cosmologically. Interestingly, unlike many agriculturalists, the cosmological scheme does not focus on the East and the rising sun, but rather on the sea – as with the sun for agriculturalists, the primary source of subsistence and ultimately status. In this case, as with the !Kung, access to basic subsistence resources

235

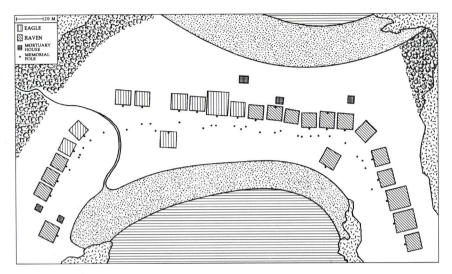

Figure 11.10 Koona (Skedans), Haida, Queen Charlotte Islands, *c.* 1860 (modified from MacDonald 1983; Smyly and Smyly 1973)

depended on membership within a house-group, and this co-operation is emphasized by the open plan of the house and the central focus of the individual domestic units. In contrast, the house is in competition with others, segregated from them by impermeable walls and cultural conventions governing inter-house behaviour.

Whether these various social and symbolic dimensions would be detectable archaeologically has yet to be determined. The deviations from the ideals, both in the relative positions of different social or status groups within the community, or even the layout of individual household symbolic space, as in the relative location of residential houses and mortuary houses, is likely to lead to difficulty in identifying, let alone deciphering, the spatial conventions, as also illustrated in the previous examples.

CONCLUSIONS

Are these simply three hunter-gatherer cultures which behave differently? I think there may be substantially more to it than that. Let me return to my original two concerns:

First, I have argued that hunter-gatherers are not necessarily simpler than other cultures, nor can their behaviour be explained simply in ecological terms. They appear to inhabit a cognized world as richly imbued with symbolic meaning as other societies; unfortunately anthropologists, particularly recent ecologically oriented hunter-gatherer ethnographers, have tended to pay relatively little attention to this aspect of their culture, and archaeologists perpetuate this myth. While attention has focused on hunter-gatherer symbolism with respect to myth and art, there have been few explicit studies of the social and symbolic basis of community spatial behaviour (e.g. Paulson 1952; Hallowell 1955; Chang 1962; Ohnuki-Tierney 1972).

Second, I have argued in each case that a functional/behavioural perspective is not in contradiction with a symbolic explanation of spatial behaviour – rather, both are relevant and essential if we are going to develop as full an understanding of the material and archaeological record as we can.

There have also been several sub-themes running through this chapter. First, I have tried to demonstrate that there is social and symbolic patterning in the material record of hunter-gatherer settlement, even though much of it may not have been recorded by standard ethnographic accounts (e.g. contrast Rogers 1963, 1972, and Pothier 1965, with Tanner 1979). The lack of interest in or discussion of such patterns in most ethnographies cannot appropriately be used as evidence to argue for the absence of particular characteristics of spatial organization among foragers (e.g. Kent 1990b), or to argue for the precedence of functional issues (Binford 1978; 1986; 1987).

Second, individuals are just that – individuals – not mindless automata blindly following norms. They follow or deviate from such norms to varying degrees, just as different individuals may understand their own behaviour differently. People, whether sedentary agriculturalists or hunter-gatherers, are not simple, and we cannot effectively treat them as if they were, either behaviourally or symbolically. When the individual richness and variability observable through anthropological and ethnoarchaeological research is simplified and presented only in terms of norms (e.g. Humphrey 1974; Tanner 1979; Bourdieu 1979; Donley 1982; Kent 1984), we lose much of the richness of the observational context, and the potential insights of a broader-based focus on patterns of variability (e.g. Moore 1986; Binford 1991a).

Third, the ethnographic record, or a normative abstraction from it, is not the same as an archaeological record of behaviour, and the palimpsests we usually must deal with. Unfortunately, the archaeological record is complicated, and we cannot develop an understanding of the past by empathy alone (Schiffer 1972; Clarke 1973; Binford 1977; 1978; 1981; 1982). As a minimal strategy, we have to know what people in the past did, before we can try to ascertain why they did it. Regardless of their merit, post-processual objectives cannot effectively be pursued without adequate attention to the middle-range concerns (Patrik 1985).

Finally, are societies simply different, as post-processualists often seem to argue, or is there pattern in human behaviour, as processualists maintain, including symbolic behaviour? In the context of hunter-gatherers, an adequate understanding of this dispute is difficult to develop, since so few anthropologists have made systematic observations of symbolic and spatial behaviour among such groups. The examples I have illustrated, and a few others (e.g. Boas 1909; Paulson 1952; Hallowell 1955; Chang 1962; Ohnuki-Tierney 1972), have led me to think that there may be common dimensions of variability, linked to major differences in behaviour. One of these concerns the degree of social and labour differentiation within the society, at the family and community level (Whitelaw 1989). Another links to mobility – I might suggest that more mobile groups organize themselves primarily with respect to other people – their social relations, and their social relations of production. Increasingly sedentary groups, more directly tied to the exploitation of a specific and limited environment, and usually more territorial, seem to be more preoccupied with fixed features of the environment. If there is patterning at such a broad, inter-cultural level, I think it is our job to try to document and to explain such differences in behaviour, not to ignore them, or simply to accept them as different.

NOTES

I would like to thank the editors for inviting me to contribute this paper, and Mark Edmonds, Ian Hodder, Susan Kent and Tim Murray for discussion of some of the points addressed.

1 These patterns were compiled by dividing the debris at the core of each of Yellen's camps into individual hut-associated patterns, aligning and superimposing the patterns for each hut-site along the hut to hearth axis, from each of Yellen's camps where the relevant family or individual was documented. Where debris from adjacent hut-sites blended into each other, debris was associated with the nearest hut.

2 One strength of Yellen's data which is not generally duplicated elsewhere is that most of his data come from the same group of related individuals, so that it is possible to distinguish context-specific and idiosyncratic patterns of behaviour from broader cultural norms. It is notable that certain pairs of individuals consistently camp closer together than others, attributable, even among brothers, to patterns of socialization and association (Silberbauer 1981: 165). Expanding his sample to include dry-season camps, Yellen and others have also noted other context-specific patterns in behaviour (Gould and Yellen 1987; Kent and Vierich 1989; Whitelaw 1989; Kent 1991). Similar contextual variation in the settlement behaviour of individuals has recently been considered by Binford (1991a) for a series of Nunamiut camps, demonstrating the role of spatial behaviour in social strategies.

3 The sex-specific seating rules appear to be followed in most of the photographs of the !Kung which I have encountered, though one cannot be sure whether the few exceptions (e.g. Marshall 1976: 80) document variations in behaviour, or have simply been printed in reverse.

4 Equally, it is not suitable to regard ethnographic normative statements as adequate documentation of variability in behaviour. In the case of the !Kung omission of any detailed discussion of gender-linked activity areas in the principal ethnographies has been used by Kent (1990b: 130–2) to support the proposition that gender-specific activity areas do not usually exist among egalitarian hunter-gatherers. None of the ethnographic studies cited in support of that proposition focused in detail either on gender-specific behaviour or, with the exception of

Yellen's (1977) and Fisher's (1986) work, documented spatial behaviour in detail. The research of O'Connell et al. (1991) also contradicts this interpretation for the Hadza.

5 Because of the nature of anthropological interest, it is usually only possible to document these patterns of interaction and co-operation though recorded kinship data; this does not mean that I presume that kinship 'determines' either social or spatial behaviour, as others have read into my work (Binford 1991a; 1991b: 256; Ingold 1992: 793; cf. Whitelaw 1989: chapters 4–5).

6 Interestingly, swiddening groups, where land is often held in common by a kin-based unit within the larger community, often have a considerable emphasis on the spatial localization of kin-groups within the community (e.g. Yanomamo: Chagnon 1974; Smole 1976; Akwe-Shavante: Maybury-Lewis 1967; Bororo: Lévi-Strauss 1936; Bradfield 1973; Simonis 1977).

BIBLIOGRAPHY

Anderson, D. (1982) 'Space use and site structure', *Haliksa' i* 1: 120–41.

Audouze, F. (1987) 'Des modèles et des faites: Les modèles de A. Leroi-Gourhan et de L. Binford confrontés aux résultats récents', *Bulletin de la Société Préhistorique Française* 84: 343–52.

Bartram, L.E., Kroll. E.M. and Bunn, H.T. (1991) 'Variability in camp structure and bone refuse patterning at Kua San hunter-gatherer camps', in E.M. Kroll and T.D. Price (eds), *The Interpretation of Archaeological Spatial Patterning*, New York: Plenum.

Binford, L.R. (1962) 'Archaeology as anthropology', *American Antiquity* 28: 217–25.

——(1977) 'General introduction', in L.R. Binford (ed.), *For Theory Building in Archaeology*, New York: Academic Press.

——(1978) 'Dimensional analysis of behaviour and site structure: learning from an Eskimo hunting stand', *American Antiquity* 43(3): 330–61.

——(1981) 'Behavioral archaeology and the "Pompeii premise"', *Journal of Anthropological Research* 37: 195–208.

——(1982) 'Meaning, inference and the material record', in C. Renfrew and S. Shennan (eds), *Ranking, Resource and Exchange*, Cambridge: Cambridge University Press.

——(1983) *In Pursuit of the Past: Decoding the Archaeological Record*, London: Thames and Hudson.

——(1986) 'An Alyawara day: making men's knives and beyond', *American Antiquity* 51: 547–62.

——(1987) 'Researching ambiguity: frames of reference and site structure', in S. Kent (ed.), *Method and Theory for Activity Area Research*, New York: Columbia University Press.

——(1991a) 'When the going gets tough, the tough get going: Nunamiut local groups, camping patterns and economic organization', in C. Gamble and W. Boismier (eds), *Ethnoarchaeological Approaches to Mobile Campsites: Hunter-gatherer and Pastoralist Case Studies*, Ethnoarchaeology Series 1, International Monographs in Prehistory, Ann Arbor.

——(1991b) 'Is Australian site structure explained by the absence of predators?', *Journal of Anthropological Archaeology* 10: 255–82.

Boas, F. (1909) *The Kwakiutl of Vancouver Island*, The Jesup North Pacific Expedition. Vol. 5(2), Memoirs of the American Museum of Natural History, New York: American Museum of Natural History.

Bonnichsen, R. (1973) 'Millie's camp: an experiment in archaeology', *World Archaeology* 4: 277–91.

Bourdieu, P. (1979) 'The Kabylie house', in P. Bourdieu, *Algeria 1960*, Cambridge: Cambridge University Press.

Bradfield, R.M. (1973) *A Natural History of Associations. A Study in the Meaning of Community*, London: Duckworth.

Brooks, A.S., Gelburd, D.E. and Yellen, J.E. (1984) 'Food production and culture change among the !Kung San: implications for prehistoric research', in, J.D. Clark and S. Brandt (eds), *From Hunters to Farmers: The Causes and Consequences of Food Production in Africa*, London: University of California Press.

Carr, C. (1991) 'Left in the dust: contextual information in model-focused archaeology', in E.M. Kroll and T.D. Price (eds), *The Interpretation of Archaeological Spatial Patterning*, New York: Plenum.

Chagnon, N.A. (1974) *Studying the Yanomamo*, New York: Holt, Rinehart & Winston.

Chang, K.-C. (1962) 'A typology of settlement and typology and community patterns in some circumpolar societies', *Arctic Anthropology* 1: 28–41.

Clarke, D.L. (1973) 'Archaeology; the loss of innocence', *Antiquity* 47: 6–18.

Cribb, R. (1991a) *Nomads in Archaeology*, Cambridge: Cambridge University Press.

——(1991b) 'Mobile Villagers: the structure and organization of nomadic pastoral campsites in the Near East', in C. Gamble and W. Boismier (eds), *Ethnoarchaeological Approaches to Mobile Campsites: Hunter-gatherer and Pastoralist Case Studies*, Ethnoarchaeology Series 1, International Monographs in Prehistory, Ann Arbor.

Cunningham, C.E. (1964) 'Order in the Atoni house', *Bijdragen tot de taal-, land- en volkenkunde* 120: 34–68.

Donley, L.W. (1982) 'House power: Swahili space and symbolic markers', in I. Hodder (ed.), *Symbolic and Structural Archaeology*, Cambridge: Cambridge University Press.

Douglas, M. (1972) 'Symbolic orders in the use of domestic space', in P. Ucko, R. Tringham and G. Dimbleby (eds), *Man, Settlement and Urbanism*, London: Duckworth.

Draper, P. (1975) '!Kung women: contrasts in sexual egalitarianism in the foraging and sedentary contexts', in R. Reiter (ed.), *Toward an Anthropology of Women*, New York: Monthly Review Press.

Fisher, J.W. Jr (1986) 'Shadows in the Forest: Ethnoarchaeology among the Efe Pygmies', unpublished Ph.D. thesis, University of California.

Fisher, J.W. Jr and Strickland, H.C. (1991) 'Dwellings and fireplaces: keys to Efe Pygmy campsite structure', in C. Gamble and W. Boismier (eds), *Ethnoarchaeological Approaches to Mobile Campsites: Hunter-gatherer and Pastoralist Case Studies*, Ethnoarchaeology Series 1, International Monographs in Prehistory, Ann Arbor.

Fourie, L. (1928) 'The bushmen of South West Africa', in C.H.L. Hahn, H. Vedder and L. Fourie (eds), *The Native Tribes of South West Africa*, London: Frank Cass.

Gallay, A. (1988) 'Vivre autour d'un feu. Analyse ethnoarcheologique de campements Touaregs du Hoggar', *Bulletin du centre Genevois d'anthropologie* 1: 35–59.

Gamble, C.S. and Boismier, W. (eds) (1991) *Ethnoarchaeological Approaches to Mobile Campsites: Hunter-gatherer and Pastoralist Case Studies*, Ethnoarchaeology Series 1, International Monographs in Prehistory, Ann Arbor.

Gargett, R. and Hayden, B. (1991) 'Site structure, kinship, and sharing in Aboriginal Australia: implications for archaeology', in E.M. Kroll and T.D. Price (eds), *The Interpretation of Archaeological Spatial Patterning*, New York: Plenum.

Gordon, D. (1980) 'Reflections on refuse: a contemporary example from James Bay, Quebec', *Canadian Journal of Archaeology* 4: 83–96.

Gould, R. and Yellen, J. (1987) 'Man the hunted: determinants of household spacing in desert and tropical foraging societies', *Journal of Anthropological Archaeology* 6: 77–103.

——(1991) 'Misreading the past: a reply to Binford concerning hunter-gatherer site structure', *Journal of Anthropological Archaeology* 10: 283–98.

Gregg, S.A., Kintigh, K.W. and Whallon, R. (1991) 'Linking ethnoarchaeological interpretation and archaeological data: the sensitivity of spatial analytical methods to postdepositional disturbance', in E.M. Kroll and T.D. Price (eds), *The Interpretation of Archaeological Spatial Patterning*, New York: Plenum.

Hallowell, A. (1955) *Culture and Experience*, Philadelphia: University of Pennsylvania Press.

Hitchcock, R.K. (1987) 'Sedentism and site structure: organization changes in Kalahari Botswana residential locations', in S. Kent (ed.), *Method and Theory for Activity Area Research*, New York: Columbia University Press.

Hodder, I. (1987) 'The meaning of discard: ash and domestic space in Baringo', in S. Kent (ed.), *Method and Theory for Activity Area Research*, New York: Columbia University Press.

——(1989) 'This is not an article about material culture as text', *Journal of Anthropological Archaeology* 8: 250–69.

Humphrey, C. (1974) 'Inside a Mongolian tent', *New Society* 3(10): 273–5.

Ingold, T. (1992) 'Foraging for data, camping with theories: hunter-gatherers and nomadic pastoralists in archaeology and anthropology', *Antiquity* 66: 790–803.

Julien, M., Karlin, C. and Bodu, P. (1987) 'Pincevent: Où en est le modèle théorique aujourd'hui?', *Bulletin de la Société Préhistorique Française* 84: 335–42.

Kent, S. (1984) *Analyzing Activity Areas: An Ethnoarchaeological Study of the Use of Space*, Albuquerque: University of New Mexico Press.

——(ed.) (1990a) *Domestic Architecture and the Use of Space: An Interdisciplinary Cross-cultural Study*, Cambridge: Cambridge University Press.

——(1990b) 'A cross-cultural study of segmentation, architecture, and the use of space', in S. Kent (ed.), *Domestic Architecture and the Use of Space: An Interdisciplinary Cross-cultural Study*, Cambridge: Cambridge University Press.

——(1991) 'The relationship between mobility strategies and site structure', in E.M. Kroll and T.D. Price (eds), *The Interpretation of Archaeological Spatial Patterning*, New York: Plenum.

Kent, S. and Vierich, H. (1989) 'The myth of ecological determinism – anticipated mobility and site spatial organization, in S. Kent (ed.) *Farmers as Hunters: The Implications of Sedentism*, Cambridge: Cambridge University Press.

Kira, A. (1976) *The Bathroom*, Harmondsworth: Penguin.

Kroll, E. and Price, T.D. (eds) (1991) *The Interpretation of Archaeological Spatial Patterning*, New York: Plenum.

Kus, S. (1983) 'The social representation of space: dimensioning the cosmological and the quotidian', in J. Moore and A. Keene (eds), *Archaeological Hammers and Theories*, New York: Academic Press.

Lee, R. (1979) *The !Kung San: Men, Women and Work in a Foraging Society*, Cambridge: Cambridge University Press.

Lee, R. and DeVore, I. (eds) (1968) *Man the Hunter*, Chicago: Aldine Press.

Lévi-Strauss, C. (1936) 'Contribution à l'étude d'organisation sociale des Indiens Bororo', *Journal de la société des Américanistes* 28: 269–304.

MacDonald, G.F. (1983) *Haida Monumental Art: Villages of the Queen Charlotte Islands*, Vancouver: University of British Columbia Press.

Marshall, L. (1960) '!Kung bushman bands', *Africa* 30: 325–55.
——(1961) 'Sharing, talking and giving: relief of social tension among !Kung bushmen', *Africa* 31: 231–49.
——(1976) *The !Kung of Nyae Nyae*, Cambridge: Harvard University Press.
Maybury-Lewis, D. (1967) *Akwe-Shavante Society*, Oxford: Clarendon Press.
Meillassoux, C. (1973) 'On the mode of production of the hunting band', in P. Alexandre (ed.), *French Perspectives in African Studies*, Oxford: Oxford University Press.
Moore, H.L. (1986) *Space, Text and Gender: An Anthropological Study of the Marakwet of Kenya*, Cambridge: Cambridge University Press.
Murray, P. (1980) 'Discard and location: the ethnographic data', *American Antiquity* 45: 490–502.
O'Connell, J.F. (1987) 'Alyawara site structure and its archaeological implications', *American Antiquity* 52: 74–108.
O'Connell, J.F., Hawkes, K. and Blurton Jones, N. (1991) 'Distribution of refuse-producing activities at Hadza residential base camps: implications for analyses of archaeological site structure', in E.M. Kroll and T.D. Price (eds), *The Interpretation of Archaeological Spatial Patterning*, New York: Plenum.
Ohnuki-Tierney, E. (1972) 'Spatial concepts of the Ainu of the north-west coast of southern Sakhalin', *American Anthropologist* 74: 426–57.
Oliver, P. (ed.) (1969) *Shelter and Society*, London: Barrie & Jenkins.
——(ed.) (1977) *Shelter, Sign and Symbol*, Woodstock: The Overlook Press.
Oswald, D. (1987) 'The organization of space in residential buildings: a cross-cultural perspective', in S. Kent (ed.), *Method and Theory for Activity Area Research*, New York: Columbia University Press.
Patrik, L. (1985) 'Is there an archaeological record?', in M. Schiffer (ed.), *Advances in Archaeological Method and Theory. Volume 8*, New York: Academic Press.
Paulson, I. (1952) 'The "seat of honour" in Aboriginal dwellings of the circumpolar zone, with special regard to the Indians of northern North America', in S. Tax (ed.), *Indian Tribes of Aboriginal America*, Chicago: University of Chicago Press.
Petrequin, A.-M. and Petrequin, P. (1988) 'Ethnoarcheologie de l'habitat en grotte de Nouvelle-Guinée', *Bulletin du centre Genevois d'anthropologie* 1: 61–82.
Pothier, R. (1965) *Relations inter-ethnique et acculturation à Mistassini*, Centre d'études nordiques, Travaux divers 9, Institut de géographie, Université Laval, Quebec.
Rogers, E.S. (1963) *The Hunting Group – Hunting Territory Complex among the Mistassini Indians*, Bulletin of the National Museum of Canada 195, National Museum of Canada, Ottawa.
——(1972) 'The Mistassini Cree', in M. Bicchieri (ed.), *Hunters and Gatherers Today*, New York: Holt, Rinehart & Winston.
Samson, R. (1990) *The Social Archaeology of Houses*, Edinburgh: Edinburgh University Press.
Schiffer, M.B. (1972) 'Archaeological context and systemic context', *American Antiquity* 37: 156–65.
Silberbauer, G. (1981) *Hunter and Habitat in the Central Kalahari*, Cambridge: Cambridge University Press.
Simms, S.R. (1988) 'The archaeological structure of a Bedouin camp', *Journal of Archaeological Science* 15: 197–211.
Simonis, Y. (1977) 'Le village bororo et le rêve des architectes: remarques anthropologiques', *Espaces et Sociétés* 22–3: 89–100.
Smole, W.J. (1976) *The Yanomama Indians: A cultural geography*, Austin: University of Texas Press.

242

Smyly, J. and Smyly, C. (1973) *Those Born at Koona. The Totem Poles of the Haida Village Skedans, Queen Charlotte Islands*, Saanichton: Hancock House.

Sommer, R. (1969) *Personal Space: The Behavioral Basis of Design*, Englewood Cliffs: Prentice Hall.

——(1974) *Tight Spaces: Hard Architecture and How to Humanize It*, Englewood Cliffs: Prentice Hall.

Spurling, B. and Hayden, B. (1984) 'Ethnoarchaeology and intrasite spatial analysis: a case study from the Australian Western Desert', in H. Hietala (ed.), *Intrasite Spatial Analysis in Archaelogy*, Cambridge: Cambridge University Press.

Stevenson, M.G. (1991) 'Beyond the formation of hearth-associated artifact assemblages', in, E.M. Kroll and T.D. Price (eds), *The Interpretation of Archaeological Spatial Patterning*, New York: Plenum.

Swanton, J. (1909) *Contributions to the Ethnology of the Haida*, The Jesup North Pacific Expedition Volume 5(1), Memoirs of the American Museum of Natural History, New York: American Museum of Natural History.

Tambiah, S.J. (1969) 'Animals are good to think and good to prohibit', *Ethnology* 8: 423–59.

Tanaka, J. (1980) *The San: Hunter-gatherers of the Kalahari: A Study in Ecological Anthropology*, Tokyo: University of Tokyo Press.

Tanner, A. (1979) *Bringing Home Animals: Religious Ideology and Mode of Production of the Mistassini Cree Hunters*, London: C. Hurst.

Tuan, Y-F. (1977) *Space and Place: The Perspective of Experience*, London: Edward Arnold.

Whitelaw, T. (1983) 'People and space in hunter-gatherer camps: a generalizing approach in ethnoarchaeology', *Archaeological Review from Cambridge* 2(2): 48–66.

——1989 'The Social Organization of Space in Hunter-gatherer Communities: Some Implications for Social Inference in Archaeology', unpublished Ph.D. thesis, University of Cambridge.

——(1991) 'Some dimensions of variability in the social organization of community space among foragers', in C. Gamble and W. Boismier (eds), *Ethnoarchaeological Approaches to Mobile Campsites: Hunter-gatherer and Pastoralist Case Studies*, Ethnoarchaeology Series 1, International Monographs in Prehistory, Ann Arbor.

Wiessner, P. (1977) 'Hxaro: A Regional System of Reciprocity for Reducing Risk among the !Kung San', unpublished Ph.D. thesis, University of Michigan.

——(1982) 'Beyond willow smoke and dogs' tails: a comment on Binford's analysis of hunter-gatherer settlement systems', *American Antiquity* 47(1): 171–8.

Wilmsen, E.N. (1982) 'Studies in diet, nutrition and fertility among a group of Kalahari bushmen in Botswana', *Social Science Information* 21(1): 95–125.

Woodburn, J. (1980) 'Hunters and gatherers today and reconstruction of the past', in E. Gellner (ed.), *Soviet and Western Anthropology*, London: Duckworth.

Yellen, J. (1977) *Archaeological Approaches to the Present: Models for Reconstructing the Past*, New York: Academic Press.

INDEX